The Real Stories behind Honour Killing

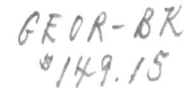

The Real Stories behind Honour Killing

By

Shahnaz Shoro

Cambridge
Scholars
Publishing

The Real Stories behind Honour Killing

By Shahnaz Shoro

This book first published 2019

Cambridge Scholars Publishing

Lady Stephenson Library, Newcastle upon Tyne, NE6 2PA, UK

British Library Cataloguing in Publication Data
A catalogue record for this book is available from the British Library

Copyright © 2019 by Shahnaz Shoro

All rights for this book reserved. No part of this book may be reproduced, stored in a retrieval system, or transmitted, in any form or by any means, electronic, mechanical, photocopying, recording or otherwise, without the prior permission of the copyright owner.

ISBN (10): 1-5275-2959-2
ISBN (13): 978-1-5275-2959-5

The Book is dedicated to

Roger Witts, whose insight, valuable suggestions and categorical support enabled me to let the world hear the stories of the unheard and unsung individuals who are victimized by the erroneous connotation of 'honour'.

TABLE OF CONTENTS

Acknowledgments ix

Foreword xi

Preface xiii

Introduction 1

Chapter One 25
The Accounts of Killers outside Jails
    Sajid 25
    Hanif 37
    Arshad 47
    Zafar 57
    Atif 72
    Adnan 85
    Usman 98

Chapter Two 113
The Accounts of Convicted Killers in Jails
    Naeer 113
    Omar 121
    Saeed 127
    Ata 133
    Ayaz 138
    Anwar 144

Chapter Three 151
The Accounts of Women at Various Shelters
    Saba 151
    Saira 155
    Sajida 160
    Irum 168
    Amna 173
    Fareeha 179
    Rabia 186

    Najma 193
    Rubina 199
    Shaheen 205
    Asma 210
    Ghazala 218
    Tahira 224

Conclusion 231

References 249

Appendix A 251
Interview questions for the female inhabitants of the shelters

Appendix B 253
Interview questions for the killers who killed for honour

Appendix C 255
The names of the interviewees

Appendix D 257
Characteristics of the female participants

Appendix E 259
Characteristics of the male participants

Appendix F 261
Biographical sketches of the female interviewees

Appendix G 267
Biographical sketches of the male interviewees

Glossary 273

Acknowledgements

My heart cries for the eighteen-year-old participant who pleaded with me to take her photograph as she was unsure about the safety of her life. Her words still make me sad: '*Baji*, take my photo and keep it with you so that when these cruel people kill me my image should remind you that I was also alive once'. I wish I could have taken her photo but the ethical convention which I had signed with the University of York prevented me from doing so. She, like all of the other interviewees, is constantly in my thoughts.

Being unjudgemental and unbiased, I would like to thank my participants for their trust in me, and for giving their time to share their life stories with me. I was a stranger to them but they respected me by answering most of my questions eloquently. I went to them with honesty and they enriched my understanding with such detailed data that at one point my supervisor Professor Stevi Jackson said that she had not seen such strong data throughout her research career. That was the time when I considered myself a selfish person who had made an unfair bargain. That was the time when I vowed to myself that I would write every single word which they had uttered and let the world hear the plight which affected their lives. I am grateful that I have been given enough time to fulfil my duty and my obligation to them.

I am extremely grateful and indebted to my husband Akbar Laghari and our children Zaryab and Sophia, without their unconditional love and support, I would have given up a long time ago. They always respected my passion for learning and assisted me to comprehend what the meaning, value and strength of a family is.

Foreword

Courage comes in many forms. This book is a remarkable testament both to the courage of many women who have survived the most terrifying ordeals and whose future is still uncertain, and to the courage of many men who are prepared to speak openly to a stranger about what they have experienced. It is also a stark and horrifying presentation of unspeakable cruelty, vicious dishonesty, greed and corruption. Dr Shoro lets the people on both sides of the phenomenon of honour killing describe their experiences, justify their actions and pour out their hopes with compassion, empathy and vivid clarity but without commenting on, analysing or judging any of the experiences which she relates. There are no heroes, no heroines in the stories which are told in this book: the men who proudly describe the murders which they have committed, the children who grow up with no access to education, the men who are falsely accused of the most appalling murders, the young girls who are forced into loveless marriages, the women who are bullied, abused, slaughtered and sold, and the forces of authority which ignore, condone, even encourage murder, slavery and corruption – they are all victims of a society in which there is no honour at all. It is also a society which knows no boundaries: although the interviews took place in Upper Sindh, newspaper headlines in countries across the world tell of honour killings but rarely explore the social background to them as deeply as Dr Shoro does in this book. The courage which Dr Shoro needed in tracking down her interviewees, meeting them and listening to their stories is admirable and the restraint which she shows in letting the voices be heard unfiltered by analysis means that the reader will be shocked not only by the stories which are told, but also by the acceptance shown, even by the victims themselves, that this is the way that things are. Anyone who reads this book will be deeply affected by the experiences which are related and by the descriptions of the everyday ordinariness of the environment in which the most extraordinary crimes are committed.

Roger Witts
October 2018

PREFACE

The purpose of this book is to let the world comprehend the phenomenon of honour-related violence and crimes and the cultural tradition of killing. The study was conducted in the northern divisions of Sindh, the second largest of the four provinces of Pakistan. The principal question which guided my research was 'What is the relationship between honour and killing?' This research was inspired by a need to investigate whether honour killing is happening to punish supposed wayward women in order to maintain cultural values and a social system, or whether acting in the name of honour implies attempting to achieve some hidden objective. I gathered the experiences of those involved in honour killings through informal, semi-structured, open-ended, in-depth interviews, conducted under the framework of the qualitative research method. The aim of my study was to present the data which I collected without any meddling in the name of analysis so that readers can explore the tradition of honour killing and to let the versions of the affected people be heard. The interviews were held with three different groups of people; women who had been threatened with death were interviewed in three different shelters, convicted killers were interviewed inside two jails and killers who were not in jail were interviewed in carefully selected locations. This book presents the divergent accounts of thirteen men and thirteen women about how they had been affected by the tradition of honour killing and their experience of living in a society which has very strict honour-related norms. In these case studies, women who have been accused of being *karis* speak out and reveal the motives behind the allegations and killings in the name of honour. The male killers, whom I met inside and outside the jails, justify their acts of killing in the name of honour, culture, tradition and religion. Their accounts reveal their childhood and education, their financial and social conditions and the impacts of these on their lives, thoughts and actions. By viewing the rise in honour killings in Sindh over the last three decades as a suspicious change, I argue that there are some notable features, such as Pakistani law, gender discrimination in every walk of life, the social and economic situation, and cultural and religious interpretations of notions about honour killing, all revealed in the interviewees' accounts. Although this was a small-scale study in a limited geographical area, its findings can be generalized more widely and can help to make recommendations for future research into this controversial and disturbing subject.

INTRODUCTION

Of all the most heinous crimes against humanity, a major crime committed in the name of culture is known as 'honour killing' and is, unfortunately, still regarded by many people as an honourable act. Honour killing as a traditional norm or cultural practice to restore tarnished honour because of the perceived misconduct of a kinswoman has been widely accepted as an honourable act in many societies and legislative systems. However, it is regarded by many researchers in the field of gender-based violence that honour killings are one of the most psychologically complex, sociologically complicated, morally distressing and legally challenging violent crimes against humanity. Hanmer (1996:12-13) explained that violence of this kind, regardless of cultural borders, includes the torture of women by men for a number of reasons such as marriage, pregnancy, the birth of children and simply to get rid of their wives, and the sexual, physical and emotional attacks and traumas which are inflicted on victims can continue for several years. If they complain, women are often told by their confidants that 'you should not make a fuss because married women are always hit': "This is especially important in understanding how much violence has been accepted, condoned, normalized and ignored by both individuals and institutions. It has been seen as a private matter" (Hearn, 1996:24).

Honour killing is not a recent phenomenon; such crimes in the name of honour have been happening throughout history all over the world in many communities, countries and cultures. The feudal and tribal concept of *karo-kari* in Pakistan is that if a man sees any of his female relatives in a compromising position with any man other than her husband, it becomes his moral obligation to kill both of them. It is affirmed that most tribal areas have no other substitutable punishment than murder for a woman who, in their view, is adulterous. Honour-related crimes against women are linked to a patriarchal society. Before the male-controlled, strong patriarchal culture existed, there are no records of such killings in the name of honour. Durant (1935), however, wrote that before the beginning of patriarchal society, the position of women was superior to that of men and that the matriarchal period lasted for 9,290,000 years of the known human history of 30 million years. Lerner (1986) stated that the patriarchal structure consistently excluded women from all creative and scientific progress but added that "patriarchy was not imposed as a single event but the subjugation, exploitation and commodification of women are ancient and widespread". Jafri (2008:27) suggested that the history of human civilization bears witness to the fact that women have been humiliated and treated brutally certainly since the rise of city-states.

It was the beginning of an agricultural society which gave birth to the patriarchal philosophy which changed the comparatively prestigious position of women. The new ideology chained women and reduced their status to that of slaves in several respects. This system began to treat a woman as a thing, a commodity or a property and denied her an identity to the level that eventually she became an easy target in the hands of opportunists, mainly because of her weaker physique, because the agricultural society was based on physical strength rather than intellectual capabilities, mental skills or the ability to give birth. As a result, women's position was reduced to a weaker being and the man-made society created its own ethical and moral masculine norms. These norms had their own male-oriented rules which were clearly visible in the way that they were made and imposed in every social written and unwritten contract, whether it was a law or a religious tenet. The physical power of men pushed aside the intellectual and artistic capabilities of women and the two genders became divided on a basis of deep inequality. Out of so many other concepts and terms, the word 'honour' also came to be used as a means of restricting the free will of women. The concepts and meanings which they associated with the word 'honour' gave the dominant males a free hand to punish, control, abuse, torture or even kill if, in their opinion, women violated the very notion of what they saw as honour. Baker *et al.* (1999:165) pointed out that "the concept of honour used to rationalize killing is founded on the notion that a person's honour depends on the behaviour of others and that behaviour therefore must be controlled". In many societies, 'the other' whose behaviour can cause shame and damage to the widely held concept of honour is 'female'. In honour killings, the victims are mostly women and the murderers are mostly men; fathers, uncles, brothers, husbands or sons.

In this Introduction, my aim is to investigate the significance of the word 'honour' in both its broad and its narrow terms from the eastern and the western perspectives. Interestingly the meaning of 'honour' fluctuates when different sources define women's honour, which undoubtedly supports the notion of hierarchy. Samuel Johnson in his *A Dictionary of the English Language* (1755) defined honour as "nobility of soul, scorn of meanness, reputation, fame and privileges of rank or birth". The *Chambers Encyclopaedic English Dictionary* (1994) states that honour is "a source of fame, glory, great respect, distinction, pleasure and privilege, a high reward and high standard of moral behaviour". From these very respectable sources, it can be seen that from the very high level to the common level, the concept of honour derives from the personal human conditions of dignity, worthy characteristics, moral conduct, and a sense of obligation to the ethical excellence which sets the rank of nobility.

Honour, although it seems a simple word from these two definitions, nevertheless sets two different responsibilities and practices for men and for women. For example, the *Chambers Encyclopaedic English Dictionary* includes among its definitions of honour that it is "a woman's chastity or her reputation", and Johnson's *Dictionary* states that honour, "in connection to women is chastity or virginity or in case of a married woman fidelity/loyalty". The classical notion of honour has obtained greater value in terms of man's superiority, which makes woman an instrument for maintaining and purifying honour and, in the case of ruining honour, she has to be punished. The notion that honour is hidden in men's dignity and women's chastity has been accepted generally all over the world.

Interestingly, the treatment of honour expands to include in eastern values the same connotations as shown in the western definitions above. Hussain (1999) stated that "the whole concept of honour is based on a tribal, pre-Islamic world view in which woman is considered as a chattel with no mind or will of her own", and therefore men have to set boundaries and limit women's actions in order to keep their family's honour safe. This concept of honour made male family members responsible for regulating and guarding not only their family's female members' moral and sexual behaviour, but also extended to their dress codes and social conduct. Because of its abstracted and multi-faceted implications related to the two gendered divisions among human beings, honour codes vary from culture to culture, group to group and person to person, and it is this concept which has nurtured and developed the culture of honour-related violence.

Research into honour killings has suggested that the history of honour killing goes back as far as 1200 BCE and was practised under the rule of Hammurabi and in other Assyrian tribes (Khouri, 2003). Goldstein (2002:12) found its roots in ancient Rome where, for the first time in history, women's sexual conduct became subject to legislation during the reign of Augustus (27 BCE to 14 CE). According to the law, the husband

and father of an adulteress were given the right to kill her to preserve the sexual purity of a woman as a way of keeping her kinsmen's level of honour high. Laws which associated insult, shame and honour with the actions of women were certainly not limited to the Roman Empire; in medieval Europe, early Jewish law mandated death by stoning for an adulterous wife and her partner (Cantarella, 1991). Under Ottoman rule, a killer would "sprinkle his victim's blood on his clothes and parade through the streets displaying the bloody murder weapon to increase his honour" (Kressel, 1981:143). In Arab societies, if a woman has caused shame to the family, a man or men must react accordingly otherwise they would be the cause of adding disgrace (Giant, 1979, cited in Baker *et al.*, 1999). This brief historical overview confirms that the concept and the ritual act of honour killing with legislative backing is very old and is not limited to any specific part of the world (Khan, 2006; Welchman & Hossain, 2005).

On 7 December 1995, the widely watched news channel CNN broadcast an intensive report entitled 'Honour Killing: a Brutal Tribal Custom'. The documentary was a compilation of data about the Muslim Arab communities residing in Israeli and Palestinian territories. That documentary made honour-related crimes and killings the topic of debate all over the world and numerous western television channels, as well as the print media, began to reveal the countries where honour killing is still rife, despite a serious horrified reaction from very many directions. The greatest numbers of reports about honour killings appeared principally in Central Asia and in Islamic countries such as Pakistan, Jordan, Bangladesh and Palestine. Jafri (2008:27) commented that "This led to the belief in the popular imagination that honour killing is somehow related to Islam". Khan (2006), however, named two Islamic countries, Malaysia and Mauritius, where honour-related killings have never occurred. Cases of honour killings have been reported all around the world; the statistics show that honour killings take place in India, in the Middle East, in Latin America, in Europe and in North America. However, more than 90% of the reported cases are either in Islamic countries or within Muslim families which have emigrated to other countries (Shoro, 2017).

Pakistan is one of the eight South Asian countries which have been in the news for their high numbers of honour-killing cases. The Islamic Republic of Pakistan comprises four mainly Muslim-dominated provinces with a population of approximately 176 million. All of the provinces have their own distinctive cultures, as their names show. For example, Punjab has Panjabi culture, Balochistan has Balochi culture, Sindh has Sindhi culture and Khyber Pakhtunkhuwah has Pakhtun/Pashtun culture. Underneath these cultures there are a number of sub-cultures which each have their own different moral and traditional values. The Pakistani community is divided into urban and rural classes; the urban population is much more privileged than the rural population. The women who live in the cities enjoy better work opportunities, education and freedom than those who live in rural villages. Khan (2011) stated that "For the past many years, families belonging to the *wadera* (feudal) classes have been ruling the country, whereas the poor and oppressed people are deprived of their basic rights. The country's fundamentalist forces and the Army Generals are the protectors of this medieval feudal system; therefore, they are against those who speak against oppression" (Khan, *On-line magazine*, 2 March 2011).

In this patriarchal culture, the significant influences on women's lives are education, class differences, the rural/urban division, tribal and feudal norms and uneven socio-economic conditions. Except for a few influential, elite groups of women, the social set-up begins with unwritten slavery for women and ends abruptly at the authoritative attitude of men. Despite some attempts made by various democratic governments to elevate the status of women in rural Sindh, the situation is not promising and there is an urgent need for a multi-dimensional change in order for ordinary women's lives to be made better. Khan (2007:94) pointed out that "Women are considered the property of the males in their family. The concept of ownership has turned women into a commodity which can be exchanged, bought and sold and killed". Hearn (1996) commented that "Men's day-to-day domination was routinely reinforced by the state, for example, in the avoidance of intervention in 'marital disputes' by the police. The position of women was also generally weak in terms of divorce proceedings and the award and receipt of maintenance" (Hearn, 1996:25).

Today, Pakistan has a high number of honour killings, both reported and unreported. Even so, it is interesting to note that from the country's creation in 1947 to the late 1980s there was no terminology such as 'killing in the name of honour' or 'honour killing' known or used by the common people. For the last four decades, the rising number of honour killings has been primarily interlinked with changes in the secular law of Pakistan introduced by the military regime of the dictator General Zia-ul-Haq,[1] who came to power through an overnight military coup and

---

[1] General Muhammad Zia-ul-Haq was the sixth President of Pakistan from 1977 until his death in 1988, having declared martial law for the third time in the country's history in 1977. He was Pakistan's longest-serving head of state, ruling

promptly imprisoned the very first democratically elected prime minister[2] of Pakistan.

"Upon independence in 1947, Pakistan inherited the common law and criminal justice system modelled after the English legal system" (Irfan, 2008:8). It was the British Penal Code (1860) which became the formal legal system (statute, secular state law) of Pakistan. According to that Code, the laws defining murder stipulated two distinct aspects. First, *mens rea*,[3] which means that if the intention of killing is there but the act is not performed, then there is no offence. Second, *actus reus*,[4] which means that if the act is performed without intention, it is *khata*[5] but not an offence. Under this law, if someone intentionally kills a person (on any pretext) it could be considered a murder.

However, in order to make Pakistan an Islamic state by incorporating Sharia[6] law into the country's legal system, in 1978, General Zia established "*Shariat* Appellate Benches, grafted onto Pakistan's four High Courts" (Hussain, 2005:400) to determine cases based on the teachings of the Qur'an and the *Sunnah*.[7] A *Sharia* council was appointed to bring the

---

for eleven years. He is most noted for his efforts to bring religion into mainstream society within Pakistan and in foreign policy, for his close relationship with the United States and support for the so-called Afghan Mujahedeen resistance against the Soviets in Afghanistan.

[2] Zulfiqar Ali Bhutto, a social, secular political leader of Pakistan, served as President of Pakistan from 1971 to 1973 and as Prime Minister from 1973 to 1977. In 1977, he was ousted in a military coup mounted by General Muhammed Zia-ul-Haq and was arrested. He was hanged on 4 April 1979 for allegedly ordering the murder of a political opponent in 1974.

[3] Latin: 'mental guilt', an 'intention'.

[4] Latin: 'a criminal act'.

[5] 'an accident'.

[6] Islamic religion-based law is called *Sharia*. These laws are derived from the Qur'an, *Sunnah* (the practices of the Prophet) and *Hadith* (sayings of the Prophet). The modern forms of *Sharia* law have been derived from various schools of legal interpretations created by four religious scholars in different periods of early Muslim history and in the context of different socio-economic and political systems, Hanafi (699-767CE), Maliki (713-795CE), Shafi (767-820CE) and Hanbali (780-813CE). In Pakistan, the state derives dominantly from the Hanafi school of thought, which is Sunni ideology (the dominant group of Muslims in Pakistan) (Khan, 2006: 229).

[7] *Sunnah,* (plural *Sunan*) is the verbally transmitted record of the teachings, deeds and sayings of the prophet Muhammad (peace be upon Him) defined as a path, a way and a manner of life.

state's legal statutes into alignment with Islamic doctrine (Hussain, 2007). The purpose of creating a *Shariat* Appellate Bench of the Supreme Court was to give it status as the final authority in *Sharia* cases.

In his bid to run the country by Sharia law, whatever ordinances General Zia implanted into the constitution of Pakistan caused great damage to women's already inferior position to that of men. To strengthen patriarchy, the far-reaching repercussions of the misogynist legal acts put women into miserable conditions where their lives were at the mercy of their male relatives. These ordinances ran contrary to human rights and totally undermined the efforts of the very first elected secular democratic political party to empower women in the newly created state.

The most controversial of the new ordinances were the *Hudood*[8] Ordinance (1979) and the *Qanun-e-Amna*[9] Order (1984). These ordinances added new criminal offences of adultery and fornication to Pakistani law and new punishments of whipping, amputation and stoning to death (Lau, 2007). The provisions relating to *zina*[10] were replaced by an ordinance with punishments of a flogging of 100 lashes for unmarried offenders (women and men found guilty of having extra-marital relations) and stoning to death for married offenders (Heng & Liew, 2010).

"More worrisome for human rights and women's rights advocates, some lawyers and politicians, was the incarceration of thousands of rape victims on charges of *zina*" (Heng & Liew, 2010:360). All of these *hudood* punishments were dependent on Islamic *hudd*[11] proof. This proof requires

---

[8] *Hudood* means 'limits' or 'restrictions', as in limits of acceptable behaviour in Islamic law.

[9] This is 'blasphemy', the act of insulting or showing contempt for God or for religious or holy persons, or towards something considered sacred, with penalties ranging from a fine to death. From 1987 to 2014, over 1300 people were accused of blasphemy, mostly from non-Muslim religious minorities. The vast majority of the accusations were lodged for desecration of the Qur'an (*BBC News*, 6 November 2014).

[10] The Arabic word *zina* means all sexual intercourse between a man and a woman who are not married to one another through a *nikah* (marriage contract). It includes extra-marital and pre-marital sex. "According to Islam, '*zina*' constituted social suicide – an entire society commits suicide over time if it allows fornication and adultery to go unpunished in the Islamic style" (Mirza, 2008). *Hudood* Ordinances are laws in Pakistan which were enacted in 1979. They replaced parts of the secular, British-era Pakistan Penal Code. Before the implementation of the *Hudood* Ordinances, the state had nothing to do with *zina*.

[11] 'The limit'.

four Muslim men of good repute to testify as witnesses to the crime in question. In practice, uncorroborated testimony by women was inadmissible in *hudood* crimes (Hussain, 2005). So in cases of rape, victims were sometimes charged with fornication and jailed whereas their rapists were freed because the women could not comply with the *hudd* requirement of having four reputable Muslim men testifying to the rape.

The irony of the situation is this: how can a raped woman produce 'four truthful' and 'abstaining from major sins' eyewitnesses as section 8 (b) of the ordinance demands? And they all "must have witnessed the penetration" (Jafri, 2008; Khan, 2006; Warraich, 2005). As a result, women preferred to keep silent even when they had been gang-raped. These ordinances were not the only discriminatory acts which paved the way for extreme violence against women in order to push them to the state of segregation in Pakistan. According to Shah (1998:56), "statutory law under the *Zina* Ordinance does not strictly differentiate between rape and fornication either; in fact, if a raped woman cannot prove that she did not consent to intercourse, she is considered to have committed *zina*, fornication, which attracts severe punishments. It does not dishonour the rapist". Both of these laws have had a devastating effect on the rights of women: "Girls as young as twelve were also sometimes jailed and prosecuted for having extra-marital intercourse because the ordinance abolished Pakistan's statutory rape law" (*Human Rights Watch*, 1999:18). The incorporation of the *Sharia* laws into the legal and judicial system of Pakistan actually authorized men to control the actions of their kinswomen with the backing of the state. After the death of General Zia in 1988, inconsistency and instability has prevailed in Pakistani laws. In fact, his death was not the end of his era. The greatest example of this was the promulgation of *Qisas*[12] and *Diyat*[13] Ordinances in September 1990 by his

---

[12] *Qisas* is an Islamic term meaning retaliation or retribution in kind, or revenge, an eye for an eye, nemesis or retributive justice. It is a category of crimes in Islamic jurisprudence in which *Sharia* allows equal retaliation as the punishment. The *Qisas* principle is available against the accused, to the victim or victim's heirs, when a Muslim is murdered, suffers bodily injury or suffers property damage. In the case of murder, *Qisas* means the right of a murder victim's nearest relative or *wali* (legal guardian) to, if the court approves, take the life of the killer (Encyclopaedia Britannica).

[13] In Islamic *Sharia* law, *Diyat* is the financial compensation paid to the victim or heirs of a victim in the cases of murder, bodily harm or property damage. It is an alternative punishment to *Qisas* (equal retaliation). In Arabic, the word means both blood money and ransom, and it is spelled sometimes as *Diya*, *Diyah* or *Diyeh* (Spevack, 2015:81). *Diyat* compensation rates, under *Sharia* law, have historically

successor as president, Saeed Ishaq Khan (Shoro, 2017). The term was defined by section 299, sub-section (k):

> *Qisas* means punishment by causing similar hurt in the same part of the body of the convict as he has caused to the victim or by causing his death if he has committed *qatl-e-amd* in exercise of the right of the victim or a *wali*.[14]
>
> a: In the case of *qatl-e-amd*, an adult sane *wali* may, at any time and without any compensation, waive his right of *qisas* (Section 309-1).
>
> b: In the case of *qatl-e-amd*, an adult sane *wali* may, at any time on accepting *badl-e-sulh*,[15] waive his right of *qisas* (Section 310 -1).

The meaning of *qisas* with reference to honour killing has two components. One is that if there is sufficient evidence of *qatl-e-amd*, it carries the death penalty. The second is that it is the right of a victim or his/her *wali* that the death penalty be awarded to the murderer. Murder is not prohibited in all the major religions but no state in the modern world allows or condones the murder of anyone on any pretext. The punishment for murder is also prescribed everywhere in the world. Thus, this ordinance has deep and far-reaching implications. It is interpreted to mean that if the legal heir of the deceased does not want to exercise his right, the death penalty cannot be awarded. And if the legal heirs of the deceased reach a compromise with the killer, they can withdraw their right of *qisas* and therefore there is no death penalty. Hence, the law has been codified in the following two sections of the Pakistan Penal Code (PPC) *Qisas and Diyat Ordinance*. In addition to this, in section 300 of the PPC, there is an exemption of "grave and sudden provocation", defined as unintentional murder: "A male relative can also kill a woman on the pretext of 'sudden provocation' or 'fit of anger' or 'heat of passion'" (Khan, 2006:175). Thus, the ordinance proved a fatal blow to the already poor status of women. Hussaini (2009:112) reported that it had been confirmed by Government of Pakistan that between 1998 and 2003, 4,101 people were killed in honour-related crimes. *Human Rights Watch*, the *Human Rights*

---

varied based on the gender and religion of the victim. Muslim women victims have typically been compensated at half the rate of Muslim male victims, whilst non-Muslims' compensation rates have varied between 1/16th to half of a Muslim, for an equivalent case (Terrill, 2012:559).

[14] An adult legal heir.

[15] 'In lieu of peace'. Compoundable offences are those in which the parties to a dispute can reach a compromise and proven killers can seek or buy pardon from the victim's family.

Commission of Pakistan (HRCP) and *Amnesty International* all produced annual reports on the statistics of killings on the pretext of honour throughout the 1990s and onwards all reported a constant rise in which, according to a representative of the HRCP (2014), 70% of the victims of honour killings were women and 30% were men.

I conducted the fieldwork for my PhD study of honour killing in northern Sindh, the hub of honour killing, where it is referred to as *karo-kari*.[16] The term *karo* is used to describe the man involved in an act of adultery whereas *kari* defines an immoral and adulterous woman. On the other hand, this term shows racist discrimination too because in the Sindhi language, *karo* literally means the colour black. This term indeed is a symbol of inferiority (Hoodbai, 2000:25). As I have discussed earlier, the word 'honour' and the meanings attached to it are largely misogynistic and anyone is free to adapt it to fit their cultural norm. The specific meaning attached to the word honour, which affects both the social and personal standing of an individual or a community, is unique in the context of the northern part of Sindh.

In general, men in the area of my research need to have control and possession over the social and sexual conduct of their female relatives. The term 'honour' is linked largely with female behaviour in this region. This division creates a kind of hurdle to family relations because it prevents family members, whether male or female, from being able to earn respect on equal footings. In this patriarchal culture, if a woman wants to be an honourable woman, she must conform to the masculine definition of honour and she should also even maintain a vigilance over the other female members of her family and go against them when the male expectation requires it.

The centre of my research was Sindh, one of the four provinces of Pakistan, which has a fascinating history of civilization. Throughout the centuries it has remained a land of poets, mystics, intellectuals, aesthetes, lovers and secular writers. The history of Sindh provides fertile ground for researchers to investigate what it was that introduced such appalling crimes in a land of peace.

Changes occurred in Sindh's geography and social life as a result of various invasions and migrations of people (Fredunbeg, 1900; Durant,

---

[16] *Karo-kari* is an act of murder in which a person or maybe two are killed for his or her actual or perceived immoral behaviour.

1935; Lambrick, 1986; LeBlanc, 2013; Wright, 2009). Hence, Lashari (1992:32) considered *"karo-kari* an immoral perception of honour" and showed his surprise by asking "how has this norm taken place on the soil of love, brotherhood and tolerance?"[17]

In today's Sindh, honour killing is one of many persistent social evils. "According to a women's organization in Sindh, in 1996 alone, 148 women were killed in the name of honour and more than 300 cases of *karo-kari* occurred. Another organization based in Sindh reported that during three months of 1999, 132 cases of *karo-kari* were registered" (Khan, 2006:150-151). A report by the Aurat foundation in Karachi (19 July 2012) stated that "A total of 8,539 cases of violence against women were reported in the country during 2011, which was roughly 6.74% higher than the number of cases reported during the previous year. The largest number (133) of cases of violence against women in Sindh was reported in Sukkur, closely followed by Jacobabad (132) and Ghotki (121)". Nonetheless, almost every research body has stated that the numbers of recorded cases of honour killing are far fewer than those of unreported or unrecorded cases.

Previous studies have suggested that honour killing is acceptable in societies which have a gender-biased structure and in which men guard women's sexual and moral actions. Along with this generalised definition of honour killing, some stereotypes which are believed to be the main reasons for honour killing have been listed as choice of marriage, refusal of an arranged marriage, choosing a marriage partner against the wishes of the family, seeking divorce from a husband, being a victim of sexual assault or rape, committing adultery and having illicit relations, getting rid of a wife or any other woman of the family, desiring a second marriage, property saving, or if a wife gives birth to a female child, brings a small dowry or maybe even presents an unsweetened cup of tea to her husband. A woman can be killed under the plea of honour if she serves food late, goes to her parents' home without seeking the permission of her husband, or interrupts or refuses any small thing to her husband. Who can stop men from killing a woman? (Thebo, 2000; Khokhar, 2002).[18] Another common trend which was identified by Noor (2000:68) is that after the first night of marriage, the next morning could be a decisive time for the future of the bride. If the newly-wed groom confirms her virginity, she will survive, but if he does not for one reason or another, she can be murdered as *kari*. In

---

[17] My translation.
[18] My translation.

this kind of murder, the bride's brothers and father sometimes also take part.[19] Honour killings may be carried out for other less usual reasons which may have not clearly been depicted, such as planned killngs for the sake of money, personal gain or personal enmity. Some murders have strange but thought-provoking reasons. For example, Hina (2000:21) stated that "a man killed his wife as he claimed he had seen her committing adultery in a dream".[20] In another case, Shaikh (2000:62) explained how a man found a young stranger offering a prayer in a graveyard. Because the stranger was standing near the grave of the man's recently dead wife, he caught him and claimed that he must have been *karo* with his wife otherwise why would he be offering a prayer over her grave? "The stranger was taken to the landowner for a decision in *jirga*, and there he was fined heavily in order to avoid being killed; he paid the money and thus saved his life."[21]

As I was researching and writing about the reasons for such killings, a Sindhi newspaper, *Kawish*, published details of three cases of honour killing in which two women were killed and a third was brutally tortured. In the first case, reported on 5 January 2012, a 35-year-old woman, a mother of seven, was killed by her brother and nephew for her second marriage after the death of her first husband. Her second husband had also divorced her two days before, after receiving death threats and the registration of a fake case of abduction by her brother. She went back to her parents where bullets killed her and her body was not received by any of her relatives. She was from Ghotki in Sindh. In the second case, in Hyderabad in Sindh, a 35-year-old woman, a mother of eight children, was tortured for about two hours by local *waderas* by calling her *kari*. Her clothes were ripped off by villagers and she had lain helpless on a road for ten hours. Later, the police took her to a hospital. This case reveals that the licence to beat and kill women had been assumed not only by the family's male members but also by the local landlords. On 6 January 2012, another woman from Ghotki was murdered on a charge of *kari*. She was at her parents' home when her husband, along with a few armed men, burst in and, calling her *kari*, tried to kill her. In an attempt to escape, she hid under the bed; they dragged her out and opened fire on her. Her younger brother and her mother, holding the Qur'an in an attempt to plead for the life of her daughter, were tortured. The dead woman's brother registered a case against his sister's husband and stated that it was because of sexual

---

[19] My translation.
[20] My translation.
[21] My translation.

abuse by her father-in-law that she had come to them and that she was not *kari*. No-one from the village interfered.

Many examples show that in a state of fighting or peace, enmity or friendship, ultimately women suffer. For example, a brother killed his sister after accusing her of being *kari* with his enemy in order to deny her the right to some property. Thus, his two purposes were served: the property remained his and an opponent was also killed. If a man's proposal of marriage is refused by a family, he kills one of her family's women and then kills any man of the family which refused his proposal in order to take revenge. In offences of this type, usually a *jirga*[22] decides that one woman from the family of a man who has been murdered as *karo* must be given to the murderer (the person who killed in order to save his honour) to restore peace. Money is given to the *kari's* husband or, if she was unmarried, then to her father, but the lion's share is taken by the members of the *jirgas*. In all situations of this kind, it is the women who suffer.

The principal question which I had to address was how to carry out research on such a sensitive subject in order to open up new dimensions on the issue. I had seen research theses and papers in which data were collected from those who were directly or indirectly involved in honour killing, including the relatives of the accused, an adulterer and adulteress, the members of the investigation team, the police and the community, eye-witnesses to honour killing and the members of the *jirgas*. For me, the most important thing was to reach those who have been directly affected by a killing in the name of honour so that the circumstances of their involvement might be heard. How do they see the tradition? What does a killer think about and then kill someone or a few people? How do those who evade a killing by chance see the issue and what do they expect of life in the future? Do women who have been threatened with death have any secure future? What are the reasons behind these killings? Most importantly, I wanted the answers to these crucial questions to come either from the killers themselves or from women who had been threatened with death in order to understand the phenomenon of honour killing. The data collected in this way were analysed but the analysis could be subject to bias as in such analyses the researcher or researchers have to scrutinise and

---

[22] The *jirga* is a local customary tribal court. It is an illegal local law-enforcing and decision-making assembly or tribal council. The informal law system which runs parallel to the state's formal law is tribal law (village courts). Its judgments come through *jirga* and are implemented by tribal/feudal leaders and their henchmen.

evaluate the findings in their own way, according to their own understanding of the issue, the culture, tradition, internalization and socialization. No matter how hard researchers endeavour to maintain the highest level of neutrality and impartiality, they have to explore the data and interpret and explain it in their own way. At this point, the researcher becomes responsible for data and the data loses its originality. The original data, in every research study, becomes of secondary importance and it is the analysis which takes the major place. The purpose of this book is to let the reader go through the original data which I gathered ... every single word of the interviews which I held can be heard by the readers and by future researchers in order for them to comprehend the actual and basic motivations, objectives and consequences of honour killing.

Cottle (1978) insisted that one of the extensively acknowledged aims of feminist research is to allow people to speak for themselves ... and in return to communicate to them, in conversation as well as in writing, that it is their words which I am seeking and not material for the generation of something which will ultimately transcend their words and hence their lives (Cottle, 1978:xii).

In terms of planning and designing an appropriate research method, Mason (1996:7) described "how researchers might determine what their research is 'really about', and what is its 'intellectual puzzle'". The main purpose of my research and, to my understanding, the intellectual puzzle of the subject being researched is the most crucial issue to be considered. It requires a passionate and careful strategy for sorting out the challenges of the topic. The intellectual puzzle for me is why the menace of honour killing exists on such a large scale but has still not been understood, and why, despite so much research on this subject, controlling and ending honour killing seems to be so difficult. My intellectual puzzle is how these elements are embedded in the lives of the women who are threatened with death and the men who kill women in the name of honour. It was vital for me to let people speak out as much as they could. In order to enable them to open their hearts, I needed the best possible research methodology. For me in this situation, informal, semi-structured, open-ended, long interviews seemed the perfect solution.

I chose to conduct qualitative research because it is a flexible and contextual technique: Mason (1996:3) stated that qualitative research does not characterise a set of techniques or philosophies but is instead the result of "a wide range of intellectual and disciplinary traditions" and that "social studies rely quite heavily on qualitative ways of knowing". About the use of qualitative in-depth interviews, Letherby (2003:84) commented that this approach is not only viewed by many as "politically correct" and "morally responsible", but is also clearly "very relevant in terms of the development of an approach which is grounded in the experience of women". Qualitative research relies on four methods, as suggested by Marshal and Rossman (2006:97): interviewing as a researcher, direct observation, in-depth interviewing and data analysis. In my book *Honour Killing in the Second Decade of the 21st Century*, I followed the method which Creswell (2003:xxiv) suggested: "collecting of open ended data, analysing of text, representation of information and personal interpretation of the findings, and report writing differ from the traditional, quantitative approach, and all inform the qualitative procedure". Along with this guideline, I was further steered by a suggestion made by Silverman (2001:11) who stated that "The four major methods used by qualitative researchers are observation, analysing texts and documents, interviews and recording and transcribing".

On preparing the framework for designing a research methodology, Creswell (2003:xxiii) advised that "This requires identifying the research problem or issue, framing the problem within the existing literature, pointing out deficiencies in the literature, and targeting the study for an audience". When I was designing the fieldwork, I visualized the whole picture of the set-up of the honour-killing cases, the perpetrators and the women survivors who had been threatened with death. Finding interview participants was one of my major concerns, along with the methodological concerns and ethical issues involved in conducting feminist research, as well as some reflections on data collection and analysis. Although some of the data which I acquired was used in the analysis and writing-up process, the untouched, unused and unanalysed data (accounts and interviews) are still there for readers to analyse and comprehend for themselves without the intervention of any researcher.

Deciding who my participants and interviewees should be was the first task. I intended to gather information from those who were directly affected by honour-related crimes. For that purpose, I thought of the two groups which, in my opinion, would be the best people to talk with: women who had been threatened with death, and perpetrators and killers. I decided that the location of the data collection was to be upper and northern Sindh, mainly the cities of Larkana and Jacobabad, the most notorious area in regard to the number of honour killings. My fieldwork research confirmed that accused women could be found in shelters provided for them (such a refuge is called a *darulaman*), and that convicted killers could be found in the jails, so my second reason for choosing districts in northern Sindh was that Larkana and Sukkur both have refuges and Sukkur and Jacobabad have jails, and these refuges and jails were where I needed to conduct the interviews. To access the shelters, the jails and the killers, I had to seek the co-operation of two trusted local intermediaries in the relevant districts of upper Sindh. Their meetings with the higher authorities of the shelters and jails to arrange and confirm a visit made my access possible. It was also equally important for me to speak with and record the accounts of killers convicted of honour killings outside the jails who had either never been arrested or had been imprisoned for only a short period and then set free. When the intermediaries contacted them with the help of their friends' network, many showed their willingness to talk to me about their honour killing experience.

I was aware of the norms of the qualitative methods which a researcher has to think about and plan in great detail in terms of the steps and the research issues, and the need to be flexible and open to change. In general, a qualitative researcher does not develop hypotheses or presuppositions and cannot anticipate all the potential issues and problems in advance, but must let the data do the explaining. "Hypotheses, measurements, samples and instruments are the wrong guidelines. Instead you need to learn about a world you understand by encountering it first hand and making some sense out of it" (Agar, 1986:12). How to devise an interview theme was a significant task. My greatest responsibility as a researcher was to focus on people's perceptions and the feelings which they expressed in order to study how the participants understood themselves and their world. For searching and researching the lives of people, interviews are regarded as the most useful method. Kvale (1996:6) stated that in order to research the lives of interviewees with respect and sensitivity, the technique of face-to-face interviewing has been widely adopted by feminist researchers.

The Interview Themes

In order to understand the circumstances behind the killings, I designed my interview questions in a flexible way, structured to be informal and open-ended so that I might cover nearly all aspects of my interviewees' lives. When I was designing the questions for the women who had been labelled as *karis* and were in protective custody in refuges, my idea was to explore the domestic and social situations which had eventually forced them to seek refuge. My questions for the women were designed to explore their lives from their childhood and their life before marriage to the mode of marriage, life after marriage, their view of the norm of honour and their hopes for their future life (*see* Table 1).

Table 1: Interview themes for women

Themes	*Sub-topics*
Life before marriage.	Tribal and parental background, siblings, childhood, favourite games, education and work.
Life after marriage.	Mode of marriage, relations with the husband and in-laws, financial situation, children.
How violence, honour and collusion are embedded in their lives.	Views about men, honour and honour killing. Reasons why and how they were threatened with death.
Future expectations.	After leaving the *darulaman*, what would they want their life to be like and what hopes do they have for the future.

The interview questions which I designed for men were slightly different for two reasons; first, according to whom a man had killed (mother, sister, wife, daughter or other kin) and second, whether the killer had killed both *karo* and *kari* or just *kari* (as the literature suggests that a *karo* is seldom killed alone). In the interviews with men who had killed in the name of honour, either a woman as *kari* or both *karo-kari*, I set out to explore their parental, tribal, social and educational backgrounds and to extend this to their family life and their mode of marriage and then to the actual killing. This included their standards about honour and women in order to explore the detailed circumstances behind such killings by asking questions about the justifications for the killing (*see* Table 2).

Table 2: Interview themes for men

Themes	Sub-topics
Life before marriage.	Tribal and parental background, siblings, childhood, favourite games, education and profession.
Life after marriage.	Mode of marriage, wife's and in-laws' attitudes, children.
How violence, honour and collusion are embedded in their lives.	Views about women, the concept of adultery and honour killing. What made them become killers?
Advantages and disadvantages of the killing.	Life in jail or life after the murder. Justifications for killing. Future plans.

Mason (2002:226) stated that interviewing is "the art of knowledge excavation and the task is to enable the interviewee to give the relevant information in as accurate and complete manner as possible". I handled this challenge by including almost all the possible questions in every interview and by varying the way in which I asked the questions in order to meet the different reactions which I encountered. I respected one of the widely acknowledged aims of feminist research which is, as Cottle (1978:xii) explained and I described earlier, to allow people to speak for themselves and not merely gather material for the generation of something which would move beyond their words and their lives.

With the extended support of both of my intermediary friends, I became able to interview convicted killers outside and inside the jails and women who had been accused as *karis* and had evaded death only narrowly. Technically, therefore, interviews were conducted with three groups of people; women who had been threatened with death and who were taking refuge in three different shelters; convicted killers in two jails of upper Sindh; and killers who were not in jail. The whole chronological process, from my fieldwork design to the obstacles which I came across when contacting the relevant people and conducting the interviews, is not relevant here as I do not want to create any barriers between the reader and the interviewees. For the same reason, no discussion of the data analysis or the writing-up will be included in this book. Because I am part of the same culture, tradition and society as those whom I interviewed, it was a big challenge for me to not to say something but to remain silent, but I think that the personal accounts which I uncovered on such burning issues should be presented unadorned to the reader for analysis. In this book, by reading the accounts of women threatened with death and of convicted killers inside and outside jail, you will come to know and realise what honour killing actually is and what the beliefs are which are letting the inhumane practice of killing for the sake of honour exist. The first chapter in this book is comprised of the interviews with those men who had killed one person or a number of people allegedly on the pretext of honour killing and were not in any jail. In the second chapter you will read the accounts of convicted men who were in jail serving sentences on charges of murder, and in the third chapter, women who had been threatened with death (as *karis*) and were living temporarily in three different shelters will be presented. The conclusion consists of my personal opinions about honour killing in Sindh on the basis of my research findings.

In this particular area of Sindh, where a person's reputation, respect and identification are strongly connected with his or her caste, it is important to explain the significance of the particular caste to which someone belongs and what it demonstrates. The significance of mentioning the caste of the interviewees is that it shows their tribal and communal affiliation as well as their social class, their financial status and their geographical origin. There is a general understanding in Sindh that honour killing is a Balochi custom. However, my data support the fact that there are killings for the sake of honour in both communities and that Sindhi and Balochi killings have a similar ratio, which is visible through their people's castes. In this book, almost fifty percent of the male participants who killed people on the pretext of honour and of the female participants who faced death threats were Sindhis, as their castes identified them. Nevertheless, the castes of the participants have been changed into the names of other castes for the sake of anonymity with a careful assessment that a Sindhi caste should be changed to another Sindhi caste and a Balochi caste should be changed to another Balochi caste.

Sardars and *waderas* are self-appointed bullies who wield enormous power over the interviewees' lives. In the tribal system, the *sardars* and *waderas* live like kings of their particular areas. Many rich *sardars* and *waderas* stand for election to political posts locally, regionally and nationally. For decades they have been elected as members of the national and provincial assemblies and the senate and have acquired enormous power. Needless to say, the democratic system is hijacked in their hands and the powerless and poverty-ridden people have no other option except to vote for them and choose them as their representatives and thus increase the powers of their enemies in the name of democracy. When these *waderas* die, their sons automatically inherit their positions and play a similar role.

All of the interviews with both genders were held in the Sindhi language. A few interviewees answered in Seriki, a language which I understand well, as its structure and grammar are very close to Sindhi and Punjabi, and I am fluent in both of these languages. However, I transcribed and translated all the accounts into English. Because of the physical, financial, moral and social situation of my participants, many of them used very emotive language including slang terms. As the only translator, there was a risk that I could have used words in English which were more emotive than that the original words used. However, to the best of my ability, I took great care in the translation to avoid any type of bias. The main purpose of translating their versions in the most appropriate way possible was my determination to let their stories be heard, complete with hesitations and repetitions, and the need to reflect something of the character of the speakers in the language style and the words which they used to tell their stories, and the need for me to communicate their actual feelings and thoughts to the reader. To respect their confidentiality and not to compromise their anonymity, not only have the names of my participants been anonymised, but also the names of their husbands, wives, parents, brothers and other relatives. The cities which they mention have been given fictitious names. Likewise, their castes have been changed, but the Sindhi castes have been exchanged with Sindhi castes whereas the Balochi castes have been replaced with Balochi castes. In addition, the reason for the detailed personal descriptions which I provide (their hair, clothes, jewellery, appearance, physical disabilities) is to make the reader feel acquainted with the participants and to add to the overall impression of a complex culture and society which I want to depict.

References

Agar, M. (1986). *Speaking of Ethnography*. London: Sage.
Allen, R. (ed.) (1994). *The Chambers Encyclopaedic English Dictionary*. Chambers: the University of Michigan.
Baker, N.V., Gregware, P.R. & Cassidy, M.A. (1999). Family killing fields, *Violence against Women*, 5(2): 164-184.
Cantarella, E. (1991). 'Homicide of honour: the development of Italian adultery law over millennia'. In Kertzer, D. & Saller, R.P. (eds), *The Family in Italy: From Antiquity to the Present*. (pp.229-244). New Haven, CT: Yale University Press.

Cottle, T.J. (1978). *Private Lives and Public Accounts*. London: Franklin Watts.

Creswell, J.W. (2003). *Research Design: Qualitative, Quantitative, and Mixed Methods Approaches.* London: Sage.

Durant, W. (1935). *Our Oriental Heritage*. New York: Simon and Schuster.

Fredunbeg, M.K. (trans.) (1900). 'The Chach-Nama: an ancient history of Sind' (*Tarekh-e-Hind wa Sindh*). Originally written in Arabic by Kàzí Ismáíl in the early eighth century, translated into Persian by Ali Kufi in 1216). Commissioners Press. India: Bazar Delhi.

Goldstein, M. (2002). The biological roots of heat of passion crimes and honour killing, *Politics and the Life Sciences 21*(2). Available at: www.politicsandthelifesciences.org/image/0209_Cover_Full.pdf. [Accessed: 13 December 2014].

Hanmer, J. (1996). 'Women and violence: Commonalities and diversities'. In Hearn, J., Fawcett, B., Featherstone, B. & Toft, C., *Violence and Gender Relations: Theories and Interventions*. London: Sage.

Heng, M.S. & Liew, T.C. (2010). *State and Secularism: Perspectives from Asia*. Singapore: World Scientific Publishing Company.

Hearn, J. (1996). *The Problem of Men's Violence*. London: Sage.

Hina, Z. (2000). 'Burning women in the intensity of honour'. In Wistro, S. *Karo Kari.* Karachi: Weer Publications.

Hoodbai, N. (2000). 'The case'. In Wistro, S. *Karo Kari.* Karachi: Weer Publications.

The Human Rights Commission of Pakistan (2014). State of human rights in 2013. Lahore: Mission Road.

Hussain, H. (2005). *Pakistan: Between Mosque and Military*. Washington: United Book Press.

Hussain, R. (1999). Community perceptions of reasons for preference for consanguineous marriages in Pakistan, *Journal of Biosocial Science, 31*: 449-461.

Hussain, Z. (2007). *Frontline Pakistan: the Struggle with Militant Islam*. New York: Columbia University Press.

Hussaini, R. (2009). *Murder in the Name of Honour: the True Story of One Woman's Heroic Fight against an Unbelievable Crime*. Oxford: Oneworld Publications.

Irfan, H. (2008). 'Honour related violence against women in Pakistan'. Available at: http: www.lexisnexis.com/documents/pdf/20080924043437_large.pdf. [Accessed: 29 November 2012]. Paper prepared for the World Justice Forum, Vienna.

Jafri, A.H. (2008). *Honour Killing: Dilemma, Ritual, Understanding.* Karachi: Oxford University Press.
Johnson, S.A. (1755). *A Dictionary of the English Language.*
Khan, S. (2007). *Zinas: Transnational Feminism and the Moral Regulation of Pakistani Women.* Karachi: Oxford University Press.
Khan, T.S. (2006). *Beyond Honour: an Historical Materialist Explanation of Honour Related Violence.* Karachi: Oxford University Press.
Khan, A.H. (2011). Women in Sindh, *Islam Awareness.* Available at: http://www.islamawareness.net/Marriage/Quran/sindh.html. [Accessed: 12 January 2012].
Khokhar, N. (2002). *Musafir Muhabbaton.* Hyderabad: Roshni Publications.
Khouri, N. (2003). *Forbidden Love.* London: Doubleday.
Kressel, G.M. (1981). Sororicide/filiacide: Homicide for family honour, *Current Anthropology 22*(2): 141-158.
Kvale, S. (1996). *Interviews – an Introduction to Qualitative Research Interviewing.* Thousand Oaks, CA: Sage.
Lambrick, H.T. (1986). *History of Sindh* Vol. I. Sindhi Adabi Board: Pakistan.
Lang, S.D. (2000). *Sharaf Politics: Constructing Male Prestige in Israeli-Palestinian Society.* Cambridge, MA: Harvard University Press.
Lashari, F.M. (1992). *Paigham* (2004) Information Department Sindh: Pakistan. Vol. XI: 5-6.
LeBlanc, P.D. (2013). *Indus Epigraphic Perspectives: Exploring Past Decipherment Attempts and Possible New Approaches.* Thesis submitted to the Faculty of Graduate and Postdoctoral Studies, Department of Classics and Religious Studies Faculty of Arts University of Ottawa: Canada.
Letherby, G. (2003). *Feminist Research in Theory and Practice.* Philadelphia: Open University Press.
Lerner, G. (1986). *The Creation of Patriarchy.* New York: Oxford University Press.
Marshal, C. & Rossman, G.B. (2006). *Designing Qualitative Research.* London: Sage.
Mason, J. (2002). *Qualitative Researching* (2nd edn). London: Sage.
Noor, S. (2000). 'Karo Kari: a curse and a crime'. In Wistro, S., *Karo Kari.* Karachi: Weer Publications.
Shaikh, A.T. (2000). '*Karo-kari* or *karobari*'. In Wistro, S., *Karo Kari.* Karachi: Weer Publications.
Shoro, S. (2017). Honour Killing in the Second Decade of the 21st Century. UK: Cambridge Scholars Publishing.

Silverman, D. (2001). *Interpreting Qualitative Data: Methods for Analysing Talk, Text and Interaction*. London: Sage.

The Human Rights Commission of Pakistan, Report (1998/2002): *Violence against Women, 11*(4). Lahore: Maktaba Jadeed Press.

The Human Rights Commission of Pakistan (2012): 'State of human rights in 2011'. Available at: http://www.hrcpweb.org/pdf/. [Accessed: 21 April 2013].

Thebo, S. (2000). 'Honour killing: a research report of Amnesty International'. In Wistro, S., *Karo Kari*. Karachi: Weer Publications.

Warraich, S.A. (2005). 'Honour killing and the law in Pakistan'. In Welchman, L. & Hossain, S. (eds), *Honour*. London and New York: Spinifex Press.

Welchman, L. & Hossain, S. (2005). *Honour: Crimes, Paradigms and Violence against Women*. London and New York: Zed Books.

Wright, R.P. (2009). *The Ancient Indus: Urbanism, Economy, and Society.* Cambridge University Press, ISBN 978-0-521-57219-4, retrieved 14 September 2015.

Chapter One

The Accounts of Killers outside Jails

1: *Name*: Sajid, aged 83

The interview lasted for an hour and eleven minutes and took place at a local hotel.

Sajid looked neat and clean; he was wearing an off-white turban and a white dress and he had a wide kerchief on his shoulder.[23] He spoke confidently. He had joined a political party named *Awami Tehrik*[24] in 1974 and told me about the time he had spent with the farmer-Marxist activist Comrade Fazil Rahu.[25]

Q: *Assalam-u-alaikum.*

A: *Walaikum-assalam.*

Q: How are you doing?

A: Very well, thanks.

Q: Would you like to talk to me, *chacha*?[26]

A: Yes. Why not? How can I say no to you? You are like my daughter. I have daughters of your age so why would I not want to talk to you?

Q: Thank you. Do you have any objection if I record what you say?

---

[23] Keeping a quite long kerchief on the shoulder is considered a sign of a respected man.
[24] A political party of Sindh.
[25] Fazil Rahoo (1934-1987) was a political leader and one of the most famous peasant leaders in Sindh. He was born at Rahuki village in the Badin district of Sindh. He had fought throughout his life and was imprisoned for several years and was finally killed on 17 January 1987.
[26] Uncle.

A: No, *Ammar*,[27] I understand your need to record our conversation. Do it. I speak the truth. I am a truthful person. You can write; you can record, whatever you feel necessary, do it. I feel proud that you need my words to use for some big work. God will make you successful in the efforts you are making.

Q: Let me tell you one thing; whatever information you give me will be used only for the purposes of my research and for any related publications.

A: I understand. I know that.

Q: May I ask your name, age, parents, community, business and so on?

A: My name is Sajid. I was born in 1929. I am now 83 years old. My caste is Aagani. I am from Larkana. My father was a farmer and I had two brothers and two sisters. My father died when I was just eight years old.

Q: Could you please tell me something about your childhood; your siblings, schooling and favourite games?

A: Hmmm, childhood! When my father died, my elder brother looked after me well. He was the one who helped me to marry. My sisters also died early. I went to a school but the Hindu teachers used to beat us very harshly. Their intentions in fact were that Muslims should not study but should leave the schools so that they would remain illiterate and ignorant. They thought that if Muslims learned mathematics, they would understand the interest system and might become as strong as they were before, so they discouraged Muslim boys and would beat them miserably. I was also tortured severely by my teachers. They gave very inhumane punishments and that was the time that parents could not complain about the behaviour of teachers. Students were left with only one option, to leave the schools, so I did like hundreds of others did; I left school with no certificate in my hand. It was a success for the Hindu teachers. However, I did learn to read the Qur'an.

Q: OK, what about games and friends?

---

[27] Mother.

A: I was not a naughty boy from the very beginning, so I remained very careful. I used to play harmless games so that no-one would be teased.

Q: What was your mother's attitude towards you?

A: Oh, my mother, she was extremely kind to me. I used to massage her head, her legs, her feet and she prayed all the time for me. She said that I would never need anything from anyone in life but that I would fulfil the needs of hundreds. My mother loved me so much that I even forgot that I didn't have a father. She was a blessing, a very loveable person. You know, it was my mother's prayer that I have been able to speak to people, before so many people, to a crowd. Speaking with you, a well-educated person, needs courage. It is not a joke. These were the prayers of my mother, and secondly I give credit to the friends who trained me. In 1974, I joined *Awami Tehreek*. I was very punctual about time. The leaders of the party would use my name as an example for my punctuality. I still care about time. I was determined to arrive here by four o'clock and I am here. I can't be even five minutes late.

Q: Good, I appreciate that. Can you please tell me something about your marriage?

A: Which one, first or second?

Q: Let's talk about the first one first.

I: I was too young when my mother and brother asked my paternal uncle for his daughter's hand for me. My uncle raised no objection. My wife was the daughter of my maternal uncle and aunt, so it was a kind of family affair. I think I was hardly thirteen or fourteen years old at that time and she was perhaps the same age or may be one or two years younger than me. It was my mother-in-law, my aunt, who told me, 'Look, your wife is a *kari*'.

Q: Who told you?

A: My mother-in-law, my wife's mother.

Q: She said this about her own daughter?

A: Yes, and I believed her and said, 'If you say so, it must be right because no-one else would accuse her but a mother. You must be speaking the truth so I must listen to you and believe you'. I had a morsel of food in my mouth when she told me this; I spat it out and left my home.

Q: How long had you been married to her?

A: Five years.

Q: Did you have any children by her?

A: Yes, a son, who died later and she was pregnant with another child. When my mother-in-law gave me the news, I straight went to a woman whom I called mother after the death of my real mother. It was seven months after the death of my mother. She knew that my mother had died and that then my brother and I had separated, so she was very kind to me and I respected her like my mother.

Q: OK.

A: We brothers fought and were separated during her life, but when she died my brother offered to live with me again but I refused as I felt it was an insult to the soul of my mother. I thought about it and said to my brother that during our mother's life we had kept away from each other, so how would we live together now? I didn't want it. It would have given people the impression that our mother was the cause of the dispute between us brothers and that as soon as she died, we had started to live together again. I wouldn't give such an insult to my mother's grave. Why would I make people laugh at her after her death? I could not spit on my mother's grave, so I asked my brother to keep his hand on my head [look after me] as an older brother, but told him that we would not live together again.

Q: But what had made you separate?

A: Women fighting. Our wives could not bear each other. All the time they were quarrelling. It was unbearable. We could not tolerate it so eventually we became separated.

Q: OK. When you were told that your wife was a *kari*, what did you do?

A: On the third night after I got this news, I killed her.

Q: How?

A: One night, I was sleeping at my home, not in my bedroom but outside. Suddenly I felt a jerk as if somebody had shaken my body and I heard a voice from nowhere. It said, 'Get up! Shameless man, are you still sleeping?' I picked up my axe and stood up ... and ... killed her.

Q: Killed her? You mean you killed her when she was fast asleep?

A: No, when I went into my bedroom, as its door was open, I saw a shadow of a man going out. 'Who was he?' I asked. 'I don't know' she replied. On that reply I did not wait another second but with a hard blow of the axe, I chopped her head off. My brother was not in the village; he had gone to Larkana. When people told him that his brother had killed his wife to preserve his honour, he came back immediately and as soon as he reached me, he put his turban[28] on my feet. At this act, I said firmly, 'Wear the turban. Put it on your head. Whatever I have done it is not a crime. I have saved our honour so don't worry'. That was a time when honour killing was not common so people all around the village deliberately came to see me and meet me. The people were curious and they were heard saying to each other, 'Let us go to that village and meet a young boy who had killed his wife to save his honour'. Yes ... I still remember. It was 27 July when I killed my wife.

Q: Did you not give your wife a chance to talk about it?

A: When my mother-in-law told me about her character, I left home and went to my spritual mother whom I told you about. She looked into my eyes worriedly. She said to my brother, 'Do something for him. He is in agony. He is not the same person who came to me last night. There is something that is burning him'. She pleaded with me to talk to her and tell her how I felt, but I could not utter a word. I could only reply, 'Nothing, mother, nothing, I'm all right. Don't worry about me please'. But you know, the *sadri*[29] which I had on my shoulder fell down and I did not notice. Wherever I went and visited anyone, I felt that people were laughing at me and talking about me as if I was the centre of their conversation. I felt as if the whole world knew about my disgrace and people were saying, 'He is the dishonoured man who couldn't do anything to save his honour'. No matter wherever I went, in shops, in the fields, outside, I felt people saying, 'Dishonourable man, you have no honour'.

---

[28] The turban is a sign of pride in tribal areas. Putting the turban on your head is an honourable deed and putting it down shows great humiliation.
[29] A large square kerchief which men (mostly in tribal cultures) throw on their shoulder as a gesture of being respectable; it is a symbol of decency.

That was the time when I pleaded before God and cried and asked God, 'Oh God! Give me courage to save my honour, to protect my honour. Make me brave to kill my wife. I should finish her and fulfill my duty'.

Q: Did you try to get your wife to confirm it?

A: When my mother-in-law told me that she was a *kari*, my wife was sitting on my right side on a *charpaee*.[30] By all means she could have said to her mother 'No, that's a lie'. Instead she remained silent and when I looked into her eyes she lowered her face, which strengthened my belief.

Q: What did she say about it?

A: Nothing, as I told you. She did not look into my eyes and she remained silent. Her own mother was accusing her, not someone else. What else was required to confirm it? If the allegation was false, she would have said to her mother, 'Mother, what are you telling my husband? What have you seen? Why are you accusing me? How could you call me a *kari*?' She could have said something in her defence or she could have denied the allegation. Actually, as I understood it she was not expecting any extreme action from my side. Because I was a simple, soft-spoken, kind-hearted and non-violent person, she thought that I might forget about it and tolerate such a thing. Then, as I have already told you, one night, in the half-moon light, the creator awakened me. I felt as if somebody shook my foot. 'Are you still asleep' were the words I heard and I found someone else in my body; I jumped up and rushed to her room. The door was opened and I saw someone running out. I entered in room; 'Who was he', I asked. 'I don't know', was her answer. 'You do not know', I said, and I smashed my axe on her head. And … she died. She was finished. I always keep an axe with me from my childhood.

Q: Didn't she shout or try to stop you?

A: No, she didn't shout. She just tried to cover her face with her hands but the first blow of the axe had finished her. I then hit her three more times with the axe and when I was sure that she was dead, I went forward, put down my axe and broke her neck with my hands. Her back was covered in blood and the clothes I was wearing also became red with blood. After killing her, I relaxed a bit. Then I took the axe and went out. It was nearly morning; villagers saw me, they came near to me to ask what had happened. Some of them tried to stop me from going out in those

---

[30] A Sindhi *charpaee* is a bed, usually with a decorated bed-cover.

clothes. I felt so much power in my body that I wanted to kill everyone who tried to stop me. Anyhow, the *wadera*[31] of the village came. He praised me loudly in front of the people, he took the axe from my hand and took me to his *otaq*.[32] But … I need to tell you that that was a plan of the *waderas*, because by admiring killers they wanted to be in the limelight and make the police feel that they were loyal to the police and that all the villagers were criminals. The *waderas* are still enemies of the common people and they have always been stronger and more cunning. When my brother reached there, he seemed very distracted. Brother is brother. How could he see me in that situation? When he took off his turban and put before my feet, I said, 'Be brave. Be a man. Tough times come and go. Wear your turban again'. The *wadera* called the police. In those days police only rode horses so it took quite a long while for the police to arrive. It was the time of Prime Minister Iskandar Mirza.[33] The Deputy Superintendent of Police was an Englishman. Although Pakistan had been created, English officers were still serving in some areas of Pakistan. The officer took me to the first-class Magistrate.

Q: What year was that, can you tell me?

A: It was 1951. The Magistrate asked me about the killing. I admitted it and said that I did it to save my honour. The Magistrate asked me 'Why do you admit the killing?' I replied, 'Then who has killed her? If I said I had not killed her then who else had murdered her. Did angels come and do it? I killed her so I need to be punished. If I don't admit the killing, some innocent person will be arrested. I don't want that. My conscience will not let me do that. I murdered her and I must be punished'. My brevity inspired him. My face, hands and clothes were stained with blood. He said quietly, 'Would you like to join the army?' 'No', I said straightaway, as I was perhaps not able to think of anything else. His face got red with rage and he said angrily, 'Nonsense, now burn your life behind bars. You seemed like a brave man to me so I offered you a great chance. If you had joined the army you would have been able to eat the sweetest grapes of Quetta. Now, die in jail'. When I heard that, I began pleading him to let me join the army but he had changed his mind by that

---

[31] Tribal leader.
[32] A drawing room for men only.
[33] Iskander Ali Mirza (13 November 1899 – 13 November 1969), was an East Pakistani (now Bangla Desh) politician who served as the first president of Pakistan, elected to this post in 1956 until he was dismissed by the dictator Ayub Khan in 1958.

time and refused me with scorn and said, 'You have lost the opportunity'. A trial was held and I was sentenced to life imprisonment under section 163 of the Pakistani Law. He was a very good officer, I believe.

Q: What was the trial like?

A: It was very simple. The Magistrate ordered everyone to leave the office. I can't remember his name. He was a Sindhi officer and he looked very decent. He even sent his senior clerk out of the office. I was the only person left in. He then asked me, 'Do you offer prayer?' 'Yes Sir', I replied. 'Do you recite or proclaim *Azan*[34] as well?' 'Yes I do' was my answer. 'Recite the first *Kalama*'[35] I was told. I recited it as I was instructed. Then he asked, 'Now, speak the truth. Was she really a *kari*?' 'Yes sir, she was', I answered. 'Now go', he sent me out and from there I was taken to a jail. I did not stay there very long. However, I remember one thing and I will never forget that during the period of the killing and arriving in the jail, I did not feel like eating anything. I disliked food. It tasted awful. But once I reached the jail, I enjoyed the food. It was so delicious as if I was offered a feast. Anyway, from that jail, I was sent to the special jail. There I met a very humble judge, who dealt with my case. He asked 'Why did you marry so young?' I said, 'It was my parents' decision. How could I disobey them? They were my masters. I did not marry for myself'. He was very kind to me. He was Mirza by caste. I was an easy case as I was a truthful person and was admitting what I had done, so he found no need to prolong the investigation. Within fifteen days my case was settled. The Session Judge called me and asked me if I would ever be a threat to the law-enforcement agencies if I was given a minimum punishment. I said that I would not and I was given a five-year sentence. I requested less but he said that he could not reduce it as he was of the opinion that he had already showed me mercy. Anyhow, in the jail, I asked the jailor to let me do some jobs. Everyone liked me there. I asked my brother to bring the Qur'an for me and I was given a copy of it. I spent three months in the central jail and then I was sent to the central jail in another city. There, I passed two years learning Urdu, four years learning Sindhi and I learned the Qur'an from the teachers who used to come to teach us in the jail. I was so keen to study that every day I used to finish three chapters of the Qur'an. The English teacher also suggested that I should learn English but I did not take it seriously. Only today, I feel sorry

---

[34] In Islamic countries, *Azan* is delivered five times a day in mosques in order to call people to offer prayer.
[35] There are seven *Kalamas* in the Qur'an.

as I am seeing you writing and I am regretting and saying to myself 'Would that I were as educated as you are'. Today, my eyesight is poor but I still have a desire to read and write in English. I call it my bad luck. God bless you, my child. My wife is too good. She is the mother of my ten children. Two of them have died. Now there are eight, two daughters and six sons. She is still alive and she loves me. Today, when she saw me wearing this new dress with *sadree* and turban, she said, 'You are looking adorable to me'. So I replied 'You too are looking so loveable to me'.

Q: What was it like being in jail?

A: In fact, because of my behaviour, honesty and upright character, I was given respect and care not only by the other inmates but also by the jail staff. I shall tell you a strange experience. I was in the second jail, it was moonlight, I was assigned there as a watchman due to my good behaviour. I was on the veranda and my job was to give a loud shout after each twenty to twenty-five minutes in order to make the other prisoners know that their guard was vigilant. So, I was walking and when I looked up the sky, I was mesmerized as if I was not in the jail but in my village like a free bird. Suddenly, I heard the voice of the jailor, who called me by my name and I turned back. It took me a few moments to come back and to realise the situation which I was in. That was the only time I remember that I recalled my past, my childhood and my village, otherwise I was quite composed in jail as I found so many sincere friends who loved me even more than my brothers. The five years of my imprisonment taught me that a friendship made on a train, in hospital and in jail is everlasting.

Q: Do you sometimes remember your first wife? How did you feel after you murdered her?

A: Never, except for one time. In 1955, I heard in a dream as if she was calling me by my name. 'Get up and listen to me. You are getting late' and I woke up. It was only a dream. I was confused for a minute, and then everything was fine.

Q: Did you love her before you were told by your mother-in-law that she was a *kari*.

A: Too much …

Q: Did she also love you?

A: Might be. Surely when I loved her she would have also loved me. But once I heard about her dishonourable deed, I started praying to God, 'Oh God give me courage to do this act. Make me get this job done. Let me kill her as soon as possible so that I should not be ashamed in my conscience, otherwise I will not be able to live with honour'. I thought of committing suicide as well. There was a river near my village and I thought of drowning myself in it. I did not want to see her again.

Q: You killed your wife as a *kari* but if she was told by someone that you were a *karo*, how would have she have reacted?

A: *Ammar*, listen to me! These days, those who are killing women just to show off that they are honourable people are not even good human beings. In fact, I consider them worse than animals. Today's Sindh is not the Sindh of the 1950s. It is a Sindh of criminals. Today, people don't like their wives but are after other men's women. In my youth, I could not even think of any other women as I loved and respected my wife a lot. She was a respected and loved daughter of her parents, a sister of her brothers, the honour of me and my family, I would have never ever have thought of such a dishonourable act. Even after my second marriage, as God is my witness, I have not seen the face of any women with bed intentions because I believe that all women are honourable for their families and that all outsiders should respect them. So many young boys were there in jail with me and I had the upper hand over them as I had to look after their personal matters, and I used to distribute food to them. But I always considered them as my younger brothers and cared for them. I did not misuse them. I know that a human can turn into a monster if he does not control his emotions. Nowadays, the people who are killing innocent women in honour killings are committing a sin. They are doing wrong. They can never be justified. I appreciate my jail friends who taught me the lesson of humanity and tolerance. In jail, I learned about the human body and its urges, right and wrong. I learned about Lenin and Marx. Every teacher in the jail loved me. The teacher who taught me the Sindhi language offered me his daughter's hand in marriage. He insisted that I should not go back to my village but should complete my studies to become a teacher and live with him as he had four daughters but no son. But ... *Amman*, in jail, I missed my village and I felt like a fish out of water. I simply asked him not to think like that as I was determined to spend the rest of my life in my beloved village. You know what, people may not realize how beautiful the world is but once you are behind the black, long, endless walls of a jail, you realise what freedom and the beauty of the world are. When I left the jail and returned to my village, I felt as if I had been freed from a cage. I flew like a bird to see my nest when the gate of the jail opened for me. Home is the sweetest thing on earth, *Ammar.* I remember my journey from the jail to my village. My journey by train began at four oclock in the morning and the train reached my village at four o'clock in the afternoon. I wished that the train had flown so I would have reached my village as soon as possible, in the blink of an eye.

Q: Who looked after your family when you were in the jail?

A: What family? My parents had already passed away. My son was dead. My brothers had separate homes. I had no family. I was in great distress in jail as I had no mother or father to pray for me but I appreciated the people in jail who became mine.

Q: Now you have passed 80 years of your life. How do you feel about your act of killing your wife as a *kari*. Can you justify what you did?

A: Oh no, it was an absolutely unjustified act, an absolutely unjustified step.

Q: How come?

A: Look, today men kill innocent women to get a younger woman, to grab a piece of land, to kill their enemies, to get rid of their neighbours, to settle an old score, to make people run from their houses so that they might confiscate their property. They simply kill their daughters, wives, sisters, cousins, aunts and mothers. They kill young children's mothers without any mercy. God will see them. Nowadays, honour killimg is not a matter of honour any longer. God forbid … the cruel killers think that they will live in this world forever. They do not think of the next world where they shall be answerable to God.

Q: So you think you were wrong for killing your first wife?

A: Yes, I was wrong. I must admit it but I learned it too late. This acceptance is the result of my learning now. My previous mind was different. There was no other option in my past except to kill her. I regret that killing. I now think that I would not have done it.

Q: What does your learning say about *karo-kari* today?

A: My learning says that human beings are equal. A woman is not a lesser human. Everyone has to answer to God about his or her deeds on earth. Let's take things like this: if a man can take a woman of his choice, a woman should also be given the liberty to marry a man of her own choice. And if she wants a man better than her husband and cannot control her urge for him, she should be able to marry him and should have the right to leave her husband. Nothing is wrong with this. A wife is not a property. You know what, now whoever invites me to a seminar to speak on *karo-kari*, I go and tell the audience that *karo-kari* is an inhumane act. It's not Islamic punishment. It is done either for greed or for satisfying men's so-called superiority complex or useless ego. Once I was invited to a seminar where an Islamic preacher was also invited. When he spoke, he said that if a girl has a maternal cousin, she is not supposed to be given to any other man in or outside the family. When my turn to speak came, I said, 'No, this is unjustified. If the cousin is a gambler, an addict or the girl does not like him, even then should the girl be given to him?' No, it should be a matter of choice and compatibility. It should be a matter of beauty and mental aptitude. Hearts cannot be bought or purchased. I have seen the world. Why are the wives of Hindus not called *karis*? Why are the wives of Shaikhs and other rich families not accused of being *karis*? Because their physical and financial needs are fulfilled; they have enough care, love, money, food and other necessities of life. The concept of *kari* is a creation of cruelty. A cruel system in which women have nothing to eat, no care, no money, no medicine; they look for the basic things for life and their menfolk declare them *karis*. The women have nothing, no clothes, no money, no love, no care; what should they do?

Q: If this is true, what made your wife a *kari*?

A: I blame her mother. My wife was too young. It was the responsibility of her mother to look after her well. I was away working in the fields. She used to live with her. She should have controlled her and not let her follow the wrong path.

Q: What is honour?

A: Honour is a passion. It is the voice of your conscience. It does not fall suddenly from the sky but grows with you and lets you know what is right and what is wrong.

Q: If you had a choice, what type of life you would like to have and with whom?

A: Everything should be available at home. Husband and wife should live with each other with respect and equal rights. I am a happy and composed man with my family. My land is producing enough to satisfy my family's needs. My children are also employed. My daughters are also happy in their own homes. My family loves me. I got my daughters married to good and sensible men and I gave them dowries as I consider it their right. I did not take any money from their in-laws, as girls are not for sale. What else could I ask of God? Whenever my daughters and their husbands visit me, I always give them respect and love. I am very content with my life. I don't believe in a second life so I am happy with this life and I thank God for whatever he has given me.

Q: Thank you for your time and for sharing your valuable thoughts with me.

A: You are welcome, daughter.

2: *Name*: Hanif, aged 36

The interview lasted for an hour and fourteen minutes and took place at a local hotel.

Hanif was a young, short, simple-looking man with curly hair. He seemed very composed. Some of his friends were waiting for him outside the room of the hotel where I conducted the interview. He managed to avoid eye contact with me throughout the interview.

Q: *Assalam-u-alaikum.*

A: *Walaikum-assalam.*

Q: How are you?

A: I am OK.

Q: Let me tell you one thing; whatever information you give me will be used only for the purposes of my research and for related publications.

A: OK.

Q: *Ada*,[36] are you willing to talk to me?

A: Surely.

---

[36] Brother.

Q: Thank you. I am carrying out a research project about honour killing and I need your views about it.

A: You may ask any question if you think I can help you.

Q: Can I record the interview?

A: No problem.

Q: Can you please tell me something about your family and your tribal background?

A: I am thirty-six years old. My father died when I was twenty-two. He worked as a bus driver. My mother died two years ago. I have three brothers and three sisters. I am the oldest. We are basically Baloch of Balochistan but now are settled in Larkana.

Q: What is your education?

A: I passed secondary [year-eight] level.

Q: Why didn't you complete your studies?

A: Sister, education is a very good thing. It gives you respect in society. I think nothing is better than a good education, but the point is, how do you get educated? Who would have supported me? I wanted to study but my circumstances did not let me study; I still feel sorry about that.

Q: Can you tell me something about your childhood; your brothers and sisters, your favourite games, your work and so on?

A: My childhood ... It was a very poor and innocent childhood. I don't remember playing any games but I always gave respect and love and care to my siblings. I was the oldest brother so I always felt a kind of obligation to keep my brothers and sisters happy and provide them with something so that they should not feel inferior. I always solved their problems. I tried to help them whenever they needed me. And, and, and ... what else can I tell you about? Only that poverty ruled my childhood and nothing else.

Q: What is your job?

A: I am a taxi driver, sister. I work for someone. I drive his taxi.

Q: Are you happy with the job?

A: Well, thank God, I am managing. What else can I say? I am thankful to God that I am not unemployed.

Q: Are you married?

A: Yes, I got married in 2007. It was an arranged marriage. Actually my brother-in-law, whom we respected as the eldest in our family after the demise of my father, chose the girl for me. She was his relative. My brother-in-law was not our relative but we gave our sister to him in marriage so we considered him as our senior and older brother. So everyone was happy when he offered me a girl from his family to marry.

Q: Had you seen the girl before the marriage?

A: No. You know our system. When somebody takes responsibility, we trust him. Because my brother-in-law took the matter into his own hands, we all remained silent and trusted him.

Q: What was the mode of your marriage?

A: I paid 80,000 rupees to the bride's parents. It was a compatible match as I was twenty-eight and she was twenty-four. We were both happy. She was beautiful, hardworking and very good at housework as well. I liked her very much. She also showed her love for me.

Q: How did you get on with your in-laws?

A: Sister, the truth is that my in-laws were not very happy with me. Their attitude towards me was not respectful. I, on the other hand, tried to make them happy so that they would respect me and feel honoured, but that did not work out.

Q: Why was that?

A: That I don't know. Maybe the reason was that they were wealthier than us. I was poor. My home was not as good as theirs so they considered me inferior or poor. They taunted me sometimes. They mocked me but I tolerated it in order to show them that I was a good and respectful person. I tried to find the reasons behind their dubious attitude but I could not find any other reason than that I could not compete with them financially. In fact they were outsiders and outsiders always feel themselves superior. That's what I can think and say about their behaviour.

Q: How many children do you have?

A: I have no children.

Q: How long did your marriage last?

A: For five years. Then the issue arose.

Q: Oh! Would you like to share it with me? How did it happen?

A: You know, sister, Islam does not permit us to go wrong and to be disloyal to our life partner. Islam does not grant us permission for such an immoral thing. Secondly, honour is a big thing. We cannot deny it. When anger, emotions and honour combine, you cannot control yourself. So that is what happened.

Q: Could you please tell me what actually happened?

A: Yes, sister, why not. I can certainly share it with you. Because I worked as a driver, as I have already told you, I had gone to Hyderabad. It was August in 2011. I came home late one night, or let's say early in the morning, unexpectedly and found my bedroom locked from the inside. And strangely the front door of my home was open. As I had never known or suspected anything before, I immediately thought that it was a mistake. However, I kicked the door of my bedroom in. As you know the latches of the doors in villages are not very strong so it broke and fell inside the room. When I entered, I saw my wife with the younger brother of my brother-in-law, I mean my sister's husband. Then, a human being is a human being. Anger is anger. Actually, no-one was expecting me at that time because whenever I go out of the city, I normally come back in the afternoon of the following day. You know the tradition. After seeing this tragedy with my own eyes, I couldn't control myself. It was as if there was a kind of film of blood in front of my eyes and I couldn't think about anything else. The man tried to escape but I didn't give him a chance to take the next breath and fired at him. My wife cried out 'Help, Help' two or three times, but I killed them both instantly and that was the end.

Q: What did you see?

A: Um, umm, so revealing, open things, I mean the situation was very open, unbearable.

Q: Who else was there at that time?

A: No-one was there at that time. My sister who used to live with us was at our neighbour's home for a marriage party. They were alone at that time. I came back unexpectedly. No-one knew I was coming. The man tried to escape but I didn't let him run; I killed both of them.

Q: How?

A: I locked the door of my bedroom from inside. I had my pistol with me and I opened fire on both of them.

Q: Didn't they try to resist?

A: I didn't give him a chance to take another breath. My wife cried 'Help, help' two or three times and that was the end of the story. If I had left either of them alive, my conscience would have killed me. Only a dishonourable person could ignore the situation.

Q: Do you always have a pistol with you?

A: How could I not? It is my defence. You know, living in this area is not easy; all the time your life is at risk. So everybody keeps his weapon with him. A weapon is a guarantee of life in this part of the world.

Q: What were your feelings when you saw the two dead bodies covered in blood?

A: Because of my anger and rage I was simply unable to think about or feel anything. I just felt a lot of anger; I was so angry that I could not think about anything else. I couldn't control myself. A man is a man. You know?

Q: How did you feel when you had done it?

A: It happened on 23 August 2011. When I killed both of them, I was really angry and felt very disgusted that I was living with a disloyal woman. I know that thinking of the consequences of honour killing is a sign of a dishonourable man and I certainly felt fear as well. I felt that if I went to jail, the opposite party, which was very influential, would surely be able to put me behind bars. To take revenge they would use all their powers but I managed to hide and I went to the *sardar*[37] because that was the only way I could save my life because I was not guilty. I was on the side of right. I knew that I would be arrested by the police and would be

---

[37] Tribal leader.

imprisoned for my whole life. I would face either life imprisonment or a death sentence. And in jail, I would not have been able to do anything to help myself. No matter how many friends would have worked for me, nothing would have happened and I would have been behind bars for the rest of my life. I thought that if I remained free, I would surely be able to help myself to save my life. Only by being free would I be in a position to ask for support and help from some *sardar* as I knew that the *jirga* system is fair and based on justice. All troubles, enmities and murders are solved in an appropriate way through *jirgas*, but through the courts nobody can find justice and the justice process is very lengthy. It kills you.

Q: How much time did you spend in jail?

A: No time, sister. I did not go to jail.

Q: How come? What happened then?

A: I managed it.

Q: How?

A: Certainly, as I said, I was afraid that I might go to jail – the opposing party [the family of the boy whom he had killed] were very strong and would surely work very hard to put me behind bars ... and if I was arrested by the police, I would face either life imprisonment or the death sentence. And from inside jail I would not be in a position to ask the *sardar* for help and support. SoI went straight to the *sardar* on the morning after the killing and admitted it to him. I said that I had killed my wife with a man and I did *haque*.[38] The *sardar* told me to recite the first *kalima*[39] and to take an oath. I did so. Then I was told to take the Qur'an and, holding the Qur'an, I said that I had witnessed an act of immorality and then killed the two in *karo-kari*. The *sardar* said that he would call the other party [the dead man's relatives] and the matter would be decided in a *jirga*. They were called. The date of the *jirga* was decided. The *jirga* was conducted. They were found guilty and I was found to be in the right so the *faislo*[40] was in my favour. They were found to be liars. My position

---

[38] A right thing.
[39] In Arabic, the word *kalima* means a sentence. There are six *kalimas* in Islam to facilitate the easy memorizing and learning of the basic fundamentals of a Muslim's *Aqeedah* (beliefs). *Kalimas* are called the first pillar of Islam. The first of them is known as the *kalimat aṭ-ṭaiyibah* or 'word of purity'.
[40] A decision taken in a *jirga*.

became clear. As the brother of my brother-in-law had been killed, my brother-in-law was furious and he lodged an FIR[41] against me as a murderer soon after the killing. He was really emotional at the time, but when the *faislo* was given in my favour, he realised his brother's mistake and he gave a statement in evidence before a magistrate in my favour in which he said that I was innocent. So there was no trial against me. The issue was settled and I was not sent to jail.

Q: Looking back on the killing, how do you feel about it now?

A: Now I feel honourable. I walk around honourably, not cowardly. People respect me. If I had not killed them I would never have been able to live with honour. You know the cruel system, the insulting remarks which kill people from within. A person who cannot defend his honour is called a pimp in this society. Now the blessings of God are on me that I am saved from such comments. I am considered an honourable man by society. I feel clean. There is no burden hanging over me. It is essential to avoid a shameful life to save honour. I believe that evil deeds invite disaster. So whoever does evil has to face the music. What I did was in accordance with Islam and *Sharia*. Islam forbids anyone to do such shameful act.

Q: Why did she do it? What do you think?

A: I think, I have to sort out this issue in my head … I really don't know why she did it. She had a cell phone and I remember that once when I was at home she received a phone call and was talking very slowly to someone. When I asked who it was, she replied that it was a call from a friend [a girl]. The way she answered was dubious. It made me a bit suspicious but then I thought it couldn't happen as we loved each other.

Q: Didn't you check the cell phone?

A: No, sister. I trusted her. I consoled myself by saying that it was not possible. She wouldn't betray me; she wouldn't lie to me. This was because of my love and blind trust in her. We used to take oaths to remain loyal to each other. I remember we took an oath on the Qur'an that we would always remain truthful to each other, never lie to each other and never be disloyal to each other. We used to exchange loving sentences repeatedly. I always kept my word. I never gave her any trouble. I never stopped her from visiting anyone's house. I always gave her enough money to spend on herself. In this tribal culture, men put restrictions on

---

[41] First investigation report.

their wives' movements. I never did that because of my trust in her. I didn't stop her from going to see anyone, attending marriage parties, meeting friends [girls] and things like that. I never said anything to her and I was never harsh to her. Believe me, I don't know why she did it. Why she broke my heart and betrayed my trust. I cannot say anything more. (*He could not stop weeping; tears were rolling down his cheeks so he wiped them with a handkerchief. He then cleaned his eyes and paused for a while.*)

Q: I am sorry that my questions made you cry.

A: No, please do not think like that. It is not your fault.

Q: If your wife had seen you in the same position, how would she have reacted?

A: She … she, I mean, she would not have been able to do the same or go to that extreme, but she would certainly have left me and would have applied for a divorce through the court.

Q: Why didn't you divorce her then?

A: What?

Q: You could have divorced her.

A: No, sister. Look, why would I divorce her? How was it possible? Am I a woman? Women cannot kill but men kill to save their honour. How could I have divorced her? How was it possible?

Q: Why not?

A: You know everyone has a different level of conscience and a different level of maturity. Isn't it so? Women have a different way of thinking and a different perspective about certain things whereas men have a different standpoint about certain things. Women cannot kill but men kill.

Q: How do you think other people view your act?

A: They … they respect me a lot. After this honour killing, the world changed for me. I am considered an important person everywhere in the society. People cannot make eye contact with me. They look downwards while talking to me. No-one can mess with me now. Honour killing and respect are the words, but in our culture they are the same thing. Killing a kinswoman is a sign that the killer is in fact a man of value and virtue. Killing a person, especially one who is your relative, needs courage. When a woman in your family is *kari* and you don't kill her, it means that your whole family is *kari*. What does *kari* mean? It simply means a dishonoured and disgusting woman. A killed *kari* brings your lost respect back and keeping a *kari* in your family means you are all disgusting. Once you have upheld your honour by killing a kinswoman who was a *kari*, you are treated like a king in your society and no-one can take your pride away from you. I am one of the most respected people around now. If I had not killed her, people would have treated me like an animal.

Q: Do you think this is the right concept?

A: If you ask my personal view on this, sister, I mean my personal viewpoint, then my answer is 'no'. In my personal capacity I say that I reject the system. I have to be accountable before God sooner or later. It is wrong, not just wrong but also absolutely wicked, sister. But, look and try to understand the strong custom and tradition of this society. The sick norms compel men to follow their pattern otherwise their life becomes like a dog's life. And they will not be able to walk around with respect. People's comments will kill them.

Q: What is honour?

A: In my opinion, honour is … that a woman is married to a man and becomes his wife. OK, understand … both parties agree and sign an agreement before the whole community … fine. In a marriage, the Qur'an is held between the bride and the groom and they take an oath to remain loyal to each other. The bride recites some of the verses of the Qur'an and so does the man. The *Nikah*[42] happens. It should be respected. It is the Islamic way. Then it is obvious that a woman after marriage becomes the honour of her husband and by having extra-marital relations with someone, she damages her husband's honour and then the man reacts. It is truly disrespectful if she gets involved in a kind of physical relationship other than with her own husband. This damages a man's honour. Honour is passion. It cannot be controlled easily and it cannot be controlled after

---

[42] Marriage Contract. *Nikah* literally means conjunction or uniting. In the Islamic legal system, it implies a marriage contract in the presence of a minimum of two males.

seeing something like I saw. Islam does not allow anyone to do such a shameful act or be disloyal.

Q: Imagine, you are in the past and the same situation has arisen; how would you react?

A: It is clear, so obvious that I would not repeat the action. I have realised that killing or murdering is a wrong thing. It is a very wrong way to treat somebody. If I could go back into the past, I would have left her after seeing the same thing with my own eyes. You know what I think now? If a husband sees his wife doing wrong he should leave her at once and try not to see her again because, if he sees her again he might not be able to control his anger, so the best solution is to leave her forever so that he should not think of killing. Actually, in the society that we live in, there is no other option. Killing has been made a mandatory and obligatory act. Killing is a sin whether one commits it under the pretext of honour or not. But I understand that human beings sometimes cannot control their emotions especially in such a sensitive matter. Sister, I feel pain. I still regret it. I wake up at night. Those killings have been a nightmare for me. When I am alone I keep thinking 'Why did she do it?' Would that she had not taken such a step so I would not have a ruined life. And … and, I miss her. Sister, I miss her. She did wrong and by doing wrong she forced me to do wrong. Consequently, everything went wrong. I became a criminal and my life is ruined. However, I still believe that she will be accountable to God for whatever she did because women should be loyal to their husbands. No matter what difficulties they come across on the way, a wife should stick with her husband. It should be an obligation for her to remain loyal to her husband.

Q: When will you marry again?

A: Now, I cannot even think of it. I loved her. She was my first love. I considered her as everything to me. I had blind trust in her. I never made her feel inferior. I did not inflict any pain on her. Even then she did it to me. My request is with God. He will do justice to me. God will listen to me on the Day of Judgment. I have killed two people, but despite all the anger and complaints, I regret what I did. Nevertheless, God will do justice to me, I believe. She deceived me. She did more than I ever did to her.

Q: *Ada*, thank you very much for talking to me.

A: Not at all. I am thankful to you.

3: Name: *Arshad, aged 36*

The interview lasted for an hour and fourteen minutes and took place at a local hotel.

Arshad was very talkative. He had a French-cut beard. He looked like a clever man and was very comfortable while talking. His bulging eyes made me feel a little scared.

Q: *Assalam-o-alaikum.*

A: *Walaikum-assalam.*

Q: How are you doing?

A: Very good, thanks.

Q: Let me make one thing clear: whatever information you give me will remain secure and will be used only for the purposes of my research and for related publications.

A: Sure.

Q: OK. So you know that I will record your interview?

A: You can record it if it helps you.

Q: Can you please tell me something about your family and your tribal background?

A: We are basically Rind Baloch from Jacobabad.

Q: OK. Where do you live now?

A: We have our home in Jacobabad. My father is no longer alive. He had fifteen acres of land which I look after now. My mother doesn't work as she is very old now. She can't even do housework. We don't let her do anything. We do everything for her.

Q: What about your family, siblings, childhood, schooling and your favourite games; can you please tell me about these?

A: I have three brothers and four sisters. I was educated in our village. My school was at a little distance from my home. I took my matriculation [year 10] in 1996. I never had any interest in education so I stopped further studies.

Q: What was your grade in matriculation?

A: Grade, I think … it was probably 'C'. You know, I was a typical Baloch child and the significance of a Baloch child is that he does not ask for food but asks for weapons, so I was a typical Baloch child.[43] A Baloch child doesn't take interest in anything other than using various types of arms.

Q: Any games you played with your siblings or at school with friends?

A: Very rarely, sister. I was not that kind of boy. I had a different temperament. I didn't have much time for my brothers and sisters. I preferred living outside. I didn't play even with my brothers. In fact, I had no interest in education, in games or in that kind of socialising. I spent most of my time on my land and after I had been on the land, I preferred to come back home. That has been my routine for years. From the very beginning I didn't enjoy playing any kind of game. Actually, when I was a child, I had an accident which hurt me badly. My backbone was affected and the accident reduced my movement and I could not play or move very much. Although I was very young at the time, I still remember that it was a man on a motorbike who hit me and ran away. I fell on my back and remained in pain for quite a long time.

Q: How old are you now?

A: I'm about thirty-six.

Q: What do you do now?

A: I just observe the work of farmers on my fields and advise them. I allocate work to them and then go back home. In fact, I just look after my land.

Q: Are you married?

A: Yes. I married my cousin, my paternal uncle's daughter, in 1999 and I have a daughter and a son. You know, in our childhood, our elders

---

[43] The Balochi nation is very proud of its identity as a martial race: 'Weapons are the Adornment of Baloch men' is a traditional Baloch saying.

and parents decide even at the birth of a child who will be married to whom. Therefore, I knew from my childhood that my uncle's daughter would be my wife. Actually, she had the same name as me, so I knew before my marriage that she would be my wife.

Q: Would you like to explain the mode of your marriage?
A: It wasn't anything unusual. The girl's parents gave her a few things for her personal use. This was not to be considered as a dowry which is normally received by the groom's family. This is not our family tradition. Whatever the parents want to give to their girl, they give it to her entirely of their own volition. There is no pressure on the parents at all.

Q: How did you get on with your in-laws after your marriage?

A: Wonderful, even till today. We have a very nice relationship with each other. I married in 1999 and have two children. I respect them and they respect me. There is no issue between us.

Q: What was that case of the *karo-kari?*

A: The matter was like … sister, it was 9 May in 2009; I still remember the date. You know the set-up in our villages; there are no proper bathrooms so men usually go outside for these things. So I woke up early in the morning and went out. There is a water channel (ditch) that passes through our village. It is hardly fifteen or twenty steps away from my home. Since it was dry and filled with some weeds and bushes, it had become a kind of dry trench at the time. I became aware that there was someone in it as it was still only a quarter to six in the morning and, of course, no-one could be there at that time with good intentions. I recognised the boy but he thought that I had not seen him as I went to the opposite side to dodge him. I went behind the house and reappeared on the other side. When I got near on the other side of the ditch, I saw that my cousin [a daughter of his paternal uncle] was with him. Actually, I had a *kalashankov*[44] over my shoulder. Earlier, when I got up, I had first put it over my shoulder before I went out of the house. It is my childhood habit; you know, with tribal enmities, you never know who will attack you and kill you. So … yes, I had been looking for him for a long time with a strong desire to kill him wherever I might see him. We actually have a

---

[44] The military dictator Zia-ul-Haq (1977-1988) made Pakistan play a major role in the Afghan war against the Soviets. As a result, Afghan refugees came to Pakistan in the name of Muslim brotherhood and brought *heroin* (drugs) and *kalashankov* (weapons) into Pakistan.

long history of enmity with his tribe. It was an obvious thing that one of us would kill one of us. It was understood that if I had seen him somewhere, I would have killed him and if he had seen me anywhere, he would have killed me. So we were after each other, or in search of each other.

Q: Why?

A: Because of a land dispute. I didn't start it but it had been a dispute for years between our families.

Q: Was he an outsider?

A: No, no, he was of our family but for many generations we had not met and the enmity was growing. You know, sister, about the Baloch. God can't make anyone Baloch. God can't let just anyone be born in a Baloch tribe. A Baloch child opens his eyes and finds arms. He inherits enmity and nothing else from the elders. God forbid. There is probably no Baloch on earth who does not have an enmity with someone, any family, any clan or any other tribe. And these enmities pass on from one generation to the next. We can't get rid of them. When we die, we pass them on to our children. You know, educated and well-off people pass on valuable things or good jobs, wealth or a good reputation to their children but we Baloch pass on enmities to our children. And the second regrettable thing is that when a Baloch child starts walking he learns to fire a gun. Every Baloch child has his own *kalashankov*.

Q: OK, then? Did the boy see you?

A: Yes, but as I told you, I deliberately dodged him, I went behind my house and I came out again on the other side. When I walked along the other side of the channel, I saw my cousin with him. He thought that I had gone back into the house and had not seen them. I still remember every tiny detail of that incident. It was a quarter past six. The boy didn't realize the situation and thought that I had not seen them. I didn't just have a *kalashankov* over my shoulder, I also had a dagger. Since we weren't far apart, I just took my dagger out and cut their throats.

Q: Didn't he try to run or shout?

A: Sister, he tried to run but he could not because he was inside the ditch. I jumped on him and didn't give him a chance to run. First, I cut his throat and then I turned to the girl and did the same to her. It was a very sharp dagger. It hardly took five or six minutes. I cut their throats straightaway.

Q: Didn't the girl try to scream or run away?

A: Not at all, no, no.

Q: Were you alone?

A: Yes.

Q: But surely it was natural for the girl to try to save her life?

A: She was too terrified. All she could say was that he had held her by force. She had just come out and the boy had caught her.

Q: How long did it take?

A: What, the killing?

Q: Yes.

A: Hardly five or six minutes, sister. It was a very sharp dagger. It cut their throats quickly.

Q: Why did you choose to kill them with the dagger.

A: You know that I was fully armed and wide awake. Future planning and the present scenario were both in my mind. Because I was determined to kill the boy any time, any day, I always remained alert. That was an unfortunate day for him and a fortunate day for me.

Q: Isn't it strange that at that very terrifying time neither of the two of them cried out?

A: Yes, strange; it is strange, I admit. But their time was up as far as God was concerned. That was their last day from God's side. When God did not want them to remain alive, how would they have resisted? They couldn't even stand up. I had the idea in my mind that if he tried to run, I would open fire on him.

Q: You killed both of them with the dagger, right? Why not with the *kalashankov* that you had with you?

A: The first reason was that the distance between them and me was not far. They were within my reach. The second reason was that if I killed them with the *kalashankov*, it would have been mentioned in the FIR against me. I realised that killing them with the dagger would be far easier to handle in court but that killing then with the *kalashankov* would mean having to be prepared for a long prison sentence.

Q: But whatever weapon is used in the murder, it has to be mentioned in the FIR and the police enquire about the weapons used in the murders.

A: Yes; you know how killing someone with a *kalashankov* causes trouble in court. It was clear in my mind. Although I was ready to kill him with the *kalashankov* as well, I preferred to kill him with another weapon such as a pistol … or… with some other ... as I killed them with a dagger. Some of my friends have already made the mistake of killing their opponents with a *kalashankov* and now they are in jail. Killing with a *kalashankov* means you are gone. A few of our neighbours killed their enemies with a *kalashankov* and now they are suffering for it. It's not like a pistol. It does not fire normally, it sprays bullets. So, this point was very clear in my mind – that the *kalashankov* would be the last option for me because it's an illegal weapon in Pakistan.

Q: So you didn't have a licence for it?

A: No, how can you apply for a licence? It's an illegal weapon, I am telling you. They are smuggled in from Afghanistan. So it can't have a licence.

Q: How old was the girl whom you killed as a *kari*?

A: Either fifteen or sixteen.

Q: And the boy?

A: Would be about eighteen.

Q: Were they both your relatives?

A: Yes. The girl was my paternal uncle's daughter and the boy was my father's cousin's son, but we had had no contact with them for ages.

Q: What exactly were they doing when you saw them?

A: When I saw them, they were wearing their clothes inside that dried-up water channel.

Q: I am still confused that they did not cry out or call someone for help.

A: How could they call someone for help, sister? They were guilty. God knows better. And let me make clear again the reason why they could not scream … as I told you, my conclusion was that their time was over from God. You know, when I jumped over the boy, he didn't take a single breath. So it was clearly God's wish.

Q: What about the girl?

A: First, she tried to cry a bit but when I threw the body of the boy down, she said quickly, 'He forced me, he dragged me and did it'.

Q: How did you feel when you had done it, I mean the killings?

A: The first and the quickest thought which came to my mind was that if the boy's relatives came and attacked me, I would kill them too. I knew that the girl's relatives would not come to fight me because I had seen her doing wrong with my own eyes. I was worried only about the boy's relatives or brothers. I also thought that if they hit my brothers or my father, I would kill them, as there is a very famous saying in the Balochi language that 'It is better to make an enemy's mother cry than your own'. I was so wound up at that time and I was ready to kill as many as I could. Who could dare to come across my path? I would say that he was acting unfairly towards us so it was my destiny to kill him. I was ready to teach his whole family a lesson.

Q: How long did you wait there for someone to come and see what had happened?

A: About an hour.

Q: How did the news spread then?

A: It was a bright morning. My hands and clothes were covered in blood stains. The villagers were passing by that way so the news spread through the whole village quickly.

Q: Nobody came from the boy's family?

A: No, no-one had the guts to face me. I went back to my house and told my family members everything. In the village, our houses are next to each other so we knew that the boy's family had also been informed.

Q: Then?

A: My village is next to that of the boy's family, so a strong reaction was expected from his family. So I left Sindh for Baluchistan and stayed there for twelve days. Meanwhile, my family members contacted the *sardar* of our area. The *sardar* had a talk with the area police officer and then told me to hand myself in to the police, so I did. I don't know what had happened exactly but I know that the *sardar* had a talk with the area police officer and then I was told by the *sardar* to hand myself in to the police.

Q: You had so much confidence in the *sardar* that simply on his assurance you were ready to be arrested?

A: Oh, yes, I still do have. The *sardars* are men of their word.

Q: Didn't you meet the *sardar* to tell him about the incident?

A: No. My elders met the *sardar*. I only had contact with him on the phone. At that time, mobile phones were very rare. I was in contact with him through various public telephone booths. The *sardar* talked to me over the phone. He told me that he had spoken to the senior police officers and that they would not harm me. Then, I went to the officer recommended by the *sardar*.

Q: Can you please explain the whole process? You were not in Sindh, right? So how did you turn yourself in to the Sindh police?

A: I came back to Sindh when I got a clearance sign from the *sardar*. As soon as I got off the bus, I called the police officer from a public telephone booth. His name was … He came and took me.

Q: What did you say to him on the phone?

A: I said, 'I have come back to Sindh and I am calling you on the advice of the *sardar* …'. He sent some policemen to the bus-stop.

Q: Did you have that much trust in the *sardar*?

A: Oh yes, I still do. The *sardars* are men of their word. A *sardar* is honourable so people listen to him and cannot go against what he says or decides. On the assurance of the *wadera*, as soon as I reached Sindh, the police officers came and took me to jail. Later, I was up before the court. The judge asked me some questions. I denied the killings and said that I was not there on the day when the killings happened. Then, there were some legal procedures and formalities. I was set free within a couple of days. The following week there was a *faislo* before the *sardar*. I said that their boy was obviously a *karo* and therefore I had murdered him. Actually, there are various systems or processes which determine whether it was a *karo-kari* or for some personal gain or for settling a dispute. My father was taken to a shrine and he swore on the holy book that the boy was a *karo*. The *sardar* was very angry at the slain boy's family and clearly said that whether he was a *karo* or not, they should forget about him. The *wadera* was very angry and called the killing a *haque* and declared me innocent. They told the opposite party to consider the killing as a dream or a lie, but that the issue was now buried. The boy is dead now so there can be no more discussions over a dead body. Actually, there are various systems or process for determining whether *karo-kari* is right or some personal score is being settled in the guise of honour killing. For instance, sometimes *sardars* order the most pious person from the killer's family to swear on oath that the killings are right or not. Right killings mean that the killing happened because of *karo-kari* and that no other issue was involved. The trials can vary. Sometimes to prove the innocence of a killer, the *sardar* orders one of his family members (the most religious, who takes responsibility for the killer) to walk across burning coals. If he crosses a trench filled with burning coals and his feet are not burned, the killer is considered innocent. Another example is that the person who has killed on the pretext of honur killing is taken to a mosque or a shrine where he has to take oath that the killing was *haque* and that he had killed the people because of *karo-kari*. *Haque* means that after seeing the worst things with his own eyes, he murdered the couple involved and there was no other enmity. I also said that the couple were *karo-kari* and that I had no other motive. I clearly said that their boy was a *karo* and therefore I murdered him. At that, the *sardar* became angry with the dead boy's relatives and said 'Enough is enough'. Only then did the male relatives of the murdered boy change their statements before the court and my case was over.

Q: How did they change the statement before the court?

A: Who can challenge a *sardar*'s *faislo*? Who cannot change their statement when the area *sardar* takes a decision? That's a final thing. You know, if someone disagrees with or refuses to accept the *sardar's* decision, then the next time he gets into trouble the *sardars* won't come forward to help him. This is just the way our social system works, which is very corrupt in fact. The tribal leaders and *sardars* are the kings of their areas. No-one can afford to disagree with their decisions. In villages, you know, all the time you are in some kind of trouble. Sometimes there is a land dispute, sometimes personal enmity, sometimes tribal hostility, I mean, you are constantly caught up in some trouble, so in these circumstances you can't afford to make any trouble with the *sardars*. In villages, in a minute a petty issue can blow up like a bomb blast. A small verbal argument ends up in a murder, so all the time we need to seek the support and help of these *sardars*. Maybe some animals are respected in foreign countries, but in Baloch culture, human beings are an extremely valueless commodity. In Baloch culture, life has no respect, in fact, life is nothing. You pass the time or you kill time in order to pass the days of life. Well, I live in Jacobabad so I can only talk about my own city. I don't know about other cities; I can only understand what is normal in my city. When we leave home to go out to work, we never know whether we will be coming home safely or our dead body will be dropped outside our home. Everybody seems like an enemy. You can't trust anyone, even whether the person who is with you is your enemy or friend. Friends will turn into enemies in no time. There is no trust in life.

Q: How do you think other people view your act of killing?

A: Well. Normally in our community, a killer is treated more honourably than a normal man. You know, in this society, if not every other person then at least every third person is a killer, so now it is kind of competition. But one thing is for sure, people are very careful not to mess with a killer because they know that the person who has killed one or two people may kill a third and a fourth as well, so dealing with people becomes easier comparatively.

Q: What is your concept of honour?

A: Honour … you mean what is an honourable thing? Well a *sardar* is honourable because people listen to him and cannot go against what he says or decides, right. And a common man's honour is that if he feels that somebody is looking at his family with a bad intention, he should kill him because this is a threat to his honour. Only then can he keep his honour safe. Otherwise, you know, those who know that something is going wrong in their families ... you know what I mean ... but do not kill the person who is bringing shame or a stain to his honour, he is the most dishonoured person in the world. You have to save your honour at any cost.

Q: If you come across the same situation again, how would you react?

A: Do you mean with the boy?

Q: Yes, I mean if the *karo-kari* situation happens again.

A: Sister, I will kill again and again. No matter how many times I need to kill, I cannot see or tolerate that shameful act. You know it is a matter of honour. Who will pay respect to a dishonoured person? Whoever I find threatening my family's honour, I will kill him, sister, at once.

Q: Thank you for your time.

A: You welcome, sister; and call me again if you need to know something more.

Q: Sure. Thank you.

4: *Name*: Zafar, aged 22

The interview lasted for an hour and eighteen minutes, and it took place at a local hotel.

Zafar had a smiling face and was very proud of himself. He shook hands with me as a gesture to pay respect to me as a sister. In some parts of Sindh, if a man does not shake hands with a woman, it means he is having an illicit relationship with her.

Q: *Assalam-o-alaikum.*

A: *Walaikum-assalam.*

Q: How are you today?

A: Good, thanks sister.

Q: Are you willing to talk to me?

A: Yes. I am.

Q: Whatever information you will give me will be used only for the purposes of my research and for related publications.

A: Sure, sure, I understand that.

Q: Can I record what you say?

A: Why not, then you will listen and write easily?

Q: Yes.

A: OK. No problem.

Q: Tell me something about your background; your name, caste, community, parents.

A: My name is Zafar. We are Rind Baloch and I live in Jacobabad. My father's name was Khizar. I was hardly five or six years old when my father died. My mother is still alive and does housework. She is a healthy woman and looks after our buffalos. I have two brothers and three sisters. And community; I tell you we are Baloch from Balochistanistan but now we are settled in Sindh, in Jacobabad.

Q: How old are you now?

A: Approximately twenty or twenty-two.

Q: Approximately? Don't you have an identity card?

A: Yes, I do. I do have an identity card but because I am illiterate I can't read it. I don't know what is written on it and what age it shows because when the people at the NADRA[45] office asked my age when they were making my identity card, I told them a random number which I can't remember now. Only a literate person can read my identity card and tell you what is written on it.

Q: May I ask you why you didn't receive any education?

A: I grew up as an orphan. No-one was there to guide me, help me or support me. I grew up in very tough circumstances. We were extremely

---

[45] National Database and Registration Authority (NADRA).

poor. My father died when I was a young child. I had two brothers and three sisters and one mother to support. I started toiling from the age of five or six to earn a living as a labourer to look after my family. The toiling … I started at the age of five … is still going on. No relief, no rest, no peace, life is like that. Who could make me study? Life is brutal here. What can an orphan learn? How could I study? Who could make me study? Life is brutal here. The toiling, I told you, …I started at the age of five and it is still continuing. No relief, no rest no peace. Life is like that. The matter of honour you are going to ask about, I have to say something on the issue. My answer is that when honour is hurt, you react very harshly and so when it happened to me, I also killed, but it was honour killing, really an honour killing not a fake drama. A man is a man; he cannot live dishonourably and cannot see anything dishonoured.

Q: Would you like to tell me some more about yourself, about your childhood, siblings, favourite games, education, job and so on?

A: Childhood? Yes, I remember I used to play with my brothers and sisters. There were various games like hide-and-seek, catching each other, running fast to touch a target in order to find out who was the fastest, games like these; simple, useless games. I still remember how badly I wanted to have a ball of my own. Throughout my childhood, I longed for a cricket ball but I couldn't have one and I used to think that one day I would grow up and have enough money to buy a ball.

Q: What is your job?

A: I drive a tractor on the area landlord's farm whenever he calls me. My job is labouring wherever I can get work. Sometimes I get work when roads are being built or a house or buildings are being constructed.

Q: Do you earn enough for your family?

A: Thank God for whatever is available to my family and me. What can I say? I can't complain. This is our fate. Whatever has been written for us by God, we have to be content with it.

Q: Can you tell me something about your married life; I mean the mode of marriage, wife, children, relations with your in-laws and so on?

A: I am not married yet.

Q: Oh, so what was the issue of the honour killing? Who did you kill?

A: She was my cousin [paternal uncle's daughter] and the man was from some other family.

Q: So you mean you killed them both as *karo* and *kari*?

A: Yes.

Q: OK. What was the issue? Why did you kill them?

A: You know these issues. We are Baloch people. We do not think about anything else other than killing for a matter of honour. We consider that only a dishonourable man thinks before he acts in sensitive honour-related matters. If we see anything wrong with our own eyes, then … it is natural that our blood boils. Who can control himself at those moments? It is not a real man's job to tolerate such humiliation. It all happens on a wave of emotion. The man was also from our caste but he was not a relative. His family tree is different from ours. We are different. They are different.

Q: What actually happened?

A: I saw, I saw, what I saw, with my own eyes, and then I said 'Surely there is something fishy going on'.

Q: What happened?

A: My female cousin used to live at my uncle's house. There was a little distance between my house and my uncle's. It was sort of my home so it was necessary and important for me to keep an eye on what was going on there and in the surrounding area to understand things. Everything can be understood through learning about surroundings. Surroundings tell you a lot. I noticed that something was going wrong. There was obviously a problem but the nature of the issue was not clear. It is not true that you kill or harm anyone without seeing anything. First, we get all the details about the problem or the nature of the problem. When we are sure that our suspicions are confirmed, only then do we have to kill. Before murdering someone, we confirm more than once that the issue really exists. Only then do we kill someone. What I saw made me sure that the boy whom I saw around my uncle's house had some malign interest. At the same time, a girl must be involved in the issue.

Q: So, you were keeping an eye on your uncle's house. Were your uncle's family members aware of what was going on?

A: No, I'm not sure as most of her brothers were drug addicts so they would get home late at night and not bother about what was going on. They were in their drugged world. You know these things demand a vigilant eye. Their mother worked on the fields of various farmers in order to earn money. When I killed the two, my uncle's wife, I mean the mother of the girl, was away from home for a few days. Since it was the time of the wheat harvest, she had gone to another village to work on somebody's farm there. Four days after the murders she came back.

Q: I need to understand the situation clearly. Was your cousin alone at home when she was murdered?

A: No, one of her brothers' wives was at home with her. Her youngest brother has gone with their mother for the wheat harvest.

Q: OK, what happened then?

A: I saw once … a couple of weeks earlier … I saw a stranger walking around our area. I became suspicious as I knew that he was from another area. Normally strangers only roam around other people's areas when they have bad intentions. I thought he must have come here for some wrong purpose but … I needed to be sure. From that day on, I started keeping an eye on the man and the situation as well. The second time I saw him, he was on his own at about ten o'clock at night, standing near my uncle's dried-fish farm. It was a dark night. Then I saw a shadow of a woman, my cousin, some way off. I noticed some sign language between them. I became sure that what I had suspected was right. I decided that if I saw them again, I would kill them. The third time, I saw the man standing near the farm at night and then my cousin started walking towards it. She reached him and then both of them went to a house. I kept an eye on every movement they made.

Q: When did you see him for the first time?

A: My uncle had a fish farm. I saw him standing on his own near that farm. He was standing there at night about ten or eleven o'clock. It was a dark night. Then I saw a shadow of a woman going towards the fish farm. She went there. I hid behind the farm. Actually, I saw them the next week again so I was suspicious, but this meeting made my suspicion a genuine belief.

Q: What did you see the next week?

A: I saw the man. He went to the same fish farm, to the same place … OK? I realised that if the man was there at that time of night, a woman would definitely appear from somewhere and most probably from our house. You know human nature and the human heart. There is a natural attraction between a man and a woman. Then, I noticed some sign language between them. I became sure that what I had suspected was right.

Q: So you killed them?

A: No, before murdering them, I followed and saw …

Q: What?

A: Before killing them, as I told you, I was suspicious because two or three times I had seen the man on his own. Twice I saw them smiling and going to the fish farm. I thought 'Enough is enough', and if I saw them again I would kill them both.

Q: So you waited for their next meeting to happen?

A: Yes, of course. The fish farm was empty at that time of year. It was deep and dry because there was no water at the time in the village. So the farm had become a kind of trench. One day, I was sitting there when I saw the man standing near the farm and then my uncle's daughter also started walking towards him from her house. She reached him and then they both went to a house. I kept an eye on their every movement. I knew that they would go and sit or hide somewhere and they went inside the house.

Q: Inside whose house?

A: There was an empty house. I think it belonged to a Rind Baloch family. They both went inside.

Q: So they went into the house. Wasn't it locked?

A: It was a kind of empty plot of someone, not a complete house. The outer walls had no gate. I followed them. They went into a room. So I decided to wait outside as I knew they would come out eventually. I had taken the girl's brother with me to see what was going on. If I had not taken him with me I would have been in big trouble from both sides. It was the sort of place the Rind Baloch used to rent out to different people but it was empty at that time. So I decided to wait outside. I was sure that however long they might be in there, they would eventually come out. They went in …

Q: Into the room?

A: Yes. I was standing outside the house waiting for them to come out. My cousin was also standing with me.

Q: Your cousin … means?

A: The girl's brother.

Q: How did he join you?

A: It was essential to take him along with me in order to make him an eyewitness. Otherwise, people might not have believed me. To justify the killing, it was necessary that one of her family members should be an eyewitness to what was going on. I told him about it and invited him to come along with me and see everything that was going on. If I had killed them without him being there, people might have not believed me. So, you know, if I had not had him with me I would have been in big trouble. You know what an ugly society it is. I would have been in great difficulty from both sides.

Q: Both sides?

A: Yes, from my cousin's house and the man's family's side too.

Q: Oh!

A: So I needed one side to be covered at least. I wanted one side to support me and to be with me. Only then I would be considered innocent, otherwise it would have been difficult for me to justify the killing. A one-sided issue is easier to deal with because with the males' families one can make a *khair*[46] easily through a *sardar*. And my speculations were right as it happened in this case. The *sardar* made a *khair* and I was safe.

Q: Let's talk about the situation. You said they both went into a room in that empty house, right? Then …?

---

[46] Agreement.

A: They were both in there for almost half an hour, then the man's cell phone rang so he came out of the room to answer the call. Yes, we had our rifles with us and we were standing just outside the boundaries of the house. Of course, they could not stay there for the whole night. I said to myself that she is a woman and she would obviously be scared. Surely she would be thinking of her home and her brothers, and that if someone woke up and did not find her in her bed at that time of night … and other similar ideas. For a woman to be scared at such a sensitive time is a normal thing, you know.

Q: Do only women get scared, not men?

A: Men's nerves are stronger than women's so it is the woman who becomes scared or fearful about her safety. It is a natural thing. This is how God made women. So I was sure that they would both come out, as different feelings would make them frightened. The boundaries had no real walls, they were hardly four feet high, so I stood outside and my cousin sat on the low wall around the house. They were both in the room. The man came out to answer his cell phone. He only said 'Hello' on the phone, then my cousin shot him. As soon as he fired, I stepped in and I also fired at him. We both went inside the room and did the same to the girl. First I shot her and then her brother shot her. She died straightaway like the man.

Q: The man came out of the room to answer a phone-call?

A: Yes, I said so. So when the man came out and said 'Hello' on the phone, my cousin shot him. As soon as he had fired, I shot him as well. Then, we both rushed into the room and shot the girl. First I shot her then her brother shot her; one shot from my cousin and one from me. She died straightaway, just like that man. Then we just went away.

Q: You left the dead bodies there and went away?

A: Yes. I told you that the shots had killed them. They both died on the spot.

Q: Didn't the woman cry out or shout after hearing the sound of the shot outside the room where she was?

A: She must have …

Q: Didn't she come out or try to run?

A: No, no, no … how could she dare to? We were standing there like a visit from death. She must have realised that her time was up.

Q: She didn't even lock the door from inside?

A: No, no … she was expecting to be killed. Because the man had come out, the door of the room was open. She wouldn't have had the courage to lock it from the inside and even if she had locked it, we would have broken it. When we shot her, she fell off the far side of the bed. He left the door open when he went out to answer his phone. He didn't know what might happen to him outside.

Q: When you went into the room, what did you see?

A: She was standing by the wall terrified and trembling with fear.

Q: Then?

A: Then we killed her, as I told you. First, I fired and then her brother. After we had killed her … I mean killed them, we went to my cousin's house and we told our elders everything that had happened and that we had done this job.

Q: How did you feel when you had done it?

A: I had been burning inside ever since I knew about it. Killing them made me feel that I had successfully saved my honour.

Q: So basically, when you were sure that they were both dead, you went straight back home with the rifles to let your elders know what you had done?

A: Yes.

Q: Who did you tell first?

A: My paternal uncle.

Q: The girl's father?

A: No, my eldest uncle, who was also the dead girl's uncle. The girl's father had died years ago. Her mother was not at the house because she had gone to another village for work.

Q: What was your uncle's response?

A: He wasn't alone; my other uncles were there too. Our elders were happy and they praised us for continuing the great saga of the Baloch nation. They said, 'You did a great job, you are honourable and understand what honour is. Your Baloch forefathers sacrificed their lives to uphold their honour. Honour is respect. You did an honourable job. You are honourable'. Then we told our other relatives around so that everybody should know about the honour killings and we should not be accused of doing something wrong. Thank God, nobody called these killings unjust.

Q: OK, then?

A: Then … within no time our relatives reached our home. They decided to hide my cousin who had killed them with me, and they took me to the police. I took my rifle and said that I had killed them to save my family's honour. The police asked a few general questions about the situation, the murder and other details. Then they locked me up. I was sure that I would be freed quite soon as my relatives had already spoken to the area *sardar*, and then the police consoled me and assured me that the *wadera* would support me. I faced only nine months' imprisonment. Nine months passed so quickly and I became free with the support of the *wadera*.

Q: Didn't the police ask any questions about your cousin who was with you in murdering them?

A: No. When they asked me who had helped me to kill them, I replied that I was the only person who had killed them; that nobody had been my supporter or had been with me. If I told them about my cousin they would have arrested him too and he would have been in trouble. I completely denied anyone else's involvement in these murders.

Q: But you are free, so he would have also been free by now.

A: No. Try to understand. When two people kill someone or a couple, the police always suspect that the killing was planned and we did not want that mess.

Q: What was it like being in jail?

A: Well, it was OK. The jail was really hot because of a power problem. Fans were there but there was no electricity. But, you know, good and bad, wrong and right go together. And second, a jail is a jail … they didn't let us go out at all. Only once a week, under the supervision of a police guard, we used to walk within the premises of the jail. And the timings of that walk were also limited. Let's say we started walking at midday and went to other locked-up inmates to say 'Hi', 'Hello', and by four o'clock we were locked up again. We could only meet other prisoners on Sundays in their barracks. There I met quite a few like-minded people and I wanted to spend some time with them, so whenever I had an opportunity I spent time with them in the jail.

Q: Any quarrels in the jail?

A: No, the police was alert all the time and if people tried to create any kind of trouble, you know like shouting or fighting with each other, the police really beat them mercilessly in order to punish them.

Q: Were you ever beaten in the jail?

A: No, no never. My case was respectful so the police paid respect to me. Besides, there were so many people from my area who knew the issue so I was treated very respectfully, not just by the other prisoners but also by the police.

Q: What did you think about how long you were sentenced to be imprisoned?

A: I was sure that I would be freed quite soon as my relatives had already spoken to the area *sardars* and the *sardars* had assured them about the *faislo*. I was confident that God was on our side. My relatives who used to come to visit me kept me informed about the on-going progress. Then God made the *khair*. The nine months in jail passed very quickly and I was set free.

Q: What did the complainants do? Did they lodge an FIR against you?

A: Yes, they did; and the murdered man's father also went to court once. They realised that their case was weak so they didn't follow it up. And he didn't go to the court a second time. Second, the *sardar* put pressure on them. And within no time the *faislo* was done. *Faislos* are easy, quick, in the village, and the *waderas* understand our cultural norms and we consider their decisions appropriate. The Pakistani court system is very expensive and it takes ages to decide a case. Also, Pakistani law does not understand our honour-related cultural tradition so we prefer *jirgas*. We know what will happen in the *faislo*, as general rules are applied in *jirgas* so the disputed groups always agree over the decision. We like it because it is much easier and cheaper justice than the courts and the police.

Q: Did anyone speak against you from the murdered girl's family?

A: No. How was that possible? No-one came forward from the woman's side as they knew the facts and I was from their own family. I saved the honour of the family. She was my cousin. Her own brother was a witness to the murder so how could they go against me? Only the murdered *karo*'s relatives created trouble at the beginning of the case but they stopped after a while. And our strength was visible as all the members of my family were united. They took an oath that they would defend me on the point that the killing was to maintain our family's honour. Although they are all poor like us, they still supported us financially and morally as much as they could. You know the real friend is the one who helps you in the difficult times, so all my relatives proved themselves to be good friends of mine and helped me more than I had expected. You know what kind of a system it is today: nobody helps others. It has become a selfish world now. But I am thankful that my relatives helped me at that tough time and I admire the stand which they took for me. They collected money and gave it to the police.

Q: To the police, why?

A: It was essential because the murdered man's family was giving money to the police to beat me, but at the same time my relatives were also giving money to police so that they would not beat me.

Q: So it was a kind of competition?

A: Of course. But I consider myself very lucky that by the mercy of God we won this battle as well.

Q: You mean your relatives gave more money to the police than the man's relatives?

A: Sure, otherwise how would the police not touch me? You know that the police are not on anyone's side. The police are related only to money. So my people gave the police more money and as a result I stayed safe from their beatings.

Q: How much money was collected and given to the police by your relatives?

A: I cannot tell you an absolute figure, but I heard from those who came to visit me in jail that money was being collected and that my uncle was asking relatives to help us.

Q: Did the police ask for money?

A: Yes, the police asked for 10,000 rupees from my relatives as the dead man's relatives had registered an FIR against me and those who were helping me anonymously. The police confirmed that they had received money to beat me. I maintained that I had killed them both on my own as an honour killing and that nobody else had been with me. To make me safe from police brutality, whatever my poor relatives could do, they did.

Q: Approximately how much money did your relatives pay to the police to save you from being beaten?

A: My elders must know.

Q: But you were not beaten by the police, true?

A: Yes, true; not at all.

Q: Looking back on the killings, how do you feel about it now?

A: If I see such a situation again or if somebody acts badly in front of my eyes, to uphold the honour of my family and my tribe, I will do the same. I would even kill more than two people. Not once, but as many times as I see this crime happening. I will work according to the Islamic teaching. I will proudly follow our Baloch tradition, as nothing is superior to honour. I can never let honour down. After all, we are Baloch not Hindus who do not believe in killing and overlook sensitive matters of this type. Baloch culture stands on this tradition. No matter whatever the circumstances are, we will keep our honour up. That's what the Baloch nation stands for. Whoever looks at our honour in a wrong way, we will kill him. Wasting time in these cases means allowing disgrace to happen. At the exact minute when you see wrong being done, not thinking but direct action is demanded, as you do not need to think like a businessman to save your thinking about honour. A bullet is needed directly in the chest of the person who brings disrespect to your family. Not thinking, as thinking is a cowardly act. Whatever tradition has come down to us from our forefathers, it is our duty to maintain it. I can never imagine tarnishing my culture.

Q: How do you think other people viewed your act?

A: Everybody congratulated me. Everybody praised my action, calling me a hero and a responsible Balochi who had fulfilled his duty in a noble manner. People gave my example to youngsters so that they should follow me and uphold honour. Everybody was saying what an honourable deed I had done. They were asking why somebody had dared to enter our house and cast an evil eye on our honour. If someone does wrong he must face his destiny, just like the destiny which was faced by the dead man and a woman who did not respect her family, culture and tradition, they must face the same end as she faced. The solution to staying safe is not to do wrong and not to face such a pathetic death.

Q: What is your concept of honour?

A: Honour is a passion. What else? What is it … it's a passion.

Q: And how does it emerge or arise?

A: It emerges when it sees that something is going wrong; a family member does wrong; a person tries to tarnish your family's respect or values. Then honour arises and asks you to take revenge. When someone with bad intentions looks at our women, then honour burns and forces us to react and kill those who challenge our honour. Will honour not burn strongly? Will honour not force us to react and kill those who are challenging our honour? Why does a stranger or a man who does not belong to our family or caste and has no blood relation with us, no family links … try to disregard our family?

Q: And if he had a blood relationship with you, what then?

A: No matter, even then he would have to be killed. Whether he had a family relationship or was even a blood relation, we would not let him toy with our honour. He would have to be killed, for sure. No doubt about it. Why should I forgive him? Nothing can provide any justification for sparing him. If any cousin, let's say a first cousin, did it, I mean whatever that dead man had done, even then, I would have killed him without mercy. It is honour, not a joke.

Q: In your opinion, killing in the name of honour is a right concept?

A: Absolutely right. Nothing is superior to honour. Without honour what is left in your life? Is there any respect in society for a dishonoured man?

Q: Let's say, if you were caught in a similar situation to that in which the dead man was found, what kind of treatment would you have expected for youself?

A: Well ... they ... I mean the relatives of the girl, then they would have the same right. They would have to kill me then. They would not let me survive if they had honour.

Q: Would that be right, then?

A: Well, as I said, the system is right and I killed ... and the killings were right. Then surely others also kill rightly or for a right cause. But, if I were to have an affair with a woman, then it would be my luck or chance if I could get away with it or maybe rescue myself. Otherwise, you know the destiny ... the end ... or if I could escape death, then I would have considered myself lucky. Then I would be hidden somewhere until a *faislo* with the other group by the *sardar* had taken place. Only then would I have appeared again. But Baloch culture is terrible. Five or six years is a normal time for hunting down a *karo*. We have not seen anyone who had been rescued after being accused of being a *karo*. A *karo* and a *kari* definitely have to be killed, no matter how much time goes by. They cannot hide anywhere on earth from a true Baloch. The guilty ones have to be found. That is essential. A *karo* has to be killed and a *kari* has to be killed ... No way out, no rescue. Today, tomorrow or the day after tomorrow, but they will have to meet their punishment. No mercy on a *karo* or a *kari*. But no-one else will kill a *karo* except the guilty girl's legitimate relatives.

Q: Imagine, you are in the past and the same situation has arisen, how would you react?

A: Do you think I would let my honour down? If I see such a situation again, to uphold my family's honour I would kill even more that two people – not just once, but as many times as possible. I will work to please God as long as I am alive! My act was and will remain in accordance with *Sharia*. I would do the same thing over and over again if it happens again, but now no-one would dare to look at our family as people have learned the lesson and have understood that an honourable Baloch lives there.

Q: Thank you for your time.

A: You are like my sister; I can help you even more.

5: *Name*: **Atif, aged 26**

The interview lasted for an hour and nineteen minutes and took place at a local hotel.

Atif was a tall, handsome man with deep-set eyes. His hair was done well. He was very confident and kept his arms crossed as he spoke to me. He offered to meet me again in case I needed more information about the issue which we discussed.

Q: *Assalam-o-alaikum.*

A: *Walaikum-assalam.*

Q: How are you doing?

A: Very well, thanks.

Q: Let me make one thing clear: whatever information you give me will remain secure and will be used only for the purposes of my research and for related publications.

A: Sure, sure, I understand that.

Q: OK. So you know that I will record your interview?

A: You will write it down, won't you?

Q: Sure, I will write it as well as record it. Are you willing to be recorded?

A: Oh, OK. Well, fine.

Q: If you have an objection, I shall not record you but I shall write down whatever points of view you tell me.

A: No, no sister, it's OK; if it suits you, I don't mind.

Q: Thank you; will you hold the recorder?

A: Sure, why not?

Q: Tell me something about your background; your name, caste, community, parents.

A: My name is Atif and I am twenty-six. We are Baloch from Balochistan but now are settled in Sindh. I am educated, a little ... not too much, just a secondary pass. My father was a policeman and now looks after his land. I have six brothers and four sisters.

Q: That is good to know. What about your mother?

A: My mother does housework and nothing else. She stays at home.

Q: And what do you do?

A: I run a business.

Q: A business?

A: I have a motor bike business. I buy and sell them. And I help my father on the land and ... just ... enough. Thank God, we are doing well. My elder brother also works on the land. We work together with solidarity.

Q: Would you like to tell me some more about yourself, your childhood, siblings, favourite games, education and so on?

A: My childhood was simple. I grew up like other villagers' children. Just roaming around, fighting, learning and cracking jokes. In Baloch culture, children don't normally play at home. They play outside with other boys.

Q: Children, you mean ... girls and boys?

A: No, not girls and boys together. Girls normally play with their cousins at home like with dolls or helping their mother with the housework. They don't go out. But boys stay out for quite a long time and come home late.

Q: Do you remember any game you played?

A: No ... not particularly. You know the common life in Jacobabad; children just kill time in order to grow up and be able to work ... to live ... that's it. ...

Q: Are you married?

A: Yes.

Q: Can you tell me something about your married life? The mode of your marriage, your wife, children, relationships with in-laws and so on?

A: I got married in 2000 to one of my relatives. My wife is my aunt's daughter.

Q: Your aunt's daughter?

A: Yes, my paternal aunt's daughter, I mean, my wife is my father's paternal cousin's daughter.

Q: OK; and the mode of your marriage?

A: *Watto-satto*.[47] We took one girl [*from that family*] and gave one girl to them. It is a common and simple thing.

Q: How much money did you pay?

A: Sister, no money. We are Baloch. We do not believe in giving or taking money for marriages. We do marriages only within the family and the only form of marriage we follow is *watto-satto*. There is no money involved at all.

Q: How many children do you have?

A: I have two daughters and three sons.

Q: How do you get on with your in-laws?

A: Very good, very nice so far; we get on very well. Well settled.

Q: And with your wife?

A: Fine, nice.

Q: Good … And what was the issue of *karo-kari*? Who did you kill?

A: Sister; the issue was that my uncles live some way away from us. I mean in the same village but not in the same area. So they live at some distance from us.

---

[47] Give and take/ Exchanging girls.

Q: How many uncles?

A: My three uncles lived near our house. One of my uncle's daughters went to a boy's house that was just two kilometres away from our house. In fact, she wanted to run away with the boy but the boy's family didn't make it possible. The boy wasn't at home at that time. As soon as she reached their house, the boy's father made the girl sit down and informed my uncle. My uncles then sent us a message to get to the boy's house quickly. When we reached the boy's house, the girl was sitting there. It was a matter of *karo-kari*, as you know. We brought our girl back. You know, this is a very strong Balochi custom that if something immoral happens we kill the person who causes insult to the family. So the girl was ours and the boy was theirs as she was one of my uncles' daughters. Right?

Q: Right.

A: OK. So the boy took the girl and tried to run away. But then ... they had no right to do that and they gave our girl back to us. They had no right to take the girl away and they understood and estimated our rights and our strength so they returned the girl back to us.

Q: What do you mean? Did the boy take the girl or did they go somewhere?

A: No, no, no. Actually, our girl went to their home one night. Right? As I told you, the boy's family live near my uncles' homes so my uncle's daughter went to their home at night. As soon as she got there, the father of the boy sent a man to us with a message to take the girl back.

Q: You mean your cousin went alone to their home?

A: Yes, she went to their home, in the same village, just two kilometers from our home. There is kind of a village system, you know. In a city, people might call it the same city, but we call it a different village. In J--, small, small villages are next to each other. My uncles sent us a message for us to go there quickly as something had gone wrong. Then, you know ... it was a matter of *karo-kari*, as you know. They were of the Jakhrani tribe.

Q: OK.

A: You know, she was my paternal uncle's daughter. She went to the boy. In fact, she wanted to run away with the boy but the boy's family didn't let it happen. When she went there, the boy was not at home at the time but his father was. As soon as she reached their home, his father made the girl sit down and he informed my uncle, and then I was informed.

Q: How were you informed?

A: My uncle sent a man to us.

Q: Then?

A: Then we went there, to the home of the Jakhrani family. The girl was sitting there and we brought her back home. You know, it is a very strong Balochi custom that if something immoral happens, we kill the person who brings disaster to the family.

Q: Can you share the details with me, please?

A: Yes, why not? What happened was this, sister … I'm letting you know everything clearly. We brought the girl back home and that same night we killed her.

Q: The girl?

A: Yes.

Q: Just her?

A: Just her. Yes.

Q: Did you ask her why she went there?

A: Yes, we enquired thoroughly. She admitted her fault, that she had left home because she wanted to marry the boy. It was clear. It was visible. She was a *kari*.

Q: How old was the girl?

A: She was about sixteen, I think.

Q: How did she come into contact with the boy? As far as I know, Baloch women cover their faces and don't usually go out of their houses, except for some emergency or important matter? Am I right?

A: No, no, no; our Baloch women don't cover their faces. They don't veil their faces. That is a city style, a city fashion. Our women only cover their bodies with a large sheet of cloth and there is no cover over the face. In our villages, sister, ... I told you that the boy's family live near my uncles' home. So they might have seen each other and met as well. Maybe God knows better.

Q: How long did the girl remain at their house?

A: Maybe for ten or fifteen minutes. She got there and the boy's father sent a message to my uncle and then straightaway my uncle sent the message to us.

Q: And within fifteen minutes you all reached the boy's home?

A: Yes, sister.

Q: Then?

A: I saw the girl was sitting there. When we asked her, she confirmed [what she had done].

Q: May I ask you what you asked her?

A: We asked, our elders asked, in fact, her father asked. My eldest uncle, whose younger brother's daughter she was, asked. We all asked her why she had gone there? Who for? She was made to take an oath to speak the truth and she openly admitted that she went there for the boy. She told us the boy's name and admitted that he had agreed and promised to marry her. She told us that the name of the boy who she had gone to was Shahid. She also told us that she and the boy wanted to run away from the village and go somewhere else.

Q: How many people from your side went there to bring the girl back?

A: There were five of us, sister, all five from one family. My eldest uncle and the uncle whose daughter it was, the two brothers of the girl and me. We took the girl to her father's home. First our plan was to kill both as *karo-kari* but, you know, a son is so adored by his parents that they hid him somewhere, but we did justice to our girl according to our Baloch custom. We gave her the punishment she deserved. We killed her. We do kill whoever is involved in any matter of dishonour.

Q: Did anyone from her mother's side try to rescue her?

A: No, no, not at all. Her mother knew the tradition. She felt hatred for her daughter. She clearly said that she was no relation of the girl because she had brought insult to the whole family. She said, 'From now on, this girl is dead for me because she has done wrong'. She allowed the male members of the family to punish her accordingly.

Q: Then?

A: Then, I told you, you know, we could not tolerate her any longer so her father said we must act then and there. We killed her.

Q: How? What weapon was used and who did it? Can you explain the mode of killing?

A: Yes, sister. We did not kill her with a gun. We gave her some drugs.

Q: Drugs?

I: Yes, sister, drugs.

Q: And how did you do that?

I: We gave her pills.

Q: Pills? Sleeping pills ... or?

I: No, no, sister, drugs, you know, addicts use them as drugs.

Q: Can you name the drug please?

I: 'Ativan' tablets.

Q: Where did you get the tablets from?

I: Oh, they are available everywhere at pharmacies and every general store. Hundreds in Jacobabad are addicted to them.

Q: How did you give them to her and how many?

I: We said 'Take this', and she took it. That was understandable, sister, as she was a Baloch child and knew what was going to happen to her. She knew. All Baloch children know our culture, tradition and custom. From their childhood they learn how strong the honour-related custom is. She knew, if someone brings dishonour to family, they need to face death so she knew just as well as we all knew the consequences of that act. We all knew what would happen. We simply said to her, 'Drink' and she drank.

Q: Was it syrup?

I: No, no, I told you Ativan tablets. We mixed the tablets in tea and she drank the tea.

Q: How many tablets were mixed in the tea?

A: A whole pack.

Q: I think that there are twelve tablets in a pack?

A: No, sister, ten.

Q: Then?

A: Then after drinking it, she became unconscious. Then we strangled her.

Q: What with?

A: With her own *duapatta*.[48]

Q: Did she beg you for mercy?

A: No, sister, nothing. She knew what was going to happen to her.

Q: Did she say anything before she drank it?

A: No, nothing, not a single word. She was a Baloch child and knew what was going to happen to her. From a very tender age, our children learn how important honour is. She knew that an immoral girl would face death. So we, as well as she, knew the consequences of drinking the tea. My father, my uncle, her two brothers, I and her fiancé strangled her with her own *dupatta*. It barely took two minutes, not even two minutes. The drug had already finished her. I mean the strangling was only a matter of

---

[48] Scarf.

ritual. She could not survive after such a drug but as an honourable deed, we all strangled her.

Q: Did you mix the tablets in the tea in front of her?

A: Yes, so that she should know.

Q: Who strangled her, you?

A: No, her own father. I was there too and I joined in.

Q: How many of you were there?

A: I was there; her father was there, my uncle, her two brothers and her fiancée.

Q: Was she engaged?

A: Yes.

Q: How long did it take to strangle her?

A: Sister, it took barely two minutes, not even two minutes, less than two minutes. The drug had already finished her. Let's say it was a matter of one minute.

Q: And she was dead?

A: Yes, she was finished. As I told you, the drugs had completely finished her. Then it was, I mean the act of strangling was, just a matter of ritual. She could not have survived after such a dose but for reasons of honour, they strangled her.

Q: Did you also strangle her?

A: It was necessary, sister. We all did it. We are honourable people.

Q: What about her mother … did she not plead to save her daughter?

A: Her mother clearly said that she was a curse so she asked us [men] to finish her as she could not bear the stink of her.

Q: How did you feel when you'd done it?

A: I felt relaxed and thought that that was the punishment for such immorality in our Balochi custom. We said, 'We have killed our child and now we will kill the person who is responsible for her death or for this disgrace. Now we will kill him'. Sister, may I tell you one thing, sister?

Q: Yes, sure, please do.

A: This all happened five of six years ago, right ... it happened in 2007 but none of us have seen him anywhere. No member of our family has ever come across him. We haven't even found any clue to where he is. So the issue is still going on. We need proper Baloch justice. Our enmity has not been settled. We have not attended any *jirga* to have the enmity settled with some *faislo*. We will not go for a *faislo*.

Q: Why not?

A: Because we have decided to kill the guilty boy. We have not seen him since then but we will surely find him sooner or later as the world is not big enough to hide him. We will get him wherever, whenever. This is a mission now.

Q: Where is he, in your opinion?

A: He must be somewhere in Balochistan but we don't know his whereabouts. If we knew, would we have left him alive? We need his address. We don't know anything about him. How long? Five or six years is a normal time to search for a *karo* couple. We have not seen any one who had been rescued after an allegation of *karo*. A *karo* or *kari* definitely has to be killed, no matter how much time passes. They cannot hide anywhere on earth from a true Baloch. The culprit has to be found. A *karo* has to be killed today, tomorrow or the day after tomorrow ... no way, no rescue, no mercy upon *karo* and *kari*. But no-one else will kill a *karo* or both except the girl's legitimate relative.[49]

Q: Before that *karo-kari* incident, how did you get on with the boy of the Jakhrani family?

---

[49] Chasing a runaway couple becomes the target of the tribe for generations. The men of the tribe whose girl runs away take an oath that they will not wear new clothes or celebrate any festival until they kill the couple. A number of stories published in magazines and newspapers tell that some couples were found as many as ten or fifteen years after and were brutally killed, along with their children.

A: The boy was our friend. We had a nice relationship with each other. We used to go to each other's *otaque* frequently. We did not know he would be a part of such immorality.

Q: After killing your cousin, did you go to the police?

A: No, no, why would I go to the police? We killed our own child. She was ours. We did what we wanted and what she deserved. We had a right to do what we did. Who could report us to the police? Who were her relatives? We killed her because we were responsible for her conduct. Why would people or the police interfere in our personal family matter? We killed her because she belonged to us.

Q: Did any *sardar* contact you over this matter?

A: No, why would a *sardar* contact us? As I told you, she was our child, we were responsible for her and we killed her. Why would a *sardar* interfere in that?

Q: Imagine, you are in the past and the same situation occurred, how would you react?

A: How? You mean, if it happens again?

Q: Yes.

A: Look, sister. Our culture, our religion, our honour and our conscience all demand that we must not put up with immoral acts. This is an unbearable thing for us to see and not be able to prevent it. We regard it as an immensely dishonourable deed not to kill the person responsible. We have killed and we will kill again, no matter how many times this happens. We cannot be dishonoured. We cannot bear it. If it is committed by our mother, our sister, our daughter, wife or other relative, we shall not forgive her whatever her caste and we would not waste any time before killing such women along with the men who would try to bring such an insult on us. But we will not kill any woman other than our family. If she is the wife or sister of our friends or neighbours, we will not involve ourselves in other people's business. But if a woman from our family is involved, we will throw out two dead bodies. But that killing happened five or six years ago. After that, nothing wrong has happened, thank God. Normally, from what I have observed, if an honour-related killing happens in one family, then the rest of the families around get the message and this does not occur again.

Q: But if it does happen again?

A: We will repeat what we did. There would be no mercy in this regard. This is not just today's culture. This is a custom which is hundreds, but not hundreds, it is thousands of years old. And we are proud of that and the whole Baloch nation is proud of that.

Q: If you had been seen or caught with a woman from some other tribe, what do you think would happen to you?

A: They should kill me; they must do according to our culture. If I act immorally, they should kill me. If I harm some tribe's honour they should not let me live. It is not a matter of me only. It is a matter of culture, respect, tradition and honour.

Q: How do you think other people view your act?

A: Nothing. People came to know that we have killed one of our female children and they thought nothing except that it was insulting for us that we only killed a woman of our family and not the other person involved in this disgrace. We told all of our relatives about it. The boy's family received the message about what we can do and how far we will go to maintain our honour. They understood. They asked about it and we openly admitted that we had killed the girl. Look, sister, I tell you directly so that you can understand it clearly: our women are our honour. If somebody looks at our women with a bad intention we will not put up with it. We are Muslims, so how can we tolerate it? We understand our religion. Nothing is better than religious belief and honour because soon we will all die. And what will enable us to survive in the world after? Our honourable deeds. Our honourable deeds will save us at the day of judgement and nothing else. God helps those who keep their honour up. But it is necessary only to kill justifiably and not to carry out any wrong killing. No killing for the sake of greed or self-interest as an unjust killing will make your life a disaster as it is a sin to kill someone for such a wrong reason. You should not trust wrong gossip or wrong allegations about others. Killing is justified only when you see something done wrong with your own eyes.

Q: What is honour in your opinion?

A: Our family women are our honour. Killing in the name of honour is absolutely right, sister. In this way, people learn what honour is and what dishonour is. You know what – those who do wrong have to be killed instantly. If you enter someone's home, if you have a wrong relationship with some respected family's woman, you should have no right to live. Everybody has his honour and has a right to save it in the way he wants. Nowadays, many people divorce their wives instead of killing their *kari* wives. This is their way of dealing with honour. Being men, our status is higher than women because we are the giver and the provider. So obedience to us is the duty of our women and in return protecting them is our duty. We shall keep a vigilant eye on their conduct to safeguard our honour. We are Muslims and understand that nothing is greater than religious belief and honour. Soon we shall all die and what will enable us to survive in the world after is our honourable deeds, which will save us on the day of judgment, and nothing else. God helps those who preserve their honour. Those who do wrong have to be killed instantly. We call honour killing a *jahad*.[50] Nothing is greater than honour. Without honour what is life? Those who do not kill the unfaithful woman and man are the most dishonoured people. In this way people learn what the difference between honour and dishonour is. The women who do wrong have to be killed instantly.

Q: Do Baloch men also divorce their wives?

A: Yes, they do. Those who have no energy or power or are scared of the police or maybe scared of others, they do not kill; only powerful, brave and honourable Baloch kill.

Q: Only the powerful kill; what do you mean by that?

A: You know, some people are frightened for one reason or another. They are scared of the police, scared of their relatives, the relatives of the women or scared of the suspected men's relatives, and so on. Only strong people who have a strong will and strong faith in God and the Day of Judgment kill.

Q: Thank you for your time.

A: No worries. You can contact me anytime.

---

[50] Fighting in the name of God.

6: *Name*: **Adnan, aged 38**

The interview lasted for an hour and twenty-nine minutes and took place at a local hotel.

Adnan was a man of medium height. He looked like a simple and respectful person; he had a French-cut beard and he spoke very politely.

Q: *Assalam-u-alaikum.*

A: *Walaikum-assalam.*

Q: How are you doing?

A: Very well, thanks.

Q: Let me tell you one thing, whatever information you give will be used only for the purposes of my research and for related publications.

A: Sure, sure, I understand that.

Q: Can I record the interview?

A: It's OK, if you like, do it. I don't mind.

Q: Tell me something about your background; yourname, caste, community, parents.

A: My name is Adnan. I am from Sukker. We are Baloch and originally are from Balochistan but about forty-five years ago my grandfather came to Sindh and settled here. I am now thirty-eight. My father has died, he was in a government job, not at an important position but you know that a government job is a secure job, so it was not a very difficult childhood and my father wanted us to be educated. I had three brothers and five sisters.

Q: Would you like to tell me some more about yourself, like your childhood, siblings, favourite games, education, job and so on?

A: I played many games in my village with friends and brothers and sisters and, you know, all the children play there. When I grew up, I started playing hockey and soon the district team accepted me; I played in the positions of fullback and goalkeeper but I could not carry on playing hockey. As far as my education is concerned, I passed my primary from a local school and went to college. That was two miles away from my village but then I stopped studying when the trouble [that is, after he had killed his cousin as *karo* with his sister] occurred. All of a sudden our lives changed and I had to leave education, hockey, home ... almost everything. But now things are settled and I have a job.

Q: What is your job?

A: It is a private job. I work privately at a shoe shop.

Q: How are you doing there?

A: It is fine. OK. Thank God ... I'm getting on well.

Q: Can you tell me something about your married life, mode of marriage, wife, children, your relations with your in-laws and so on?

A: I married my paternal uncle's daughter in 1990. I have three sons and one daughter. I got on really well with my in-laws from the day of my marriage. We have 100% understanding. My wife is very humble so I am blessed that I am comfortable.

Q: May I ask you what was the issue of *karo-kari*?

A: He was a cousin of my wife so he had an easy access to our family and used to come to our houses frequently. But he was actually my cousin too [father's maternal uncle's son]. Besides, he was also my friend. He used to come to our home being a relative but then gradually it was not a secret that he had a love affair with my younger sister. Since I was an educated person, I understood my society, our Balochi norms, tradition and custom, so for everyone's sake I asked the boy to marry her. I wanted the issue to be settled quickly before it became the talk of the town. I offered the solution to the boy himself, his father, his mother ... as I thought marriage the only reasonable, peaceful and logical solution. But the boy's parents, instead of listening to me or thinking about the severity of the matter, insulted me and said that I was accusing their son. They called me greedy and accused me of asking for my sister's marriage with their son because of their wealth. I said, 'I admit that we are poor and you occupy a better place in this society, but don't forget that you are at fault. Your son had started the game and you know in our culture how such issues are tackled. Do you understand? Otherwise, you know, we also need to survive as part of this culture. We cannot tolerate relationships like this'. I had the idea that if the issue was not taken seriously then killings would happen and that's what I wanted to avoid. I knew these things travel very fast in our tribal areas so if we did not kill the two who were involved with each other, our society would not let us survive. We would be the target for insults; people would spit in our faces. In addition, the boy's intentions were highly dubious. He just wanted to be out of the scene. His elders and parents were insulting us and he stopped coming and talking to me. Eventually his family told me that I should forget the issue. I now say that the boy's family deliberately put me into the worst situation and asked for the disaster which ... later became almost impossible to sort out. I understood my society, our Balochi norms, traditions and customs, so for everyone's sake I asked the boy to marry her in order to sort the problem out.

Q: Who did you make this suggestion to?

A: To the boy himself, then to his father, his mother ... as I wanted the issue to be sorted out in a decent way. I told them, 'To me this seems the only possible and reasonable solution and it will be better for both of our families. In this way, neither you nor we will be insulted by society. Let's finish the matter here and give it a logical conclusion'. I told them that it was not a big issue so just accept the fact and let them marry to solve the issue. I was educated and I wanted a peaceful solution to the problem but the boy's parents, instead of listening to me or thinking about the severity of the matter, started insulting me. They subjected me to mental torture. They said 'You are making a wrong allegation against our son'. They called me greedy and accused me of asking for my sister's marriage with their son beause they were wealthy. I said, 'Yes, we are poor but money is nothing to do with it. It is a matter of respect and pride. Your son has been involved with my sister and honour demands that he should marry her now. It is a simple thing and we all will be saved from trouble'. I said, 'I admit that we are poor and you occupy a better place in this society, but don't forget that you are at fault. Your son started it and you know how such things are treated in our culture. These are not acceptable things in our society. You have to realise that'. Otherwise, you know, being part of this culture we also need to survive, because, sister ... our society is not an urban society where these issues are tackled differently. Our society is a tribal society. We are not liberal or bold people. We cannot tolerate relationships like this with the women of our house. I had the idea that if the issue was not taken seriously then killings would happen, and that's what I wanted to avoid, because I knew that these things travel very fast in our tribal areas and if we didn't kill the two who were involved, people wouldn't let us survive peacefully... So being a member of the family, I had sympathy with both sides and the only sensible idea I had in my mind was that the boy and the girl should get married. I now say that the boy's family deliberately put me into a difficult and even worse situation; they deliberately brought trouble down on us and asked for this disaster which ... later became almost impossible to repair.

Q: Did they refuse the proposal of them marrying?

A: They not only refused it, they remained very stubborn and stern even though it was a simple matter and my proposal had no hidden motives.

Q: What were the boy's intentions?

A: His role was very doubtful. He just wanted to be out of the scene. His elders and parents were insulting us and he stopped coming or talking to me. He didn't dare to speak to his family or to justify his position. And his family eventually told me that I should forget it.

Q: Can you explain why did they do that?

A: Hmm ... simple, they had power, they had money. They were more influential than us. I tried to contact the boy to convince him but he didn't even try to contact me. So I had no choice – I took the extreme step.

Q: Did you talk to your sister about it?

A: Yes, I asked her as well and she admitted it. She accepted that she had had illicit relations with him. She said that he had a relationship with her and had promised to marry her.

Q: At your home, in the presence of so many people, how did it happen? I mean how did they keep on meeting each other?

A: It did not happen at our home, sister. I was in Balochistan, as I told you earlier. I was studying and doing some work as well. My sister used to pay me frequent visits. And you know, sister, mothers normally keep an eye on these things, but our mother was working in Jacobabad so we only got to know about it later. If my mother had been there, I would have known about it earlier. But anyway, I told you that the boy and my sister both admitted having relations with each other. I advised the boy to take the issue seriously and settle it in a sensible and decent manner. He took no notice. I was berated by his relatives. I was under pressure from my own family! When I had no other option, only then did I decide … to … do it. The boy was … dead.

Q: How?

A: One day, I saw him in Balochistan. When he saw me, he became scared. We were standing facing each other. I had a pistol in my pocket, I had been waiting for this day and I didn't waste a single minute, I fired at him. He … he was instantly … dead.

Q: Were you determined to kill him, or was it when you saw him that you killed him?

A: No, I was determined. See, at first when I was trying to sort it out peacefully, I hated the idea of killing any one. But when it was made worse by the boy's parents and other relatives by refusing the marriage option and insulting me, I started thinking about other options as well. And it was in my mind that whenever I saw him I would kill him. They really drove me to kill him because I was basically a peaceful person and I was a young student at the time. I wanted to complete my studies and to become something. I realised that if I killed him, my life, my studies, my family, my future and everything would be badly affected, but I couldn't do anything to save my future.

Q: When did it happen?

A: It happened in 1993.

Q: How old were you then?

A: I was hardly twenty or twenty-one at that time. I knew my future would be ruined. You know our Baloch customs and our culture. I discussed with myself that if I killed him, my future would be ruined and if I didn't kill him, my whole family's future would be ruined. You know that in our culture, childhood marriages are common. I was married too, and it was also a great concern for me that my family would suffer a lot. I was very worried and could not decide what to do. I tried to sort it out from every possible angle. I even told the boy and his family that if they thought that marriage was not the only solution, then they should give me another solution for how I should handle the issue, but there were no positive words, just more and more insults. They seemed to enjoy the fact that I was begging them every week and thought that I would not go so far as to take any extreme action. They just took no notice and didn't take me seriously. From the other side, my family also put pressure on me to get the issue settled. And, you know, all these related issues disturbed me a lot. There was no other way except to kill the boy.

Q: Oh!

A: Yes, I simply made my mind up and shot him down.

Q: Did he shout or tried to run?

A: No. He couldn't do anything at all. I killed him in the middle of a busy market and he couldn't run. He died straightaway.

Q: How did you feel when you had done it?

A: I had very strange and mixed feelings. I felt really sorry and blamed the stubborn attitude of him and his family. I felt sorry that they had forced me to kill him. Why didn't they try to help me to sort it out peacefully? If he hadn't done anything wrong, I wouldn't have taken the crucial step. They punished me for being peaceful and honest and they pushed me to respond with full force. They were testing my power. I didn't want to kill anyone. I didn't want him to be killed. For me, seeing him dying was a painful experience. He was my friend. I really felt bad but I couldn't endure all that. I thought many times about it all and then decided that killing him was the only option. Before killing him I was sad and then after killing him I was sad too because, as I told you before, I wasn't the murdering kind of man. I wanted everything to be resolved peacefully. Before killing him, I was thinking, 'OK, he's made a mistake but why doesn't he realise that and try to accept his mistake and correct it'. I wanted him to talk to me and discuss the matter positively to sort it out. After killing him, I was really sad and I asked myself why he hadn't realised the situation. I had talked to his family in good faith, but they ignored me and insulted me. What was left for me to be able to live an honourable life in this tribal society? He was my friend; we lived together; we spent quite good times together. I wished I couldn't have killed him. After the killing, the police arrested me. I explained everything clearly, everything that had happened. My case continued for seven years. For two years, I was in the district jail. Then I was transferred to a death-cell in the central jail after the government of Pakistan sentenced me to death. Later on, my family members, including my father, went to the boy's family to convince them to withdraw the case. My parents also did a *niani mer*[51] in order to put pressure on them so that they would change their statement before the court and withdraw the case against me. My father and other relatives went to the area *sardar* and asked him to settle the matter. The *sardar* understood the issue. He called the boy's side and explained to them that the murder was right as their son was at fault. He clearly told them that they were responsible for the consequences, not me. The *sardar* explained everything to them. So the *faislo* was made in our favour, and that made them obliged to change their statement in court. They withdrew the case and I was set free. If they had not agreed to the *sardar*'s *faislo*, I would have been hanged.

Q: As you said, the opposite party was strong, but they accepted the *faislo* of the *wadera*?

A: Who can challenge a *sardar*'s *faislo*? Who can dare not to change his statement before the court when the area *sardar* has taken a decision? A *wadera*'s words are the final authority. No one can afford the hostility of the area *sardar*.

Q: What happened to your sister?

A: As the police arrested me soon after I had murdered the boy, I could not kill her. Otherwise I had intended to kill both of them, as, you know, if only a man is killed then people from the tribe will think that there was some enmity or some other motive behind the killing, so I wanted to kill my sister as well. It was a busy market where I killed the boy, so the police got there quickly And I had no way or time to get back home to kill my sister; that was something which went in favour of the boy's family as they lodged an FIR against me claiming that I had killed their son for some financial gain, and because I could not prove that it was an honour killing case, I was given the death penalty. I was sure that whenever he crossed my path, I would kill him first and then my sister.

Q: What happened to her?

---

[51] In Sindhi and Balochi culture, *niani* means a girl and *mer* means a group. To make someone agree on some point, a group of girls/women is taken to his home. The group is treated very respectfully and in most of the cases the opposite group agrees on the issue as in the two cultures a girl is considered equal to seven Qur'ans.

A: She is not with us now. She was given to the *sardar* and the *sardar* ... gave her in marriage ... to someone ... in a faraway village. We don't know who. As a cultural taboo, we cannot have any further relationship with her, with *karis* like her.

Q: So she was given to the *sardar* as she was declared a *kari*?

A: Yes.

Q: How did she go to the *haveli*; I mean who took her there?

A: As soon as I had killed the boy, the news spread all around the village. It was understood that she would be killed so she ran and took *panah*[52] at the *haveli* of the *sardar* as *sam*[53] and later the *sardar* gave her in marriage.

Q: Where?

A: The *waderas* do not tell people or the relatives of the *karis*. Once declared *kari*, she should be killed, but if somehow she escapes from being killed, then it becomes the business of the *sardar* and he is responsible for her. *Sardars* do not tell anyone where, in which tribe, or to whom these *karis* are given in marriage ... I mean, we then consider a *kari* a dead person and do not discuss her at home at all. As a cultural taboo we cannot keep any relationship with these *karis* and the *karis* also have no right to contact us.

Q: How much money did you receive for her?

A: Nothing, nothing at all.

Q: How much money did the *sardar* sell her for?

A: I don't know. This is only known to the *sardar*. I have no idea.

---

[52] Shelter.

[53] *Sam* is a very respectful word in the Sindhi language because a number of folk sayings and tales are associated with it. Its metaphorical meaning is to provide shelter to a weaker person and not hand him/her to his/her enemies, whatever the consequences, or to keep somebody's precious thing with care for some time. However, in today's context of honour killing, Shah (2004: 46) suggests that 'In fact, *sam* means keeping a slave. A *wadera* has a complete authority over the *sam* woman'. Doud Poto (2000: 75) explained: 'The *karis* who reach the *havelies* by any means are misused by the *sardars*, their sons and other relatives'.

Q: Was any of the money received by your father?

A: No, nothing.

Q: Who looked after you or supported you and your family while you were in jail?

A: My father. My poor father suffered a lot as a result of this unexpected trouble. We were living a good life. My father was a civil servant and the poor man was paying money to the police and to lawyers and to many other people so that the police wouldn't beat me and that my life would be saved. He took early retirement and spent all his money on me. He was a jubilant person, a lively man, but this issue finished him. When he came to the court in Islamabad and heard as I was given the death penalty, he had a heart attack. While he was in a hospital, he had another attack and that one took his life. This is what happened. The killing brought endless misery to my family.

Q: What was it like being in jail?

A: A very difficult time, a very painful time indeed. I spent the time as if it was a curse from God. I was very worried there. I was gloomy about my lost future, education, life … everything. Some people live happily in jail but I found it the worst place on earth. It is not a place where people will learn how to be better civilians but rather they will turn into the worst criminals. If a trivial lawbreaker is sent to jail for some time, after the training which jail gives you he would become a dangerous criminal because in jail he would only meet offenders. Why would an innocent person be in jail? But if an innocent person ends up in jail, there is a 99% chance that he will become a criminal because he will come across a very dirty world. Jail is a very dangerous, ugly and disgusting place where every type of crime, sin and other vandalism is at its peak. The atmosphere in a jail is the worst atmosphere. In my opinion, a person who comes out of jail could never live a normal or peaceful life.

Q: Did you face some torture as well?

A: Torture? … if someone starts a fight or gets involved in fighting then the police really beat him without mercy. And when a new prisoner arrives and his relatives don't pay money to the police, then he gets beaten up by the police so that he will plead with his family to arrange some bribe for the police to stop beating him.

Q: Were you ever tortured?

A: I was in an eighteen foot by twelve foot cell which also contained a toilet. For 22 hours a day, I was locked up. I was only allowed out of the cell for two hours a day under the custody of the police. If I or someone else was rude to the police, then they would certainly have beaten us, but I wasn't that kind of person so I remained safe. Secondly, I had a strong hope that I would be set free because I had a firm belief in God and I said to him, 'God! I didn't want to kill anybody. I was driven to do it. My intention wasn't bad and I didn't want to harm anyone. I was left with no other option and only then I opted for the killing. I tried to solve the issue but no-one listened to me'. When I was in jail, somebody told me that a relative of the slain boy, someone with a good position in society, said that if the issue had been brought to him, he would have settled it in a reasonable way. But ... it was too late then. Actually, the boy's family did not want this relative to know about the issue so he only got to know about it later.

Q: Looking back on the killing, how do you feel about it now?

A: It is all very sad. My time was destroyed. My family suffered a lot of trouble. My parents suffered a lot. My friend had been killed by my own hands. The two families had been parted for ever. My paternal grandmother and my paternal auntie were the close relatives of the boy, and now we cannot see each other, neither on a happy nor on a sad occasion. I see that much has been ruined. My son, who was just a few months old, is now growing up but does not recognize me and still lives with his maternal grandparents as they looked after him when I was in jail. My wife was very upset and couldn't look after him. I was eventually set free but even then I felt that I am the loser. My life, my peace of mind, my education, everything is ruined. I had a dream of completing my studies successfully and getting a good job. I lost so much in those seven years. I now work for a small private company where I can hardly earn enough money to live on. But at that time I could have become something. I could have been able to live a better life. You know, there could be many options for a successful life. You see how much I suffered because of that killing? How much my family has suffered? My wife has suffered? My son was a few months old at the time and he was deprived of my love and care. I didn't see him growing up. He spent his childhood without his father. My family lost a lot. The boy's family also lost. Who won? Nobody could win in the battle of their senseless pride. They lost their child. My sister ... entered an endless world of misery. Actually, what I feel now is that it is a fault of our tribal system. If a bit of attention were given to these issues, the problems would not have been aggravated to this level. Nobody takes the right steps to resolve things peacefully and as result killings happen. I assume that once people start to think about sorting these issues out in a gentle way or a humane way, there would be no cases of *karo-kari*. In my case, the boy's family members knew the system very well but they ignored the basic reality. They were proud of being rich and they underestimated my family and me. They refused my sister and that was unjust. Eventually, before murdering the boy, I even gave them an option that he should marry my sister and have nothing more to do with us, but they weren't willing to listen to me. These are the issues which aggravate and increase the number of murders. If someone sees his kinswoman with some stranger in a highly objectionable situation and he kills both of them, that is an understandable instance. A situation like that can invoke aggression in a man, but if the situation is different, like the one I faced, I don't think that killing should be the last option. There are some cases where marriage between the two people involved could be the best solution and we should opt for that solution. In my case, there was a lot of time for thinking, sorting out and resolving the issue, but nobody tried to do it. The main difference between city life and rural life is that urban people sort these issues out whereas rural people tangle them up further. In cities, if wives are involved with someone other than their husband, they divorce, right? But in our tribal culture, they kill, as after killing the woman, a man is regarded as honourable. This is unjustified.

Q: Do you sometimes remember your sister?

A: Yes.

Q: Then why don't you try to find her?

A: How is that possible? Now none of us can ever have contact with her.

Q: You don't want to know how she is?

A: The villagers know and tell us that she is fine and getting on well with her in-laws.

Q: How do you think other people view your act?

A: Most of the people who understand the system admired it. After this honour killing … you cannot imagine how people felt about me. They appreciated and praised me not only to my face but also when I wasn't there. And I feel that because of this honourable act, my respect and value has increased in our society. But ... Oh God! Those who have not killed their family's women or those who have been involved with them over such allegations are considered cowards and their value is less than a dog or a cat. The system, the culture, the tradition is so dangerous. You can't imagine the insulting remarks people pass about those who don't kill. People laugh at them. They spit at them behind their backs. They are considered dishonoured to the extent that people do not want to talk to them and cannot eat with them, saying that eating with these besmirched men is a curse. Their names become obscenities. You cannot mould and fold your system. You need to be part of it and obey and surrender to its rules. You are bound to kill; otherwise people will kill you with their attitude and sharp words. That's what I have learned so far. In this tribal system, if you can't kill someone, you are dishonoured and if you kill someone you are a highly honourable and respectful person.

Q: What is your concept of honour?

A: Well, saving honour is a good thing. OK? If you see something and you immediately can't control your emotions, and in that anger if you kill both of them or your woman, then it is justified. That is honour. Emotions make you kill because your honour is your conscience. When your conscience is dead, it means that your honour is dead and then you become a body without a soul. But what I say about honour is that, if two persons of the opposite sex are involved with each other, they should be given the right to marry each other. And at that time, cultural, tribal and other financial or social differences should be overlooked. That is the right way to save your honour. If everybody takes or handles the issue with a cool head, then the curse of honour killing will be no more. As you know, killing one person or two does not bring an end to the issue but becomes the beginning of another issue. Enmity begins and grows between the two families and for generations they remain enemies. Both families suffer from various directions. The involvement of the police, the *sardar* and other people ruins the members of both families. So my advice is to tackle all the issues with a clear mind. My wife was also a relative of the slain boy so she was under pressure to divorce me, but she remained steadfast and did not leave me. They raised the condition that they would withdraw the case only when my wife divorced me. She had trust in me and in God. I was told about this condition put to my wife by my father-in-law. I told him that life and death are in the hands of God. The boy's family knows well that I had had no intention of killing their son. I gave them the best solution. If the couple had got married there would have been no problem, but they didn't listen to me and they insulted me. So as part of our tribal society, my family and I also had to survive honourably. Our cruel society would not have let me survive. I would have been the target of insult and abuse. I admit that it was not a sudden provocation but I thought about it over and over. I was the target of continual abuse and threats from the boy's family, so I killed him. Right to the last moment I kept telling them that the consequences of all that would be dangerous not only for me, but that they would suffer too, but they didn't listen to me. I suffered from many angles. Once, my father took my son into the jail so see me. I asked him never to bring him there again as he would hate me because he will grow up one day and will understand that jails are made for criminals. Then, he will hate me. He will consider me a criminal. They didn't bring him again, but I assume he remembers it. He has to live in a society where people must be telling him more than what the actual issue is and I am helpless, as I cannot make him understand anything, because he lives with my in-laws and does not want to come and live with us and I cannot force him. My mother's life has become a constant trouble, pain and misery. My father had been a happy man but because of that killing he got involved in a lot of trouble which eventually took his life. I spent five long years in a death cell. I was a student. My studies were ruined. My future became dark. Those seven years were very tough for me. I used to offer prayers and I remembered God. It was somewhere in my mind ... I hoped that I would be out of jail one day, but every single day I spent there was a curse. Many human rights' organizations visited the jail. Asma Jahangir[54] also came once. And ... when I was set free, my feelings were absolutely changed. It was like the door of the cage was opened for me and I was transformed into a bird. For a nice, humble man, life in jail is hell but it is heaven for criminals. For criminals, the jails are their second home, they keep coming and going, but a nice man thinks of home, family, the present and the future, and is always gloomy there. These feelings and the helplessness all mixed together makes you very upset.

Q: Thank you very much for sharing your life story with me.

---

[54] Asma Jahangir (27 January 1952–11 February 2018) was a founding member of the *HRCP* and served as Secretary-General and later Chairperson of the organization. On 27 October 2010, Jahangir was elected President of the Supreme Court Bar Association of Pakistan and played a prominent role in the Lawyers' Movement. She co-chaired the South Asia Forum for Human Rights and was the vice-president of the International Federation of Human Rights.

A: I feel good because I think you will share my story with the world and they will do something to stop this menace.

Q: I will try my best to let people hear your voice.

A: Thank you, sister.

Q: You're welcome.

7: *Name*: **Usman, aged 29**

The interview lasted for an hour and thirty minutes and took place at a local hotel.

Usman was a confident, athletic, strongly-built young man. He looked like an innocent man and it was difficult for me to believe that he could be anything else. He looked me directly in the eye while speaking.

Q: *Assalam-u-alaikum.*

A: *Walaikum-assalam.*

Q: How are you doing?

A: I am good.

Q: Are you willing to talk to me?

A: Sure.

Q: Let me tell you one thing; whatever information you give will be used only for the purposes of my research and for related publications.

A: You can use it wherever you feel necessary.

Q: Can I record your interview?

A: I don't mind. You can.

Q: Thank you. I am carrying out a research project about honour killing and I need your views about it.

A: You may ask if you think I can help you.

Q: Can you please tell me your name and something about your family, your community and your tribal background?

A: My name is Usman. We are basically Sindhis and have been living in Jacobabad for centuries. We are Lohar by caste. My father is a famer so we work as farmers. This is our profession from our forefathers. I have four brothers and two sisters. I am the oldest brother, my four brothers are younger than me.

Q: Would you like to tell me some more about yourself, like your childhood, siblings, favourite games, education, job and so on.

A: Childhood ... good and nice, it was a happy childhood. We enjoyed that time. In the mornings I used to go to school. I played cricket a lot. Cricket has been my passion since my childhood. One of my brothers is also a good cricketer. But we didn't play with our sisters. Sisters have to do work at home and have, you know, girlish activities like playing with dolls and doing embroidery.

Q: Even when you were children, didn't you play with your sisters?
A: When we were children we played together.

Q: Give me some examples; what games did you play with your sisters when you were children?

A: Ha, ha, ha, ... like ...I forget ... it's ages ago and I can't really remember. It was a kind of ... we drew a line between an imaginary sea and dry land and we tried to pull each other onto the other side. We used to measure the strength and the length of each other's long jumps. But from very beginning, I used to play cricket in the evening. I played cricket with friends and other villagers. I have a matriculation pass [grade 10] and this year I took the first-year exam and I am waiting for the result.

Q: OK. Good. May I ask your age?

A: It is about twenty-nine. During Musharraf's[55] time, we had a huge financial disaster, so I left my education. When he took power as a military dictator, I abandoned my studies and when he moved out of office I was readmitted and I continued my studies. Honestly speaking, I had no

---

[55] Pervez Musharraf (born 11 August 1943) is a Pakistani dictator turned politician; a retired four-star army general, he was the tenth President of Pakistan from 2001 until he resigned to avoid impeachment in 2008.

money to submit the admission form for grade eleven. Besides, I failed two papers in my matriculation exam. Poverty, disappointment, anger; all these emotions made me feel that education is not for poor people like me. You know, education needs money ... money for the uniform, shoes, books and copies. And you even need money for going to the school. Isn't that so? We were poor peasants so I gave it up. That was indeed a very tough time for me. Then, you see, 2010 was the year of the floods, so our troubles never stopped; but life is moving ahead now.

Q: Now you are studying in grade 11, called the first year, right? What about those two matriculation papers which you failed?

A: I passed them. You know what ... I took admission into the ninth grade first. In two years, I completed my matriculation and now I have completed the first year [grade 11] and I am preparing for the inter-exam [grade 12]. In the evenings, we play cricket but not in this hot weather. In the winter we all gather and play. There are four villages and we have two teams. All players get equal chances to play. I am captain of my team.

Q: Good, are you a bowler or a batsman?

A: Both. I am an all-rounder.

Q: Can you share something about your married life; I mean the mode of marriage, wife, children and your relationship with your in-laws?

A: I got married in 1997 to my cousin, my paternal aunt's daughter. From that wife I had two sons and one daughter. My eldest son got an electric shock and died while he was at his maternal grandparents' home in Shikarpur. He was picking blueberries near their house and some berries fell into some water; when he put his hand in the water he was electrocuted and died; he was only five. Then God gave me another son, so now again I have two sons, luckily. You know, when we are children, we are engaged [to be married] by our elders, so while we are growing up, each one of us knows who he or she is going to marry. So I knew it as well; my wife was my paternal aunt's daughter. My aunt's family was supposed to give two girls to us.

Q: Was the mode of your marriage *watto-satto*?

A: No sister, it wasn't a *watto-satto*. We got two girls from a family for me and my brother, as around fifteen years ago my aunt had been given to that family in marriage and it was decided that in return her two yet-to-be-born girls plus another girl would be given to us. Altogether, three girls for one marriageable girl; got it, sister?

Q: Why three girls for one girl?

A: Because my aunt was mature and was of marriageable age and surely we needed something in return. So my grandfather decided that at least one small girl of that family should be reserved for us and be given to us when she becomes mature and when my aunt would deliver two girls, they would also be ours. Because, you know, you cannot predict a child who is not yet born, so it was necessary that one already-born girl be taken. This process is called *pet likhi dean*.[56] You see, I got married again last year and I followed the same tradition. I took a young girl from a family in marriage and promised the family to give them my daughter and my uncle's daughter to their two sons in marriage, when the girls become mature.

Q: OK. Let's talk about your first wife. How did you get on with her and your in-laws?

A: Great, well, right up to today, I get on really well with my in-laws. My mother-in-law is my paternal aunt, that is the main relationship, and most of the family understood my situation and blamed my wife for what she did wrong. My father-in-law died in an accident. He was getting on a bus and when the bus driver started the bus, he fell on his back and the bus ran over him. As I said, my first mother-in-law is my paternal aunt, so that is the main relationship between my family and her, and most of the people in her family understand the situation.

Q: Sad to hear that! What was the issue of *karo-kari*?

A: You know, as the well-known proverb says, 'You invite troubles for yourself', and that's what happened. Look at me? Is there any problem with me? Am I not handsome? Not smart? And if my wife deceives me and goes after a man who has lesser qualities than me, then naturally will I not react?

Q: Can you please explain what happened and how?

---

[56] In Sindhi and Baloch cultures, the custom of *pet likhi dean* literally means 'writing stomach'. In this tradition, when a family gives one girl to another family in marriage, there is a condition that when they are born, her daughters (one or two) will be given back to the girl's family.

A: Yes. One night, my daughter who was one-and-a-half years old at the time cried in the night. I called to my wife to feed her but she did not reply. My older son, who was about five, told me that she was not there. I got up, switched on the light and saw her coming in from outside the house. When I asked where she had been, she said that she had gone to the toilet. You know, it was not a big thing but I was suspicious. I said 'OK'; I believed her. We all went back to sleep. In the day time, you know, everyone is busy so I completely forgot about what had happened that night. If you remember, in 2010 there was a great flood; it was a great disaster. I used to go to catch fish to eat and to sell. The fish in those days were very large and heavy – it was a very good season for fish. Every day, I went along with some other villagers to fish. I was coming and going and working, meeting people and I had no idea what was going on behind my back. I didn't ask who was coming and going because in villages, you know, each one of us has a small house and we live like a family. In my heart, I considered everyone like a brother or a sister so I thought everyone would be like me. I didn't know that a man was creating a problem for me in my own house. His intentions were known only by God, not by me. So the same story was repeated. My daughter started crying at night. I called to my wife but she was not there. I woke up and saw her coming in from outside. I asked her where she had been and she replied that she had been to the toilet. Then I asked her why she had gone outside for the toilet. In my house, there was a covered area which was used for the toilet, so I questioned her and became suspicious. During these arguments, I went outside and searched here and there and I saw the form of a man going away. It was a moonlit night. I went inside quickly to get my rifle and then went out again. I searched everywhere, even a long way from the house, but I didn't find anyone so I went back home with the intention of keeping an eye on the situation. I consoled myself by asking myself where he would go. He must surely come back another day. When I got back, my wife was feeding our daughter. I didn't say anything to her; I just kept my rifle by my side and lay down. Three days passed. I was worried and my heart was disturbed. Suspicion was killing me from inside and I was really very upset. I started thinking about my wife and the other man. When she had come in, I had seen him going away, so I told myself that there must be something wrong. I remembered the two nights when had I called to her and she was out of the house. I lost interest in everything. I went fishing but instead of spending a lot of time fishing, I came back early. I didn't spend much time playing cricket; I was either batting or bowling and then again going home early. I was not following my usual timetable for going back home. When people asked the reason for this change in my routine, I made something up and said that I was not feeling well, or something like that. One Friday, first I went out to catch fish and then I went home and after having a bath, I asked my uncle whether anyone had visited my house while I was away. My uncle told me that nobody had come in my absence. I asked him to stay at my house while I went into town to get groceries because I had become suspicious. While I was still in the market, I saw the uncle whom I left at home coming towards me. I was surprised and I asked him why was he there. He told me that he also needed to buy a few things so he had gone out. I said nothing because I knew that everyone has domestic responsibilities. My parents were in another city because of the floods, so I was there with my three uncles' families, although everybody had a separate home. One day I was in the marke when suddenly I noticed the man I suspected. He saw me while I was busy talking to a shopkeeper. He was sitting outside a small tea shop, and he finished his cup of tea quickly and got on a bus which went to a bus-stop near my home. He thought that I had not seen him but I kept an eye on every move he made. As soon as he had caught the bus, I told myself that he must be going to my house. I took the next bus. When I got off the bus outside my village, I could see my home from a distance and I saw that beside the dry water channel, he was sitting with my wife. Since the ditch was on the left side of my house and my house was straight ahead from where I was, I kept walking without letting them notice that I had seen them. I pretended that I hadn't seen them. I went into my house, got my rifle and a box of bullets and went straight out again; but they had seen me coming and by then my wife was entering the house, and when I went out, the boy was walking away on the other side of the channel. I put five bullets in my rifle and followed him. I fired at him and hit his leg. He fell into the dry ditch. I was walking along the edge of the ditch. By now, people had gathered and one man held me tight and another tried to snatch my weapon.[57] I could not be controlled. When I shouted at them, they left me and split up and I ran after the man. When I reached him, he asked, 'Why are you killing me, tell me what I have done wrong?' I called his wife a whore and said 'You are asking what your crime is as if you haven't committed any fault'. And I fired at his body and forehead. He fell

---

[57] "Illegal weapons are being smuggled into the province from Punjab and Khyber Pakhtunkhwa. Often the police seize these weapons but do nothing to control this growing menace. Regrettably, the illegal business of weapons has polluted the entire society. As a result, fratricidal killings, kidnappings for ransom and tribal feuds have alarmingly increased in Sindh" (*Abro*, 6 March 2011). "There are estimated 20 million illegal arms in circulation in Pakistan" (*The Express Tribune*, 17 May 2012).

over. Lots of people gathered and tried to pull my rifle off me. They were saying 'Leave him alone, leave him alone'. I said, 'Look what he has done to my family!' One man said 'OK, now leave it'; I called his mother an abusive word and said, 'Get away, or I'll kill you too'. He went away. After killing the man, I rushed home ... My wife was hiding in my neighbour's house. She was in a small room which didn't have a latch inside it. I called to her. I told my neighbours to bring her out immediately. They were reluctant to throw her out for about fifteen to twenty minutes. I kicked them, hit them, and swore at them and said 'If you don't let her come out, I'll shoot as many of you as I can'. Eventually, they realized that I would not leave her no matter what they did. Then they said, 'OK, take her to your house and kill her there'. They forced her to go out but, as you know, life is very dear to everyone and she would not come out. They almost pulled and threw her out. She tried to run towards my house. I fired at her and she fell in between the two houses. My second bullet hit her in the chest. Then I put the rifle to her head and shot her for third time.

Q: Did nobody forcibly try to stop you from killing her?

A: Men and women were forcing me; begging me not to kill her, to forgive her. They were guaranteeing that she would not do it again, but I was in a rage and was not able to hear anything else other than to kill her. Someone tried to snatch the rifle from me, another person wanted me to sit down and think it over.But they didn't hand her over and just kept on repeating these things for fifteen or twenty minutes. I kicked them, hit them and swore at them and told that that if they didn't send her out, I would shoot as many of them as I could. They asked me just to forget her this once. I said that I had killed the *karo* so how could I leave this *kari* alive. Eventually, I was prepared to kill some of them too and told them that anyone who tried to stop me would be killed. Only then did they realise that I was absolutely determined not to let her live. Then they said, 'OK, but don't kill her in this house otherwise the police will disturb us, so take her to your house and kill her there. They tried to force her out, but life is very dear to everyone and she would not come out. Then the owner of the house said, 'Now you have the right. Do whatever you want'. They pulled her and threw her out. Then I shot her as I told you before. After killing her, I called the police. Everybody knew me there. All the policemen were like my brothers. I explained the matter over the phone. I always kept good relations with everyone in and outside the village. The SHO[58] said that he was sending the police-car, but then he called me again

---

[58] Station House Officer.

and told me that there was no fuel in the car, so he sent a policeman on a motorbike. I took my rifle, the bag of bullets, the licence for the rifle and I went with him to the police lock-up. It was a highly emotional time. I was absolutely not able to think anything. My eldest son was crying over the dead body of his mother. I handed everything over to the police. When the police took me, I was bare-foot, so they gave me slippers. I washed my face. They made me sit and enquired about the incident. I explained everything as I have been explaining it to you. They wrote down the details of both of the killings. I was in the police officer's room. They did not lock me up, but then the policeman who had written down every detail of the killings told me to go to the lock-up, so I was locked up. The *sardar* of the area came as soon as I went to the police. He listened to me carefully, consoled me and said, 'Don't cry over spilt milk. God is great and he understands your intentions, that you killed them to save the Islamic tradition, so God will help you'. He told the police not to lock me up and he took responsibility for me. The police agreed and arranged a *charpaee* for me outside the lock-up. I slept there. That night, about eleven o'clock, the head of the lock-up got there and asked about me. The two dead bodies had been taken to Jacobabad for a post-mortem so he had come from there. He was told that the killer was sleeping outside as the *sardar* had directed. The officer became angry; he berated the police and ordered them to lock me up. He said that the killer had killed two people but that they hadn't locked him up yet. He asked if that was what they called their sense of responsibility. He stated that he was not prepared to listen to anyone as he had already had to deal with a criminal who had run out of the jail after killing two policemen, so he was not ready to take any more risks. So I was locked up. I spent seven days locked up. The police renewed my remand three times. Each time, they were expecting money. I told them straight that I was a poor man and that I had no money to give them; I said to them 'You are talking of millions of rupees; if you just ask for thousands of rupees we could sell some cattle and pay you'. Every time I was taken to court, the police told the court that they wanted to arrest my partners in the murders and I always denied the involvement of anyone else in the murders. These were the tactics which the police used so that my parents would provide them with some money. I was in the lock-up for twenty-one days and then I was sent to the district jail. On the first day in the district jail, when I saw all the new faces of the policemen there I shivered. They were very rude. They asked many questions. My head was down and my heart was trembling. They ordered me to hold my slippers in my hands and then go into the lock-up. I followed the order. Luckily, I found that many of the prisoners were from my city and the next day they asked the SHO to lock me up with them. They offered him a good bribe so he agreed to their request and then I was moved into their cell and we had a good time together. Meanwhile, because he was very angry, one of my brothers-in-law who had lodged an FIR against me changed his statement before the court and told the judge that I was with him on the day of killings, and that his sister and the other man were killed by someone else. He said that it was the job of the police to find the actual killer. On his statement, the court released me. As far as the boy's family was concerned, they were pressured by the *sardar* who told them plainly that their son was guilty so he was rightly killed. Therefore they could not dare to go to the court or lodge an FIR against me. They were guilty, so they tried to bring a *niani mer* as well, but my father told them to speak to me because I knew what to do. My father wanted me to decide whether to forgive them or not. However, nothing was proved against me so I was acquitted of the murders but I was not set free because there was another case of 13/D against me.[59] So we needed money again. My father was poor but he used his contacts and collected a decent amount of money to bribe the police. Then on the thirteenth of the next month, I was released from jail and by the evening of the same day I reached my home. That's what happened, *Adi*.[60]

Q: Who looked after your family while you were in jail?

A: My father, of course. My mother was looking after my kids. They were both there. My brother and my uncles were also good supporters for them.

Q: How did you feel when you had done it, I mean the killings?

A: Soon after the killings, I felt great pain. I saw my little children crying loudly over the bullet-ridden body of my wife. I wondered who would look after my children, who would cook for them. My heart was broken. Everything seemed dark and gloomy. However, I spoke to myself and tried to be composed. I said to myself, 'What is done, is done. Time does not come back'. Whatever was written in destiny had happened. What could I do? It was a cruel joke of nature upon me. The son of a bitch [the *karo*] had ruined everything. I thought that I had lost my home. My children had lost their mother. I would be in jail, for how long, I could not predict. What could I do? I asked my neighbours to look after my children

---

[59] A 13/D case means owning arms illegally.
[60] Sister.

because they were too young to look after themselves. My younger son could not sleep without me, he was so upset. When the police took me, he used to bring lunch for me every day.

Q: How old was he at that time?

A: He was about three. He used to come everyday to see me in the lock-up. At the beginning, for two days he was too scared and didn't want to come into the cell where I was locked up, but later he got used to it. The first time he saw a policeman opening the gate of my cell, he started crying. When he cried, my eyes were full of tears as well. So I put some of his favourite food near me to attract him. Gradually he got used to it and started coming into my cell every day and eating food with me. My older son came too. The police knew me there so they were very kind to me. I was very upset in the jail but had no other options. My youngest son is very attached to me and he still does not want to let me go anywhere without him. He sleeps with me. Whenever I come home, he is the one who offers me food and water before anyone else.

Q: When your son was crying over his mother's dead body, how did you feel?

A: What can I tell you about it? She was my cousin. It was very a painful situation. The ** [*he used an abusive slang term*] had ruined everything. My family was finished. My children had lost their mother. I had lost everything, home, wife, freedom, peace of life, and I was about to face the vicious circle of the police, jail, courts, and had everything to lose.

Q: Why did she do it?

A: Well, what can I say? Although I was poor I provided her with everything, everything, like food, clothes and other things. All her needs were fulfilled nicely. That was the time when the government was giving out funds and there was quite a lot to eat, like chicken, fish and other stuff. I always asked her to let me know what she needed and I gave her everything she wanted. I had almost everything at home. She smoked, so I used to buy her good-quality cigarettes regularly.

Q: Did she express her love for you?

A: Not just once, but we repeatedly used to express our love for each other. I remember one day when I came home after fishing, I had a severe fever and when she saw me in pain she changed my clothes and made me sleep. In the same way, I looked after here. She fed me with her own hands …

Q: Then?

A: Then, what she did to me later you already know about. What could I do? I saw her disloyalty with my own eyes. I did not do anything that was unjust. I need to be answerable to God one day so I swear that she was guilty. Those who have done wrong will answer to God on the Day of Judgment. Allah asks us to do justice, so I did. The holy prophet says that those who do not kill their wives after seeing the worst thing on earth with their own eyes are the most dishonourable men. Either you kill her or you put a disloyal wife aside.

Q: Why didn't you divorce her instead of killing her?

A: I didn't feel like it. If I gave her a divorce, then I would have been the target of mockery from the whole society for being so weak and dishonourable that I couldn't kill someone who had attacked my honour and so helpless that my wife had ruined my honour. The same people who now consider it an honourable thing to sit and talk with me would have spat in my face. That would have been the worst thing for me to endure. I decided to kill them and then whatever would happen, I was ready to face it; I was even prepared to be hanged. I was burning inside and I could not endure the pain of being betrayed. I thought that I had given her a lot of love, affection and care and that in return she had disrespected me for a lame man who was even poorer than me. If he was a *wadera* or a rich man, it could have made some sense at least. The wretched woman lost herself and ruined my life.

Q: How long were you in jail?

A: Twenty-two days in the district jail. Then eight days more, then another twenty-two days for the 13/D case, so let's say it was altogether one month and thirteen days. I was acquitted of the killings as there was no proof against me.

Q: If your wife had seen you in the same position, sitting with a woman, how would have she reacted?

A: She had said many times that she would kill me if she saw me with another woman and I always replied, 'Do kill me if you see me even talking to someone'. Some relationships are different but I gave her the right to kill me even if she saw me just talking to a stranger. We trusted each other.

Q: What was it like being in jail?

A: Jail ... prisoners are prisoners, you know. It was a kind of a cage where people like buffalos have to be counted and kept in. A prisoner is always stuck in a kind of uncertainty. He doesn't know whether he will be set free or be there forever – it could be a matter of days, months or years or for his whole life. But that was a place where all the time you remember God. We all offered prayers, recited the Qur'an there at all the right times. This was all we could do. But I felt that a prisoner in jail is in less trouble than his dear ones outside the jail, because the prisoner knows that he is restricted and can't do anything in jail, but his parents and brothers or other relatives keep thinking about whether he has anything to eat or not. Whether he has soap, tea, food, money or other stuff or not. Outside the jails people keep busy collecting and borrowing money to keep the prisoner safe and healthy. They are constantly worried about the prisoner's well-being more than the prisoner himself. There were nine of us friends in the jail and we had a very nice time together. We cooked together, we ate together. Actually, the feelings of brotherhood made you connected in jail.

Q: Were you not getting food from the jail?

A: Yes, we were provided with food but we didn't like the taste of it as it was not cooked well, so we prepared our own food. We didn't eat beef so we had to arrange our own food. We even preferred our prepared potatoes to their mutton.

Q: How much punishment did you expect for these killings?

A: I was sure that I would get out of the jail sooner or later as there was no proof against me. My wife's family didn't lodge an FIR against me. The *karo*'s family was at fault so they also couldn't go to court against me because the *sardar* had told them plainly that if they lodged an FIR against me he would lodge an FIR against them, so there was no pressure from their side. My wife's older brother was very angry to start with but then he realised the situation and is still my friend. Even today he was asking me to pay them a visit. But my wife's younger brother is always saying that he will kill me. He still says that he will kill me whenever he gets a chance. I answer him, 'If you think that the killing of your sister was unjust, kill me; but if you kill me, my children will kill you'. I keep asking my children this question, 'Your uncle wants to kill me. If he kills me, will you take revenge or not?' They reply confidently, 'How long shall we remain children? We shall grow up one day and kill him if he kills you'. So my children console me and I am sure that if my brother-in-law kills me, he will be killed by my children in return.

Q: And how old are your children?

A: My older son is now nine but he looks bigger than his age and talks about these issues like an adult. They both promise me that 'We will grow up one day and kill him'. What I did was justice absolutely, but his killing me would be an absolute injustice.

Q: Looking back on the killings, how do you feel about it now?

A: Well, whatever had to happen has happened. But what I see is that *karo-kari* is increasing. One of my uncles bought a television recently and we watch on it that every day there are approximately four to five cases of honour killing. So instead of decreasing, the tendency is on rise and, you know, not all cases are linked with honour. There are many wrong cases, such as somebody wants to get hold of someone else's land; someone wants to grab a home or a shop or some other property; some women persuade men that if they kill their husband and their wives or girlfriends, they will marry them, so they do so. Greed is the source of these 'honour' killings. People kill their enemies and any unwanted woman of their family, maybe the wife, sister, mother, daughter or any kinswoman, and claim that it was an honour killing. I can tell you that many cases like that are faked honour killings. In my own area where we have been living for ages, I know many people have killed more than two people in the name of honour and are still living there safely, and interestingly, they have never been approached by the police as they are powerful and can hand over handsome bribes to the police not to arrest them. What happened to my father-in-law? He had a sixteen-acre plot of land. His neighbouring landowner accused a farmer of my father-in-law's land as *karo* with one of his kinswoman, and ordered my father-in-law to leave the land immediately. My father-in-law became very upset so I offered my help and told him that we would fight them. My father-in-law said that they had said 'We will kill the woman of our family along with your farmer and then you will all be in a jail. As a result you will all be turfed off this land. If you create any trouble for us, you will be deprived of your homes as well', so my father-in-law became scared. He went to the *sardar*. As they were powerful people, the *sardar* told my father-in-law in a *faislo* to give them the land, otherwise there would be great problems. Since my father-in-law was a humble person, he was forced to sell the land to them for a very low price. He had no other option so he accepted the money and he was deprived of his land, and they didn't kill the accused farmer or their own woman. Just to show that there was some honour-related cause and that their accusation was based on fact, they gave one of their women to the *sardar* who later sold her somewhere else. I witnessed this story myself, so I can say that there was no issue of honour involved, but the justification of honour killing was used to intimidate the weak party to serve their own greedy purpose, and they succeeded in it. But, please, I assure you that in my case there was no greed, no property or money was involved and it was purely an honour-related case. I killed them to save my honour. I saw everything with my own eyes and only then did I kill both of them. I am a very straightfoward, honest man. You see now, I got married again last year and I did the same thing: I took a mature girl as my wife from a family and gave my daughter [from the first wife] as well as my uncle's daughter to them in return. The promise was made that when the girls reach marriageable ages, they will be given to them.

Q: How old are the girls now?

A: Mine is about four and my uncle's daughter is about three.

Q: Is it a written agreement?

A: No. It's only verbal and was agreed on by the most respected men of both families so now nobody can deny it. We are men of our word.

Q: How do you think other people view your act of killing; I mean your family, others in the community, people in general?

A: People appreciate it. The police were very sympathetic. The police did not disturb any of us. Otherwise, you know, the police just need any excuse to enter our houses to find money, gold and other valuables. But in my case, no such thing happened. No policeman went inside my home because they have respect for honour-killing cases and, second, they were told by the *wadera* not to touch or harm me.

Q: What is your concept of 'honour'?

A: Honour means killing for honour. Honour killing is a right way to stop wrong-doing. It is the parameter for judging the honour of a man, a culture and society. If not honour killing, then what? What else can you do to prove how to remain honourable? Honour means that a man should preserve it above everything else in the world. For saving his honour, an honourable man should cross every limit. But my wish is that a husband and wife should both be loyal to each other, as both parties get ruined in this immoral business. Honour killing is a terrible thing. Today people appreciate me as I killed my wife and the person whom she was involved with to save my honour, but tomorrow will the same people not give *tano*[61] to my daughters and sons that their mother was a *kari*?

Q: Thank you for talking to me.

A: You are welcome, *adi*. If you need to talk to other genuine killers, please let me know and I will arrange for you to meeting them.

Q: Thank you very much. I shall certainly let you know.

---

[61] An insulting and provocative remark.

Chapter Two

The Accounts of Convicted Killers in Jails

1: *Name*: Naeer, aged 65

The interview lasted for an hour and twenty-seven minutes; it took place at the district jail.

Naeer was wearing dirty clothes and had a wide kerchief on his shoulder. He had a brown Sindhi cap on his head. He was wearing white-framed spectacles. His beard was untrimmed. He spoke gently.

Q: *Assalam-u-alaikum.*

A: *Walaikum-assalam*, daughter.

Q: How are you doing?

A: God knows better.

Q: Would you like to talk to me, *chacha?*[62]

A: Yes, *amman.*[63] I am ready, so I have come to talk to you.

Q: Thank you. Do you have any objection if I record what you say?

A: No, *Ammar,*[64] I understand that you need to record it. Do it. I speak the truth which I have already spoken, so carry on.

Q: Let me tell you one thing, whatever information you will give me will be used only for the purposes of my research and for related publications.

---

[62] Uncle
[63] Mother
[64] Mother

A: OK.

Q: May I ask your name, age, community and parents?

A: We are basically Baloch but about forty years ago we settled in Sindh. My name is Naeer and I am sixty-five. My parents were poor and they were farmers but they had a few buffalos so we had our own milk. Then, you know, it was an honour-related matter so I killed and I have admitted the killings.

Q: OK. How many brothers and sisters did you have?

A: I had three brothers and seven sisters.

Q: Would you like to tell me some more about yourself, I mean about your childhood, siblings, favourite games, education and job.

A: Our childhood was very poor and full of problems. We didn't have enough to eat but our parents were extremely kind; they looked after us well. They didn't scold us or beat us so we were happy. It wasn't a kind of troubled childhood, because we knew that we were poor so we had to face the troubles of life. As brothers and sisters we used to play with each other. None of us went to school … ever… mainly because of our poverty. We used to play common games such as hide-and-seek and wrestling; we couldn't afford to play any significant games such as cricket as it required a ball and bat which we couldn't afford, but we nevertheless had a very good relationship with each other. My father was a farmer and as we grew up we also began working with him on the land of the landlord. First, we had one buffalo, then my father bought another and we started selling the buffalo milk. Then we moved to Jacobabad about forty years ago.

Q: Why did you leave Balochistan?

A: Because of the terrible state of the law and order there, we needed to move from there to Sindh. After the move, we started to sell milk and after a struggle we were able to establish our own small dairy farm. I was a young boy when I came to Sindh with my parents. We did some labouring work here as well. We worked as farmers on the land of the local landlord. Here in Sindh we improved financially. Our dairy farm grew bigger and we became established.

Q: Can you tell me something about your married life; the mode of your marriage, your wife, children, relations with in-laws and so on?

A: I married my paternal uncle's daughter about thirty-five years ago in exchange. You know our Baloch culture: whenever and whoever our parents want, we get married to, but before deciding on my marriage, my parents asked me. The girl had also seen me as I was her cousin, so I liked her and gave my consent to my parents and then we were married. The mode of the marriage was *watto-satto*. We took one girl and gave one girl to my in-laws. There was no money exchanged in that marriage. She was indeed very good. She knew how to handle happy and sad moments. She was very decent. I have three sons and four daughters from her.

Q: How did you get on with your in-laws?

A: Very respectfully. I believe that our parents and the parents of our life partner are equally deserving of respect; they are like second parents. I always respected them and they loved me. They were my uncle and aunt so they were always good to us. I was just like a son to them.

Q: Why are you in jail?

A: Because I killed ... my wife ... and ... it was like a written scroll of destiny. It was written in her fate, so it happened. She was living the life of a queen. Many servants worked under her command. She had her home. We lived together happily. When I saw her with another man absolutely naked, I killed both of them at once because of my honour. Our Islam does not permit us to see such a shameful act with our own eyes and then let them live. It would have been the worst act of dishonour if I had left them alive.

Q: When did it happen?

A: Four years ago now.

Q: How old was your wife at the time of the killing?

A: She was about fifty or fifty-five.

Q: What was the approximate age of the man?

A: About forty-five or fifty.

Q: Had you ever been suspicious about her conduct?

A: Never. She was the homeowner; everything was in her hands. She was the mother of my children and she deserved respect. But there is something in the hands of nature which neither you nor me can change, so that was her destiny.

Q: Can you please explain the whole situation, what did you see and how did you see it?

A: It was an evening; suddenly, I noticed that she was going out of our house. She left home and went away. Before she left, I said to her 'Don't go out'. She said, 'You stay at home; I'll be back soon'. I followed her when she left the house. I am a human being so I suspected that something was wrong as it was a very odd time and she had done the same thing some days before as well. So I followed her. She went to an inn not very far from our home ... I saw her going up the stairs. A man who was standing near the stairs like a guard latched up the staircase door. When he saw me unlatching it, he shouted at me 'Don't go there!' But ... I just went straight up ... and opened the door to the room in which ... How shall I tell you ... I found my wife and the man naked. As soon as I saw them, without wasting a single moment, I fired at them and killed them.

Q: Was the door to the room which they were both in open?

A: There were two types of door. One was at the top of the stairs and the other opened into the room where they both were. He was a bus-driver, so he must have instructed his bus-cleaner colleague not to let anyone come in, so the cleaner had latched up the stair-case door from the outside and was standing guard. When the cleaner saw me unlatching the door, he gave me a shout 'Don't go there and don't you dare to go into the room', but I went up the stairs and opened the door to the room in which I found my wife naked with the driver. You are like my mother or sister; I cannot lie to you and I feel embarrassed to be describing the situation, but as I kicked the door of the room, it flew open and they were both there without their clothes on. I didn't wait a single moment; I fired at them and killed them.

Q: Why did you take a pistol with you when you followed your wife?

A: I had caught her going out once before at a very odd time. At that time I didn't suspect anything, but this time I saw her going and asked her not to go out, but she refused to obey me and went without letting me know, so it was natural for me to think that something was up, so I took my pistol with me. It was a very unusual time, and when I saw that she was going towards an unbelievable place, I mean to an inn, I suspected something bad. For example, when you come and go to and from an office, nobody suspects anything, but if you go out at a time when normally no woman goes out, then it means that something is wrong, so I became suspicious, *Ammi,*[65] and I followed her. It was getting darker. Night was about to fall and I wondered where and why she was going out alone at that time. And when I had asked her not to go, she had replied that she was just coming back soon. Last time, when she left home almost at the same time, she returned, let's say, after forty or fifty minutes. I felt puzzled but I hadn't said anything to her. But the second time, I took my pistol with me even though I wasn't sure about anything. Islam doesn't let us allow a life partner to behave in such an immoral way. The room was as small as this office where we are sitting now.

Q: Was there any shout, any request, or any discussion with them when you were about to kill them?

A: No, it wasn't like that. Yes, when the man saw me at the door he swore at me rudely and shouted 'Why have you come in?' But I responded by using a slang word about his wife with all my hatred, and I fired at him, and then at my wife, and I shouted 'You won't get away from here today'.

Q: What was your wife's reaction?

A: Nothing; when she saw me, she just looked down. She didn't say a single word. She had a life like a queen. She ruled over everything and her servants. If you go to my neighbours and ask people, they will confirm the way she was living. Even when the children were little, I looked after them and did not let her work hard. It was a passionate love. I loved her completely. I never gave her any pain. I loved her, I respected her and I always cared for her. Then … it's my destiny … what fate had written in my future. I now have to face these torturous days in this hot jail. I have to face the burning agony all my life now. That was somewhere in my destiny and I was not aware of anything that was going to happen. Look at my situation. I can only shed tears. I am in jail, in a miserable and helpless condition. My children were inexperienced and couldn't manage the business and they ruined everything. A mysterious disease spread and all my buffalos died. My daughters keep crying all day and night. My youngest daughter is now fifteen or sixteen. She is very sensitive and has almost lost her sight from all the crying. What happened? We had money, love and children. God's blessings were on us. What was missing?

---

[65] Mother.

Everything was going well. Look at my age ... at this age my hair had gone grey, hers too ... was this the time to go for such immorality and disloyalty?

Q: How did you feel when you had done it?

A: Was I in my right mind? Was I able to think about anything after seeing that day of judgment on earth? A dark pall was spread before my eyes. It was a trauma that I had had to suffer. It was the beginning of an unending tragedy that ruined everything I had made after such a long struggle. But all I could remember was that I killed for the sake of God in compliance with the instructions of my prophet Muhammad (peace be upon Him). Our Islam does not permit us such immoral behaviour. To see such a shameful act with my own eyes! If I had closed my eyes and had not killed them, how could I have shown my face to God on the Day of Judgment? Could I prove that I had followed my beloved Prophet (peace be upon Him)? My daughters and sons have all been doomed; they are working as road labourers in these chilly afternoons.

Q: Why do you think she did it?

A: Only God and she really know best why she did it. God may rest her soul in peace. I still pray for her. She had everything a woman can dream of. She had millions of rupees all the time in her care. She was the voice of authority in our home. Whatever she wanted to buy she was free to have. See, even the clothes I am wearing were bought by her.

Q: If your wife had seen you in the same position, how would she have reacted?

A: Look; being human she would have also lost her mind like I did. It was natural.

Q: Who is supporting you and your family while you are in jail?

A: No-one. Who helps you when you fall? Everybody is busy minding his own business. No-one looks after you when disaster strikes you. No-one is there for my family except for God. My children tried to manage things but they were not experienced or clever enough to handle all that. My sons are now working at various places to earn a living. One is working as a farmer and the other is working here in this jail as a labourer. See the front part of the jail is under construction, and he is working there on a daily wage. This is what I have to see with my own eyes and look at my misery... how helpless I am and I have to face what destiny has brought me. My children were innocent. Clever people outsmarted them and they did not understand anything. See how much this incident has affected us?

Q: What is it like being in jail?

A: Very painful. The world of the jail is absolutely different. I ask myself ... how I am feeling and how I am passing my time. God is great. My case is continuing. Let's see what happens. I don't know how long I will be locked up here. This is my fourth year in this jail and I haven't seen any of my daughters since I came here. Only my sons come to visit me over here.

Q: Looking back on the killings, how do you feel about it now?

A: What can I say? I built a big bungalow for her, better than even the area landlord's house, but I regret to say that she brought her own fate from God. I still wonder how she had got involved with that man. When did God make them feel that they could do it? How did it happen? If it had happened when we were young, I might have not thought so desperately and would have taken the issue some other way; but, now, at this age? I understand that youth is like a storm and without any real intention someone can behave like this and might get involved with someone other than her husband, but ... at this age? I cannot understand that at all. Surely at least she would have thought for a bit what her children would think of her?

Q: How do you think other people view your act? People in the family and others in the community, people in general?

A: People in the area condemn what she did completely. My house was the most respected house in the whole area. Everybody says how she ruined her own and her family's life. People are surprised at the way she could just abandon so much pleasure in her life. Her dishes and her clothes were washed by her servants. People are confused about why she did it. People accuse her of ruining everything. I wasn't like other men in my society; I used to prepare her breakfast and her tea every day and set it out on the table for her.

Q: What is your concept of 'honour'?

A: Islam does not teach us to accept dishonour. The message of Islam is to kill anyone who brings dishonour to your family. Can an honourable man bear his wife to be naked with any other man? Honour means defending your honour and killing those who attempt to defile your honour. I assume she did it because, since she was married to me, she had not seen any days of difficulty. She only saw peace, love, care and affection. She did not know what hard work is. She enjoyed wearing nice clothes and wearing make-up. If one of the children sometimes made her angry, I always scolded the child, never her. I always told my children to ask their mother nicely and never be rude to her. I discouraged my children from talking loudly to her.

Q: Let's say, if you were found in the same way that you found the man you killed, what punishment would you expect?'

A: Well ... the woman's family would have the same right. They too would not have let me survive if they had honour.

Q: Would that be right then?

A: Well ... as I said, honour killing is a true punishment. Then surely others would also have the same right to save their honour, but it would be my luck or chance if I could evade that or rescue myself somehow. Otherwise, you know, destiny ... the end ... and if I avoided death, then I would consider myself lucky. Then I would have to be hidden somewhere until a *faislo* with the woman's family was made by the *sardar*.

Q: Do you think that honour killing is the only punishment in cases like this?

A: Killing for honour is absolutely right. The only way to save your honour is to kill those who attack your honour – whether he is your blood relative or not. I cannot let anyone play with my honour. It is honour, not a joke.

Q: Thank you for sharing your sensitive story with me.

A: *Amman*, keep praying for me so that this tough time of my life will soon be over.

Q: Sure. I will.

2: *Name*: **Omar, aged 16**

The interview lasted for an hour and nineteen minutes and took place at the district jail.

Omar was wearing very dirty, torn and patched clothes. On his head he wore a black sports cap. Throughout the interview, he kept wiping the sweat from his face with his right sleeve because of the very hot weather. He was continuously moving his right leg.

Q: *Assalam-o-alaikum.*

A: *Walaikum-assalam.*

Q: How are you doing?

A: Thank God.

Q: Would you like to talk to me?

A: Yes, sister. Ask me whatever you like.

Q: Let me make one thing clear: whatever information you give me will remain secure and will be used only for the purposes of my research and for related publications.

A: Research means?

Q: I am studying *karo-kari*, so I will share your story with others, but they will not be able to recognize you.

A: Please do.

Q: Thank you. Do you have any objection if I record what you say?

A: No, why? I speak the truth as I always have, so carry on.

Q: May I ask about your name, age community, parents and the reason why you are in jail?

A: I'm a Shaikh from Sindh. My name is Omar. We are basically Sindhi. My age is about sixteen or seventeen or ... maybe ... God knows better but I have not got my identity card done yet which means that I am under eighteen. My parents are alive. My father does not do any work.

Actually we do not let him do any work because he is an elderly man now so he stays at home. We are five brothers who work for him.

Q: Would you like to tell me some more about yourself, about your childhood, your brothers and sisters, your favourite games, your education and your job?

A: We are five brothers and three sisters. As far as games are concerned I never played any games. I work at people's houses. I do sweeping, mopping and other jobs for the family. I wasn't the sort of person who has friends or falls in with anyone.

Q: Didn't you even play with your brothers and sisters?

A: No, *bajee*.[66] I understand but, you know, my sisters are much older than me and are married so they live in Larkana. So I had no chance to play with them.

Q: Did you play any games with your friends at school, or outside school?

A: I never liked any of that. Right from the start I worked outside. And you are asking about school ... I went to school but I didn't study there. Actually, once there was a fight between me and some other children in the school. They belonged to a different caste and were rich so they didn't want me to be there. You know boys ... they were the fighting type. After that fight, I was badly beaten by one of my teachers so I left the school and didn't go back any more; but that happened long ago ... a lot of time has passed between then and this incident. You know, the situation in my city is that there was no teacher and no school the very day I left the school, and I didn't go again.

Q: Where do you work?

A: They are rich people in my city and I do housework like sweeping out, mopping and cleaning. I prepare rice, chop vegetables, buy fresh food for them ... and I earned four thousand rupees a month until two months ago. But now I have left the job because... you know... because of the case. Since I am locked up, how can I continue with the job?

---

[66] Older sister.

Q: Are you married?

A: No, not yet. Can I tell you what actually happen in the matter of honour?

Q: You can. Yes. What was the reason for the honour killing?

A: As you know, in our Islam it is clearly stated that we are the guardians of our women and if someone treats them in a dishonourable way, we must deal with those people with an iron hand. Also, we have a strong tradition of defending our honour. We have to kill or be killed for honour, which has been a strong value for centuries and it is the instruction of our Prophet Muhammad (peace be upon Him). This strong passion does not allow us think when we see a threat to our honour and, without losing a second, we will kill straightaway to save our honour.

Q: So what did you see?

A: What did I see? OK. I need to explain it to you in the right order. It was one o'clock in the morning. There was a marriage ceremony in our neighbourhood and I was going home after the party with one of my cousins, the son of my paternal aunt. We all live near each other so I first left him at his house and then went on to my own home. I killed that boy. Yes, I killed him with my own hands. That's what I did.

Q: Can you please explain what actually happened and why you killed him?

A: Yes. As I told you, I was with him on the night when the killing happened. I left him at the door of his house and went on to my own home. On the way, I got a call on my mobile from another cousin, my uncle's son who worked in Karachi as a house-servant like me. He asked me if he could talk to his wife. My uncle lived with us along with his family. So his daughter-in-law, I mean the wife of the cousin who had phoned me, was there at home. As soon I reached my home, I gave my phone to my sister-in-law and told her to keep it and that I would get it back from her the next day. Then I went to my room. I was trying to get to sleep when I noticed something unusual. What I saw was that after half an hour, the cousin who I had just left at his house, came on to my home and went straight to my sister-in-law's room, the one who I had lent my phone to to talk to her husband and then give it back to me the next day.

Q: Was your home not locked?

A: No, you know the village system. There are only low walls around the houses like fences. We are poor people. Do we have proper houses? How can we arrange doors or a proper home and all that? The recent flood and heavy rains had made us even poorer. There is no concept of doors in our homes. I knew that some of my family members, such as my father and my uncle, had suspicions about an illicit relationship between my cousin and my uncle's daughter-in-law, but I had no such doubts. But when I saw him coming in in the dark, I got suspicious. He entered and thought everybody was asleep, so he went straight into her room.

Q: Was she alone in her room?

A: No, she had a daughter sleeping besides her. She was very young, let's say seven years old, I reckon, God knows better. I saw what I saw, and when I saw it, I was completely consumed by thoughts about honour.

Q: What did you see?

A: What I saw was that they were sleeping together. You know there was no door to that room but I peeped in through the window.

Q: Can you please explain more explicitly what you actually saw?

A: *Bajee*, how can I tell you about a bad deed?

Q: Well, you know, to let people know about things, we have to describe them clearly.

A: OK. Are you married?

Q: Yes, and I am a mother of grown-up children, brother.

A: OK. Then you know what a husband and wife do? The usual process … both of my sister-in-law's legs were up in the air and he was doing … what husbands do. After I saw this, I went back to my room and got my pistol. Her room's light was off even though there was electricity. When the boy saw me inside the room, he held his hands over his lower body and ran away. There was an alley just by our homes. He was running along it when I shot him. He was killed instantly. I came back. Meanwhile, my sister-in-law had put her dress on and was lying on another *charpaee*. I went in and fired at her but I missed and she was unharmed. Meanwhile, my father, my uncle and other relatives had all gathered and they held me and tried to save her, and also I didn't have another bullet. My missed shot did not cause her any harm but we handed her over to her parents and kept her little daughter with us, as the daughter was our blood. She went to her parents because we couldn't keep her anymore. We don't know whether she was given to someone in marriage or not as we don't keep any information about *karis*.

Q: How old was she?

A: About eighteen or nineteen.

Q: What was her husband's reaction?

A: He appreciated what I had done and my uncle also appreciated me. It was an honourable deed that I had done, so I was appreciated.

Q: How did you feel when you had done it?

A: How did I feel? I felt nothing … but yes, I understand now. When I saw it, I got really emotional. My whole body started shivering. I became emotional. But after killing him and deciding to throw the woman away, everything appeared normal to me. You know, I did the act in accordance with the teaching in the Qur'an, so I was satisfied that I had performed my duty honourably.

Q: Who is looking after your family and supporting you while you are in jail?

A: *Bajee*, it is God who supports and helps everyone. God is there to look after my family. As the boy's father and uncles have lodged an FIR against my father and me, the police arrested me but my father got away successfully. Although they are our relatives, you know, their son had been killed, so for them it was normal to be upset, but I believe soon they will understand the situation and change their statement in court in my favour and I will be released from jail.

Q: If you had been seen in the same position with someone else's wife by her husband, how would he have reacted?

A: It is certain that I would have been killed. But the question is, why would I challenge someone else's honour? If someone threatens someone else's honour, whether it is someone else or me, he has to be killed instantly. Mercy in this regard is just another word for dishonour.

Q: What is it like being in jail?

A: My jail experiences ... see so far ... I am new so it is fine. Not too bad. Electricity is a big problem. You see that we have been talking for about two hours and there is no power. The other day, I heard the policemen saying that they will arrange light from another phase, so let's see. Other systems in jails are fine. Food is also very nice and from the very beginning I've lived with everyone here like a brother, so I am also liked here like a brother.

Q: How do you think other people view your act; your family, other people in the community and people in general?

A: All around, people appreciate my act of killing and call me an honourable person. In jail even the policemen and the other prisoners see what I did as an honourable act. Now people are suggesting that we should do *khair* with the boy's family, so our elders are doing that, and hopefully things will be settled with them, and the case will be over soon. As it was a case of honour, I don't expect a long punishment. God will help us. We will succeed.

Q: Looking back on the killing, how do you feel about it now?

A: I believe that whatever happened was right, and that it was written in the fate of my family. God chose me for this righteous act. Now I am thinking about the future and I pray before God for his mercy on us. My peace of mind is a gift that I received from God after the killing. I killed him in accordance with the Qur'an's teaching, so I am satisfied that I carried out my duty honourably. As you know, in our Islam it is stated that we are the guardians of our women and that if they mistreat our honour, we must punish them for their dishonourable actions. Also, we have a great tradition of defending our honour. We have to kill or be killed for honour, and we have been doing it for centuries and it is the instruction of our Prophet Muhammad (peace be upon Him). So now it is in the hands of the honourable judge of the court to make a decision. I have no clear idea how long I'll be here, but I assume that soon I shall be released as our elders are having talks with the murdered boy's family to withdraw the case against me.

Q: Why do you think she acted as she did?

A: I think that she had been having shameful relations with the dead boy even before her marriage, and they might have been doing it for years. It was the first time they had been caught red-handed. We call them *karis* and all *karis* must be killed on the spot, but she was lucky that I missed her and that I had no more bullets in my pistol, so she was not killed.

Q: What is your concept of honour?

A: Honour is a passion, it is power and emotions. No-one teaches you what honour is, but it is in your blood. Her parents gave her to a man in marriage so it became her responsibility to look after her husband's honour. When she violated it, then a man's honour is harmed and he kills. Those who have honour and respect an honourable life kill, otherwise many dishonoured people see this immoral behaviour with their own eyes and leave the guilty ones alive. They do not kill because they do not have honour.

Q: But you were not the woman's husband, so do you think you had a right to kill her?

A: Every single man of a family has a right to kill a wayward woman; it might be the daughter, a mother or a wife or anyone else.

Q: OK. Thank you for sharing your life story with me.

A: You are welcome, *bajee*. May I go now?

Q: Yes, you can. Thank you again.

3: *Name*: Saeed, aged 26

The interview lasted for an hour and fourteen minutes and took place at the district jail.

Saeed had long hair. There was a dark black dot on his forehead, which is considered a sign of a pious Muslim. It is earned by offering continuous prayers because when someone's head keeps touching the ground while offering prayers, this sign appears. He was wearing a black thread around his neck and a yellow thread round his wrist. Saeed could hardly walk without the help of his walking stick; his leg had been crippled by childhood polio. He asked me whether he could kill and run away from the police with only one leg, as was claimed in the police report. He wept continuously for his elderly parents, his wife and his two young children.

Q: *Assalam-o-alaikum.*

A: *Walaikum-assalam.*

Q: How are you doing?

A: I am OK.

Q: Are you willing to talk to me.

A: Yes, sure.

Q: Can I record what you say too?

A: Yes. I won't tell lies and you look trustworthy to me.

Q: Please note that I will use the information which you give me in my research and in any related publications.

A: OK.

Q: Thank you. Tell me something about your background. What's your name, caste, community, parents and so on?

A: My name is Saeed. By caste I am Mangi. Our profession is begging. We basically play drums and earn money, but if there is no opportunity for us to play our drums, we beg for our living. We are principally Baloch but we are settled in Sindh so we now call ourselves Sindhi. I'm not sure about my age. It is … I think it is written on my identity card but the police have it at the moment so I can't show it you. I think I am twenty-six. I remember it vividly only because here in the jail they made me an ID card. I didn't have one before.

Q: Would you like to tell me some more about yourself, your childhood, siblings, favourite games, education and job?

A: I wasted my childhood. I lost the use of my leg when I was a child because of polio. After that, I was unable to walk properly and my parents told me not to play outside very much as the naughty children used to push me over and run away all the time. But I learned drumming and I'm good at it. These days, people don't often call for us because they like modern singers, so those of us who play traditional classical music can't earn our bread and butter with this art anymore.

Q: OK. Are you educated?

A: No. I went to school but, you know, I was my parents' blue-eyed boy and I didn't like going to school, and my parents said that I didn't need to go to school as they would provide me with everything at home. And our system of life ... you know... it's a kind of gypsy life-style. We move from one place to another so study was not possible, and study means that you have to have an interest in studying. I hate books. I had no interest in studying. My father was a beggar so he said it was his duty to collect food for us and I just had to eat it. Because I had polio in my left leg, I couldn't walk properly, so my parents were extremely kind to me and they looked after me very well.

Q: What about your brothers and sisters.

A: I had one brother and one sister. My brother died when he was young and my sister also died soon after her marriage. When she died, my maternal uncle created such havoc and as the result of that I am in the lock-up. My father is a very old man. He is also in the lock-up with me. My mother and my wife are at home. I was the only breadwinner in my family. I am very worried about my family. I have a three-year-old son and a daughter just eleven months old. I have no other relatives, there are no maternal or paternal uncles who will look after my family. Whoever is there in the name of our relatives are no support at all. They don't even come to visit my father and me in the jail. Only my poor old mother comes to see us along with my young children. My paternal uncles put me in this disaster. God witnesses everything, how when my children come to visit me here in jail, I really suffer, and I have requested the honourable judge that because I and my father are innocent, he should kindly have mercy on us and release us so that we can be free and request some honourable people like a *sardar* or a *wadera* to intervene in our problem so that we can come out of it because we are suffering here in jail without ever having committed any crimes. The honourable judge replied that God would help us. My mother is a very old woman, she can't bear it all. My uncles did us a great wrong; they lodged an FIR against my father and me. We didn't know anything about what had happened so we didn't run away from the place where we were and the police arrested us. I was the only breadwinner in my family. I used to beg from people to help me because I am a cripple. From dawn to dusk I used to go out to beg. Some people were extremely kind; some used to give me one, two, five or ten rupees but some richer people could give me fifty to hundred rupees as well. I always prayed for their long life, prosperity and good health. Even when people had not given me anything, I still did not disrespect them. Whatever people gave me, food, money, clothes or other useful things, I used to take back home to distribute among my family members and I ate the food with my family. I played with my son and lived nicely with my parents. Except for God, no-one was with us, but I was happy with my family.

Q: Can you tell me something about your married life; the mode of marriage, your wife, children, relationship with your in-laws and so on?

A: My grandfather married twice, so one of my step-uncles gave his daughter to me in marriage without asking for any money as he was very kind to us. My father-in-law has passed away now but my mother-in-law is still alive and we have a very good relationship with each other. I told you about my children: my son is three and my daughter was just six days old when my father and I were arrested. My wife is a very good woman; a simple and innocent woman. I didn't want to kill her without any reason.

Q: So was there any pressure on you to kill her?

A: Sort of.

Q: Could you please explain it to me? What kind of honour killing was it?

A: It is a long story, sister, you know. My father was made to marry a woman (my mother) by my uncle (my father's older brother) with the condition that after this marriage the first baby girl would be given to them, right. So my mother had a girl (my only sister) and when she grew up, to fulfill the promise, we gave her to my uncle. My uncle's son married her. When my sister was pregnant, her child died in the womb and my sister then died from an infection. When she died, my uncle forced my father either to buy or get a girl for his son, or to give him money so that he could buy a girl for his son himself. My father took a stand and said that he had fulfilled the promise by giving them a girl but that he could not stop her dying as it was God's wish that she had died. My father also told me that when his brother (my uncle, the one we had given my sister to so that his son couldould marry her) got married, my father had paid him 30,000 rupees. But my uncle would not listen to or respect my father's previous good faith and kept on asking for either money or a girl. Where could my father get another woman for my uncle's son? My father had no money. So my uncle then asked for a small plot of land which I had bought after saving up the alms which people had given me. My uncle is a very clever and cruel man. With his other brothers, he keeps creating issues and troubles for people. In one case, he had a four-year feud with a family whose daughter had been abducted by his younger son. The family was asking for their girl back or a *faislo*, but my uncle and his sons refused to listen to them. About thirteen months ago, most probably they or some other people (as I said, my uncle keeps creating problems because of his troublesome nature) ... one night some people broke into their house and killed the son who had kidnapped the girl. We live quite far away from my uncle's house and we didn't know anything about the killing. Later, we got to know about it because people told us. One day after the killing, my uncle whose son had been killed came to us and suggested to me that if I killed my wife as *kari*, he would stop asking us for money and instead would give us some money and blame the other family's man as *karo* and earn some money from him in a *faislo*. I flatly refused to kill my wife as she did not know anything about the murders and was entirely innocent. Why would I accuse her of being a *kari*? First, my uncle insisted that my father and I should kill her, but when we both refused to do so, he lodged an FIR against us two months ago in which he accused us of killing his son. Because we didn't know anything at all about this plan, we were arrested by the police. When the police came to arrest us, our neighbours told them that we were peaceful people and that we had never disturbed anyone in the area. My uncle's statement was recorded with the police in which he accused my blind father and me of killing his son. You look at me: I can't walk properly, my blind father can't see anything, so how could we break into somebody's house, kill someone and run away? But the atrocity did not end there. When the police arrested us, they beat me a lot so that I would confess to killing my uncle's son. I wouldn't confess because when I have not committed such a sin, why should I admit to it? But because I refused to confess, they began beating my old blind father in front of me. I couldn't stop them so I begged them to not beat my father and said that I would admit what they had accused me of. The SHO who had beaten us both mercilessly, my father and me, took us to the court and before the honourable judge he asked me about the killing. Because I was very scared, I lied to court and said that because the boy had been *karo* with my wife, my blind father and I had killed him. This was the version that the SHO wanted me to give to the court. To save my father's life and to avoid the third-degree brutal torture, I admitted the killing, but God knows I am not a murderer, and neither was my father involved in any murder. Now I am really worried about our safety and our future as the other prisoner brothers are asking why I admitted it before the court. That means that I had confessed to the killing so the punishment and the imprisonment could be long. We might be hanged or be in prison for ever, or … I just can't predict what might happen. I don't know anything. I am not a clever person, I am just a simple beggar. My only crime is that I bought a small plot of land, which was not liked by my well-off relatives who couldn't bear to see me having my own small house. My second fault is that I did not kill my innocent wife as a *kari*. And the third fault is that I have no money to bribe the police to stop them beating us and accusing us wrongly as murderers. What should I do? I am not a person who understands what law is and how people use it. Now my uncle will grab the plot and I don't know what they will do to my innocent wife, as my mother and my grandfather are too weak to stop them from any wrongdoing against my wife and children. I just don't know what will happen. I can only pray to God. Could you please help us? We'll be extremely thankful to you.

Q: I am very sad to know about this. Is there no-one out there to look after your family while you are in jail?

A: Who can look after my family? I have told you the whole story. I used to beg to be able to feed my family; we all relied on alms. Now, I don't know how they can survive. This is my story. I haven't committed any crime. I can't imagine killing anyone. You can meet my father; he is blind, so how could he kill someone?

Q: Did you let any other officer know that you had admitted to the killing because of the third-degree torture?

A: I am very scared of the police. They are heartless people. They show no mercy to old, crippled and powerless poor people. You do something – you are educated. They might listen to you.

Q: I promise you that I will let your voice be heard by as many people as possible. I shall write your story and share it with the world.

A: I need justice.

Q: I know; it is your right and it should be the priority of every state to provide its people with justice.

A: Pray for my family and for me.

Q: I will, and thank you very much for sharing your story with me.

A: Please come again to see me.

Q: God bless you.

4: *Name*: **Ata, aged 22**

The interview lasted for an hour and eighteen minutes and took place at the district jail.

Ata had curly hair; his eyes were big but he was looking very pale. His shirt was buttoned up to the collar. He had a red thread around his wrist. The significance of this thread is that it is either taken from some shrines or from some religious clerics with the purpose that it will keep them safe from evils. People wear them around their neck or wrist as a safey measure. His hands were shivering.

Q: *Assalam-o-alaikum.*

A: *Walaikum-assalam.*

Q: How are you?

A: You can see, what shall I say about how I am?

Q: Would you like to talk to me?

A: I was told about your visit. At first I had decided not to meet anyone but then they told me that you write books and that my story will be in your book, so I changed my mind and decided to talk to you.

Q: Thank you for talking to me. I am a researcher and I am working to know what honour killing is, so I am interviewing those who have been involved in honour-related violence either directly or indirectly.

A: Does this mean you will write my story in your book?

Q: You are right to some extent, but let me make one thing clear: whatever information you give me will remain with me and will be used only for the purposes of my research.

A: In your research book?

Q: Yes, you can say that.

A: I will tell you everything with honesty.

Q: Thank you very much. May I record your talk too.

A: Yes, otherwise you might lose some important things.

Q: Thank you. Can you tell me your name, caste, community, parents and your background.

A: My name is Ata, I am Mugal by caste. Basically we are from Balochistan, but about fifty or sixty years ago we settled in Sindh. My father had an insignificant government job. He had two wives so I have four brothers and three sisters from both of my mothers.

Q: Would you like to tell me some more about yourself, your childhood, siblings, favourite games, education, job and so on?

A: My childhood was good as my father had a government job. Even though it was a very minor job it was a good source of regular income. Second, we have seven acres of land and we grow rice on it. I worked as a shepherd in my childhood. I always played nicely with my sisters and brothers; we lived happily and enjoyed spending time with each other. The games we played were simple, like pushing each other, hide-and-seek, throwing and catching a ball – things like that. I just went to school, let's say, for hardly two years. First, my responsibility in my family was to take our buffalos, cows and goats to graze in the fields. Second, I had no interest in studying and, to be perfectly honest, there was no education in our schools so I couldn't learn anything. You might know that in villages like ours, if there are schools and teachers, do they actually teach?

Q: May I ask how old you are?

A: I am twenty-two.

Q: Can you tell me something about your married life; I mean the mode of your marriage, your wife, your children, your relations with your in-laws and things like that?

A: I was getting on really well with my wife and my in-laws. We visited each other's homes and looked after each other in difficult times. I married my paternal uncle's daughter when I was eighteen. My uncle gave her to us and we promised to give him our future baby girl. In addition, I paid him 25,000 rupees, and we, I mean my father and I, promised my in-laws that I would give them my first baby girl. Actually, he was my uncle so there was no trouble over that; he just put down these two conditions for my marriage and we accepted them.

Q: And if she did not give birth to a baby girl? What then?

A: God is great. God understands intentions and promises. I was sure to have a baby girl and, you see, most women deliver girls not boys. You see, now I am the father of a daughter and two sons.

Q: What was the cause of the *karo-kari*?

A: You know, I lived with one of my brothers and his family and my father. A few years ago, some people migrated to our village from Balochistan. They were actually forced to migrate by their own relatives. When they came to our village, they asked us to help them to stay and to build their cottages. We took pity on them and let them establish themselves there. One day, when I came from outside into my home, as you know our villages have just low fences around the houses and there are no proper gates or doors, so as I was going in I heard voices talking. When I went in, I saw my older brother's wife sitting and talking to the boy of the family who we had let live in our village. As soon as they saw me, they got up, but I had overheard part of their conversation. I slapped my sister-in-law and the boy, and said to him 'Look, we took pity on you; we let you live in our village when you had no place to live. Your own people were your enemies but we gave you honour and respect and now you are dishonouring us'. I shouted at him but I let him go. I didn't let anyone know about this incident, but I did go to the boy's father and told him plainly to keep his boy under control. You know, things like this are very delicate in our society. Even on a small suspicion many killings can happen, so I was treating the matter sensibly. The boy's father asked me not to tell anyone else about what had happened and he promised to send his son back to his own village and said that the boy would leave the area as soon as possible as he understood that his son had acted in an unjustified way. The boy's father did as he had promised. He himself was a poor and decent man so he sent his son to some of his relatives for four months. Nothing wrong happened during that time and I didn't see the boy around again. But after four months, one day when I was walking towards my house, I saw the same boy standing talking to my sister-in-law outside the fans of our house. I straightaway went inside the house and told my older brother about it. He called his wife inside and questioned her and he abused her physically and verbally as well. At night-time, my brother used to go to our fields to look after the water supply. We didn't want our father to work hard so to give him time to take a rest at home, we brothers divided the responsibilities of work between us. He came in late from the fields, but the next morning we needed to go out earlier, so we finished our breakfast by six o'clock. When we reached our fields, we saw our father coming towards us and he told us that my sister-in-law had killed herself with the pistol that we had at our house. My father advised us not to go back home as the police would arrest us. You know how this kind of news spreads rapidly in villages, and for making money the police, journalists from various news channels and reporters from different newspapers get together. My brother and I both went to our maternal uncle's house to hide. The police came to our house in our absence and threatened my father and my uncle (the father of the dead girl) to either hand over a culprit as the killer or an innocent person as a killer so they could produce someone as the murderer. Eventually the police forced my uncle to lodge an against my brother or me with a promise that after filling up the stomach of the filing system they would release us. My uncle did this and the police arrested me while I was sleeping at my maternal uncle's house. My uncle came along with the police and I was arrested. The police accused me, charged me with the murder and tortured me for a week or more. Eventually, they asked for 100,000 rupees to release me. My family is very poor. We could only offer about 25,000 rupees but the police refused to take that amount. They tortured me a lot to make me confess to the killing but I denied it. My father and older brother came to visit me once a week. The police charge 170 rupees a person to visit a prisoner so even meeting with relatives is expensive. What else can I tell you? I haven't killed anyone. God knows everything. I don't know how long I will be in jail. The police put pressure on my uncle to force me to confess that I had killed his daughter. My uncle couldn't go to such an extreme level because he knew that I didn't kill her, so he didn't say anything against me. However, since we are unable to pay the bribe to the police, they are angry now and want me to admit to the charge of murder. Now everything depends on my uncle: if he manages to get the case against me withdrawn, then I will be released, otherwise I don't know what might happen.

Q: Who is supporting you and your family while you are in jail?

A: Who else can support my family except for my father and my brother? Whatever remains after bribing the police, they spend on me and my family. I don't know how long I'll be in jail. Please pray for me.

Q: I will. Have the police taken you before the court?

A: No. They just keep on putting pressure on my father and brother to collect a huge amount to give them as a bribe, and in return the police will let me go, but they just can't collect that much money. Whatever they can get their hands on they have already given to the police. You know, every time to take me to their torture cell, they beat me more than before and do inhuman things to me so that I will break and admit to the murder, and my family are all heart-broken about not being able to bribe them with the amount they have demanded. As I keep saying, I haven't killed anyone but I don't know how much longer I can bear this much violence.

Q: Do you have help from a lawyer?

A: We are poor labourers, how can we afford to hire a lawyer? Only God is our lawyer.

A: Who had actually killed the woman?

Q: I told you, she committed suicide when nobody was home. My father heard the shot when he was sitting outside our home. When he went inside, he saw her lying on the ground, stone dead, and the pistol was lying beside her. No-one else was there.

Q: Where were your family then?

A: You know we live next to each other; although it's a combined house, everyone has a separate area and separate rooms and so on. My wife also went out after she heard the shot.

Q: And what about your mother?

A: I told you, my mother and my step-mother have both passed away.

Q: Do you think your uncle will withdraw the case against you?

A: He is supposed to – but he is scared of the police. He told my father that the police would kill me if he withdraws the case.

Q: I hope your tough time to be over soon. Thank you for sharing your story with me.

A: Madam, please do something for me. You are an educated woman.

Q: I will try my best to let people know what is going on with you and in the jails.

A: God bless you.

Q: Thank you.

5: *Name*: Ayaz, aged 45

The interview lasted for an hour and twenty-seven minutes and took place at a district jail.

Ayaz was the only prisoner who was wearing very clean clothes. His head was covered with a clean, white cap. His nails were neatly cut. He had a small moustache but for some reason his lips were shivering. He also wept many times during our conversation.

Q: Assalam-o-alaikum.

A: Walaikum-assalam.

Q: How are you?

A: What shall I reply to this question, *Adi*?

Q: Would you like to talk to me?

A: Yes. The police said that you would write our story so that people can read it.

Q: Yes. That's true. I shall share your story with people in my research paper.

A: Is this your job?

Q: Not strictly, it is my study.

A: That means you will write in a newspaper?

Q: No, not in a newspaper. Let me make one thing clear: whatever information you give me will remain with me and will be used only for the purposes of my research.

A: Tell everyone so that I can be freed.

Q: OK. Tell me something about your background; your name, caste, community, parents and so on.

A: My name is Ayaz and I am forty-five. I am Kori by caste and I live in Sindh. My father was a farmer. I have eight brothers and three sisters. We and our parents sometimes worked here and sometimes there. It all depended on where my father felt better. You know the life of a poor peasant in our country. My father wanted always to provide good food for his children but he couldn't. We were very poor and we still are. We have nothing, no land, no property and no home. Wherever my poor father thought that his children would be able to get twice as much food at least, that's where he started to work.

Q: Can you tell me some more about yourself – about your childhood, siblings, favourite games, education, your job and things like that?

A: School? Our poverty didn't even let us think of school. We had to move from one place to another in search of food. Besides, you probably know that teachers in upper Sindh do not teach in the villages. They just take a salary, and a large number of schools are ghosts[67] so education was a kind of different and difficult thing ... at least for us. But when we moved into the city, my younger brothers started going to school and they studied, and now my sons are also studying. I can't remember any games that I played as a child. Like every child I might have played some games, but I can't remember any because from a very young age, let's say from the age of five, I worked as a shepherd. In the city I worked as a labourer. The landlords in our areas don't want people to study because the *waderas* know that if people study, they would learn how to maintain a record of their income and then they would not let the *wadera* and his people exploit their labour. This is highly unacceptable for the landowners so they want illiterate people. So you see the schools buildings are converted into *otaques*[68] for the *waderas*. So I worked as a labourer. I used to carry heavy

---

[67] The term 'ghost school', meaning fake schools, became notorious during the rule of the military dictator General Zia-ul-Haque (1977-1988), when entire institutions started to become chaotic. The signs of educational deterioration began in the villages where influential landlords turned schools into stables and rest-houses and people had no organized structure within which they could react or get their voices heard. Teachers stopped going to the schools and the attendance of students reduced. Despite a change in government and various articles written to save education, no visible change was seen in the rural educational structure. These remarks of the Chief Justice of Pakistan, Iftikhar Muhammad Chaudhry, were published in the newspaper *Dawn* on 11 February 2013: "There are animals kept in schools and the buildings have been turned into stables. The government has failed to provide any answer or details about the state of ghost and non-functional schools, while apparently funds and salaries were being disbursed as buildings remained abandoned or occupied by animals". He ordered district judges across Pakistan to survey fake schools and submit a report.
[68] Living room.

sacks of rice on my back and load them onto trucks for a daily wage, but when there was no laboring work available, I was in trouble so I always kept an eye out for any available work. My brothers studied and two of my younger brothers became tailors.

Q: Can you share something about your married life? What was the the mode of your marriage? Tell me about wife, your children and your relationship with your in-laws.

A: I married about eighteen or nineteen years ago. I was about twenty-four or twenty-five and my wife was maybe fourteen or fifteen at the time. We do not keep a record of ages. It was a *watto-satto* marriage. We got on really well with each other. I became a father of one girl and one boy. There were no problems with my family or my in-laws; they are really good people.

Q: What was the cause of the *karo-kari*?

A: I was in the fields one day. When I was on the way home, some neighbours told me that there had been some killings. When I went into my house, I saw two dead bodies; one was my sister-in-law and the other was a man who was Jat by caste. I was confused and asked those who were there what had happened. They told me that my brother had killed his wife along with a man who was our neighbour. Within a few minutes, the police arrived and the landlord of the area came with them. He told the police to arrest me because I had killed them. The police didn't let me speak, they just arrested me. They arrested my father as well and didn't let me say anything. They also took fifteen of our neighbours' buffalos which were at our house as I used to take them to graze in the forest. In the lock-up, the SHO demanded money and promised that when he had been given the money he had asked for, he would let us and our cattle go free. We gave him 70,000 rupees and my father, the buffalos and I were freed. After paying the money, I thought that my troubles were over but I was unaware of the depth of the conspiracy. The police arrested me again and this time there was no possibility of paying a bribe to be freed. The police officer told me that the area landlord had put pressure on them to make a strong case against me so that I should not get out of the jail. I admitted to the murders because I was badly tortured by the police, but when the case was presented before the court, I denied it. Since the police report was strong and included a statement by the *wadera* that he had witnessed the murders, nobody listened to me. So I was sentenced to life imprisonment on the charges of double murder because of the conspiracy between the landowners of my area. My father died as he could not endure the troubles. This allegation and jail experience threw me into a world of great poverty, pain and debt.

Q: Did you admit to the murders before the judge?

A: I did admit it because I was tortured, but when the case was presented before the court I denied it. But the police report bore more weight than what I had told the court because it contained the landlord's assertion that he had witnessed the murders. Nobody listens to the poor people here in Sindh or anywhere in Pakistan, so I was sentenced to life. The truth is that my older brother had murdered his wife with a man, but he had run off and instead of trying to find him, the police arrested me because the landlord had told them to. After paying the bribe I really thought that my troubles were over, but after the police arrested me again, there was no chance of paying another bribe. The police presented their report to the court that I had murdered my sister-in-law along with a man even though I had denied the charges. The police did admit to me that the area landlord had put pressure on them to make a strong case against me so that I should not get out of jail.

Q: What was the reason for the *wadera*'s enmity?

A: The *waderas* are really full of their own importance. They think that all the villagers are their slaves and should work for them unconditionally. I twice refused to work on the *wadera*'s land because I needed to provide both bread and education for my children. Also, my younger brothers were studying, which was not an acceptable thing for them to do as far as the *wadera* was concerned. *Waderas* do hold these grievances in their hearts and wait for the right time to show their supremacy over poverty-stricken and helpless people like us. These are very old tactics used to pressurise and harass the villagers. The *waderas* make their peasants work rigorously for them for eighteen hours a day without any wages. How can a family live like that? *Waderas* are the main reason for the illiteracy in the villages. They have turned the schools in their areas into stables for their animals. They are into politics. They are ministers and members of national and provincial assemblies. They are very powerful. They live like kings. They do not want common people having food, education and the basic necessities of life. I was the only person who had refused to work on the *wadera*'s land for free. These self-serving *waderas* keep their grievances in their hearts and then take revenge to show their power over others and terrorise common people so that they will never challenge their powers in any way.

Q: Who is looking after your family while you are in jail?

A: My mother also died as she was very upset, but now my younger brothers who I helped with their studies and then helped them to learn to work as tailors are helping and supporting my wife and children. My daughter is married now and my son is studying. I make Sindhi caps in the jail; I earn about two hundred to three hundred rupees each by selling these caps. From that money I buy my everyday groceries and other essential things and try to save some money to send to my children as well. What else can I tell you? Home, family, life and everything has been ruined. Just dark shadows of life are following us. In Sindh, criminals live a better life than innocent, hard-working honest people.

Q: Don't the prison authorities provide you with these basic necessities?

A: They only give us food that is very tasteless and sometimes it is impossible to eat it. So we cook our own food, and for that we need gas and gas cylinders are expensive, but we have to pay it. Then we need tea, medicine, cigarettes, soap, grocery, clothes … many other things are needed. A living person needs so many things.

Q: What is it like being in jail?

A: It's my thirteenth year in jail. My total sentence is twenty-five years. I am by nature a peaceful person so I don't get involved in any trouble with anyone in the jail. Because of my kind attitude, nobody creates problems for me. I know that I am a prisoner so I behave like a prisoner. I know some prisoners are very evil but I don't get involved in any issues with them. Jail is a cage. No-one can live here happily. I remember my children and my wife all the time, and how my children are growing older. How do they feel about me, that their father is in jail? The worry makes you sick and mad. All prisoners live on their memories and get sick because of their worries. There is a saying that 'a man is stronger than a cliff', and when a man endures unimaginable circumstances and survives, he believes this saying. Then you move with the automatic waves of time and life passes. The early days here were very horrible but they have passed. I pray that God should not make anyone a prisoner. The world stands on hope. The first time I was arrested, I hoped to be released. Then I was arrested again and I hoped that the court would free me but I was convicted. Now, again I hope that the government will forgive us and release us as soon as possible. Hope, hope and hope is life. My mother and father died because of this strange and horrible tragedy. My brother who killed his wife has not been seen by anybody, neither has he contacted us again. My children grew up without my love. My wife weeps all the time and keeps praying for my safe return. My other brothers sometimes come to visit me. They bring my son too but my wife never comes here. Visits are expensive because you have to give money to the police. Half of my life has been spent in jail. I haven't been able to give love to children. What is in jail? There is no freedom, no happiness, no peace. It's an awful life. I don't know when these painful days will be over.

Q: Why is it expensive for your relatives to visit you in jail?

A: It's the police; the Pakistani police. They have no heart. For them money is their god. They ask for money whether it's a weeping eighty-year-old woman who wants to see her son or a young child who needs to see his father. The police demand money. It has nothing to do with human feelings.

Q: How much do your relatives pay to the police to visit you?

A: The rate is always the same: every single person has to pay two hundred rupees for a meeting of ten to fifteen minutes.

Q: Why do you think this has happened to you?

A: All this is a punishment for wanting my children to have an education. To give them an education, I needed to work hard for money and I did. I worked at three different places to give my family a better life. I was not ready to live a slave's life at the doors of the area landlord. They consider themselves gods. Anyway, when I was arrested my father and mother went to him. They begged him to save my life and help me to get out of jail but he refused, just saying arrogantly that he had asked police to arrest me and to draw up a strong charge-sheet against me, and now he couldn't take his words back. He suggested that my parents should beg God, but it seems that God is also on the side of the *wadera*. Everything is in the hand of *waderas*. They are the gods of the land. But still I hope, I have hope. I cannot surrender. God will surely take me out of this trouble, as he is the most merciful and benevolent.

Q: Is there anything else that you want to share with me?

A: I have said what I wanted to. I hope that people will understand how the cruel *waderas* are playing havoc with the lives of poor people and making their lives miserable. Tell people that they must get an education and get rid of the slavery.

Q: Thank you very much for sharing your story with me.

A: Please pray for me and thank you for recording my story. I hope that people will learn from it.

Q: I hope so too. God bless you.

6: *Name*: Anwar, aged 34

The interview lasted for an hour and sixteen minutes and it took place at a district jail.

Anwar was a clean-shaved, tall, soft-spoken man. He was very critical of the tribal system in which landlords behave as kings and the other official authorities work as their personal enforcers.

Q: *Assalam-o-alaikum.*

A: *Walaikum-assalam.*

Q: How are you?

A: The blessings of God on you.

Q: Would you like to talk to me?

A: Will you ask about *karo-kari*?

Q: Mainly yes, but we shall discuss some other things too.

A: OK.

Q: Would you mind if I record your talk?

A: You can.

Q: Are you ready to talk to me?

A: Yes.

Q: Thank you. Tell me something about your background; your name, your caste, your community, your parents – things like that.

A: My name is Anwar. I am thirty-four. We are Sindhi. By caste we are Korai and we live in Ghotki. My father was a policeman and my mother was a housewife.

Q: Would you like to tell me some more about yourself, I mean about your childhood, your brothers and sisters, favourite games, education, your job and so on?

A: Our childhood was very nice and peaceful; my father was an educated person and was in a government job so the way that our house ran was very decent. I have six brothers and six sisters. We all played together at home, not any particular games but we always played with love and care … outside our home, life was also good. From school, I went on to college and completed my second year there. Then I passed the test for an Artillery Centre Academy and as a result I was selected for the army. I went to Lahore for the army training. It was a wonderful experience.

Q: Can you tell me something about your married life? I mean your mode of marriage, wife, children, and your relationship with your in-laws.

A: After my second year at college, my parents had me married to a nice girl. My in-laws were good people. The mode of the marriage was *watto-satto.* My older sister was already married to the brother of my wife so as part of the agreement they were obliged to give me a girl in marriage. Our marriage didn't last long; we had hardly been married for six years when she died. However, I had a very nice relationship with my in-laws as they were kind to our own family. They used to visit us regularly because my sister was married into that family. I have four children; three sons and a daughter.

Q: What was the issue of *karo-kari*?

A: After passing the army test, I was sent to Lahore to train. One day, I received a call from one of my brothers to tell me that my wife was dead. I took compassionate leave and returned to my village. As soon as I reached my village, I was arrested for the murder of my wife. My wife's mother had lodged an FIR against me. The police made a strong case against me and then presented me before the judge in the court. In court, I asked the judge not to punish me as I was not a murderer, but no-one listened to me and I was convicted for murder and was given life imprisonment.

Q: Why did the police make a report against you when you did not murder her and you were not even in the city?

A: The police fabricated a report against me with the support of the *wadera* of my school. The *wadera* bribed the police and paid them a lot of money to make the kind of report in which they should prove me a murderer. I was also asked by the police to pay a handsome amount as a bribe to be released but I had nothing to pay it with. So I was tortured brutally. The terrible torture and my poverty have made me a convicted killer. It is all in the hands of the police. Every innocent person has to admit as many killings as the police ask for. Nobody in the world can resist the Pakistani police.

Q: What was the exact allegation against you?

A: That I had killed my wife as *kari* but, as I told you, I was not in the village or even in the province. I was on training in Lahore.

Q: What about your family? Didn't they hire a lawyer?

A: My brothers tried their best but no-one was there to listen to them. The fact is that, in Pakistan, everything is possible if you are rich. Like in my case, my mother-in-law lodged an FIR against me and told my relatives that if they paid her money she would withdraw the case. The police asked for money. In the court, people and lawyers asked for money and threatened us that if money was not paid to them, they would give me a life sentence. The judge said 'Well, if you didn't kill her then give us the man who did. How could I have produced that man?

Q: What about the army? You were training with them, you were a recruit, a member of the army. Didn't they help you and give the police enough evidence that you were with them at the time of your wife's death?

A: They came to my village. They came to visit me in jail. They said 'Sorry about the situation but you know the army cannot interfere in civil matters'. There were so many issues for army. They were occupied with the Kargil war[69] and lots of other things, so they didn't do anything for me.

Q: But who really murdered her?

---

[69] The Kargil War, also known as the Kargil conflict, was an armed conflict between India and Pakistan which took place between May and July 1999 in the Kargil district of Kashmir and elsewhere along the Line of Control (LOC).

A: It's still not clear. But may I tell you something absolutely right, the truth behind all this trouble, the murder and my death sentence? There was a conflict between the *wadera* and my family because my father wanted his sons to be educated, which was not acceptable to the *wadera*. Consequently, the *wadera* used to create problems for us. Then he accused my nephew of stealing his cow. We paid him some money even though my nephew was innocent. Next, he accused my brothers of theft and had them arrested. So when he heard that I had joined the army, he could not tolerate it. He might have thought that with the support of the army I might be able to fight back, so he decided to kill my wife and get me arrested so that no-one in my family would be strong enough to stand up to him. That was how he showed his power. These things are very common in Sindh. The *waderas* of Sindh behave like gods. They cannot bear to see anyone having a better life than them. In the matter of this killing, my family said that the *wadera*'s people attacked our house at night-time and because of their gunfire my wife was killed. In fact they came with a plan to kill one of the women in our family so that they could accuse me of a murder and have me arrested.

Q: Why did the *wadera* want you to be arrested? Why not one of your brothers?

A: The *wadera* wanted to get rid of me because I could have been stronger than him. That's what he thought. I was getting an education. I had joined the army. Things like this are very common and are going on in Sindh all the time. The *waderas* of Sindh behave like kings. They cannot bear to see anyone getting a better life. Thousands have been killed and have died for no reason in Sindh. The *waderas* kill those who they think could be a threat to their kingdom and their tyranny in any way. I am a witness in a case of a dispute over a small packet of cigarettes in which twenty-five people were murdered. This is Sindh. On a very small, trivial matter, a dozen people can be murdered because no law exists in the villages. As I told you, there had been antagonism between him and my family since the time he accused my nephew of stealing his cow, so when he heard that I had joined army he couldn't tolerate it because he realised that with the support of army I might be able to fight and finish the cases against my brothers which had been registered by the *wadera*, so he decided to kill my wife and get me arrested so that no-one would be strong enough to stand up to him. And another thing; the complainant plays the most important role in these types of case. As my mother-in-law was the complainant in this case, she was asking for a very substantial amount from my family for withdrawing the case, but we had simply nothing to pay, so the case was further strengthened. That family divorced my sister as well and she lives with my brothers now.

Q: Did your family contact the *wadera* for a *faislo*?

A: We were left with not a single penny to go for a *faislo* and we have no girls to give in *faislo* either. Because I have been accused of killing my wife as a *kari*, in a *faislo* I need to show someone was a *karo* or give money or women. I am sorry, but my situation didn't allow me to request a *jirga*. The other thing that was also very clear was that the *wadera* would be feeling triumphant and he would not leave any stoned unturned against me and my family. These *waderas* are the worst kind of people. They are inhuman. I cannot go for that.

Q: Who looks after you, or is supporting you and your family while you are in jail?

A: My mother died because she was very ill and heart-broken as she could not visit me behind bars. My father died of a heart attack on the same day that I was arrested. My wife was killed. My three sons are studying, but you know we do not send girls to school. It is considered an insulting thing in our tribal culture, so they just do housework ... I am behind bars for twenty-five years accused of killing my beloved wife. My brothers come to visit me and give me hope, but I know that the web is difficult to tear.

Q: What is it like being in jail?

A: It is a very good experience indeed. The police here, in this jail, show the best attitude as I have also been a government servant. I am not a criminal, a bandit or a thief so they respect me because my conscience is clear that I have not killed anyone. Even though I am suspended from my job, I have appealed to the High Court against the decision on my case. I appealed from jail. And about the question how I spend my time in jail ... I make Sindhi caps and other embroidered things to be sold in the market in order to earn some money. We give what we have made to the police and then they give these items to middlemen who sell them and give us some money after taking their share.

Q: Why do you think it all happened to you?

A: I consider it my fate. It was written in my destiny and who can fight against destiny. But I have hope that the High Court will listen to me and I will be freed from jail soon. I wish I could rejoin the army as I had already worked for them. God will help me because I am innocent and I believe that everything is in the hands of God.

Q: Is there anything else that you want to share with me?

A: I am happy to talk to you. I know that everyone has limitations but I believe in the power of a book. If you write this interview in your book, people will understand what the *waderas* do and how they deliberately try to keep people ignorant and terrorise them if they dare to get education and try to become successful.

Q: Yes. I will let people read your life-story so that they can understand your situation.

A: Please keep me in your prayers. I am innocent.

Q: God bless you.

Chapter Three

The Accounts of Women at Various Shelters

1: *Name*: Saba, aged 25

The interview lasted for an hour and fourteen minutes and took place at a darulaman.

Saba seemed a bold and determined woman. She called honour killing a routine matter. She used the word 'friend' for her boyfriend, which was a highly unlikely thing for me to hear.

Q: *Assalam-o-alaikum.*

A: *Walaikum-assalam.*

Q: How are you?

A: Not bad.

Q: Would you like to talk to me?

A: Yes, but can it help me?

Q: Well, certainly it can. I am a researcher and I am collecting data by talking to people who are affected by honour killing. The information which you give me will only be used in this research work and in any related publications.

A: So my story will be in the newspapers?

Q: Not in the newspapers but in a book, for sure.

A: Yes. Tell people to do something for us. If their own daughters were in our place, how would they feel?

Q: OK. Can I record your interview?

A: Why not? Will it be on television?

Q: No, it is only an audio recording in order for me to be able to transcribe every single word you utter.

A: Sure.

Q: Can you tell me something about you; your name, age, community, parents and so on?

A: My name is Saba and I am twenty five. My caste is Burro. I am from Sindh. My father's name is Ali Sher and he works as a labourer – he used to work as a labourer for companies building roads. I have two sisters and one brother. My parents loved me and cared for all of us.

Q: Could you tell me about the family you grew up in, your childhood, siblings, school and the favourite games you played?

A: My childhood was good. My parents were kind and we brothers and sisters had a good relationship with each other. I never went to school. There was no system of education in our village and my parents did not want their children to go far away, so none of us ever went to school. We played various games when we were children, such as catching and throwing a ball at each other, hide-and-seek … just games like these.

Q: Tell me about your marriage, the mode of the marriage and the process of getting married. What was life like after you were married? How did you get on with your family, your husband, your children and your in-laws?

A: My parents made me get married to my paternal uncle's son. I did not want to marry him because from the very beginning I loved another cousin. So I disagreed with their proposal and told my mother clearly that I did not want to marry the person who she wanted me to marry, but she didn't listen to me at all. She refused my choice. It was not *ado-bado*[70] but he was a son of my father's brother so my father wanted me to marry him. It was a forced marriage. I agreed eventually because my mother firmly refused the man of my choice. When I married my husband, he asked me if I had had any kind of relationship with anyone else. I lied to him and denied my involvement with anyone. However, he knew that my father

---

[70] A*ado-bado* is another term for *watto-satto.*

had forced me to marry him, so from the first day, my husband's attitude to me was not good. He used to beat me mercilessly. Although my parents-in-law were my real aunt and uncle, they always encouraged him to beat me. I stayed with them for four years. In all these years, there was hardly a day when I was not beaten or abused by my in-laws. I have no children.

Q: Can you tell me the reason why are you here?

A: My boyfriend used to live in our neighbour's house. He used to come to my parents' home because he was my cousin too, but then we became even more involved. My husband and my in-laws didn't know anything about this at the beginning, but later, after my marriage, some of my friends who were also my neighbours told my in-laws about my affair with my other cousin. Then the news spread everywhere and my in-laws made a point of beating me. To start with, they slapped me, kicked me and hit me with sticks, and then they started calling me *kari*. One night, one of my friends who lived in our neighbourhood came to me and told me secretly that I would be killed as *kari* by my husband and in-laws. I found an opportunity and ran away from my in-laws' home and reached the police station. The police believed me and sent me to the court and through the court I have reached here. The police know that killings as *karo-kari* are routine occurrences in Sindh.

Q: Did you leave home on your own?

A: Yes.

Q: Didn't your in-laws pursue you?

A: They tried to find me and they got to the police station as well. There they asked the police to talk to me and to force me to go back with them but I was really determined not to go with them, so I clearly said 'I have lived for four years with you. What forms of brutality have I not suffered while I have been with you? I do not want to be killed as a *kari*'. They had no choice but to go back. I was sure that they would kill me that night because on the day before, my father-in-law had kicked me and slapped me hard and said that I was *kari* and that that was a deep insult to them so they needed to get rid of me.

Q: Did you still have contact with your boyfriend?

A: Yes, but you know, when I was forbidden to marry my cousin, I had said to myself that now I would not think about him any more, but my in-laws' and my husband's continuous verbal and physical abuse and torture made me think about him again and I kept in touch with him through my friends.

Q: How would you have dealt with this issue if you were a man?

A: A man? You mean, if I were a man? You know to be a man means a grand thing. How can a woman think and feel like a man? Things like this make men angry and when they are angry they can do anything. I would also have taken up the issue as my husband did. I might have also thought of killing of my wife, as this is our system and culture, because to prove yourself an honourable husband, a man has to punish his wife.

Q: What do you think honour is?

A: You know, honour is a big thing and women are the honour of their man and a man has honour. A man will kill a woman to save his honour. A woman has honour too but since she is under a man's control, so the man has all the honour. Men are supposed to respect women; if a man, I mean a husband, does not respect his wife, then what's the honour of that woman? A woman's honour is in the hands of a man.

Q: How is life at this shelter?

A: Here it is all right. I want to live here until protection is provided for me by the court.

Q: How do you see your life after you have left the shelter?

A: I can't say anything definitely, but I have decided not to leave the shelter until the *faislo*. You know, when I left my home, my father-in-law tried to kill my boyfriend, but instead he killed his brother and nephew because my boyfriend was not at home at the time. So my boyfriend's family wants a *faislo* against my husband and my father-in-law. Then I will apply for a divorce in the court and get married to my boyfriend. My husband has called me *kari* so I must not go back to him.

Q: Do you have any support from your birth family in this shelter?

A: Neither my mother nor my father is looking after me. No-one comes to visit me here except for my boyfriend's relatives. So I don't want to go back to my parents or my in-laws. I want a divorce from my husband and to marry my boyfriend.

Q: If you had a choice, what kind of life would you like to live?

A: I want a life partner of my own choice. I want to marry someone who loves me. I'm sure his family will accept me. The best life is that a girl has to be given the choice to select her own husband. The marriage should not be forced. In forced marriages, many problems occur. Hundreds, rather thousands of those women have been killed and so have the men. Why don't parents let girls marry and live with the men of their choice? The best life is that every girl should marry her boyfriend.

Q: Is there anything else that you want to share with me?

A: Just one thing: that you educated people should say to the government to make a law that forced marriages should be stopped and that the people involved in making forced marriages for their daughters and girls should be punished.

Q: Sure. I shall write that as well.

A: Thank you, *bajee*.

Q: You are welcome.

2: *Name*: Saira, aged 18

The interview lasted for an hour and twenty-one minutes and took place at a shelter.

Saira was a brown-eyed, very beautiful young girl. She was wearing a brown and yellow dress. Her look was very confident.

Q: *Assalam-o-alaikum.*

A: *Walaikum-assalam.*

Q: How are you?

A: Blessings of God, and I am OK.

Q: Would you like to talk to me?

A: Yes, *adi*.

Q: Let me tell you one thing, whatever information you give me will be used only for the purposes of my research and for related publications.

A: You will write my story?

Q: Technically yes. I am carrying out a research project about honour killing and I need your views about it. Are you willing to talk to me?

A: I will tell you everything you ask me.

Q: Thank you. Would you mind if I record what you say?

A: No, *adi*, you can.

Q: Can you tell me something about you, your name, age, community and parents?

A: My name is Saira and I am eighteen. Our caste is Aaganani. We are from Sindh. My father had passed away before I was born. My mother was sold by her paternal grandparents.[71] I never saw my father. I have one sister and one brother. I am the oldest. I lived and grew up with my grandparents and our uncle, that is, the husband of my paternal aunt earned money to keep the whole family. Along with my grandmother, I used to make Sindhi caps and we gave them to a man who sold them in a market.

Q: Your father died before you were born, but what about your mother?

A: My mother was sold and she was given in marriage to a man of another tribe for money by her paternal grandparents. We came to know that with that man, she had two other children: I consider them as my brother and sister.

Q: Have you seen them?

A: Not yet.

---

[71] When women are accused as *karis* by their husbands and go to their parents' home for shelter, they risk being sold to a faraway village by their parents in order to avoid the shame of harbouring a *kari*.

Q: Could you tell me about the family you grew up in, about your childhood, school, favourite games and things like that?

A: I went to school as a child but learned nothing because the teachers didn't turn up or teach. Our school was just nothing. No-one was there to look after it. So whenever we went, we usually found it closed. I didn't learn anything from the school. My childhood was good. I played with my cousins, my neighbours. Our games were like, hide-and-seek, finding each other with your eyes covered up. I liked playing every game.

Q: Tell me about your marriage, the mode of the marriage, the process of getting married?

A: I was in love with the son of one of my paternal uncles. Not the son of the uncle that I was living with, but with another cousin. When my grandmother got to know about it, she was very angry because she wanted to sell me to a Baloch tribesman for 100,000 rupees. She got me engaged to a man whom I had not even seen and told me to marry him. One day, I left my house with the cousin whom I loved, but my grandmother got the support and help of the *wadera* of our village and had me returned to our village.

Q: How come?

A: Both of us, me and my cousin whom I wanted to marry, went to Karachi by bus. But then we realised that we had no friend there to stay with. So my cousin contacted one of his friends in another city, closer to my village. That friend invited us to go to his place and said that he would protect us, so we went to his house. When we got there, my cousin's friend asked me to go inside the house with the women of his family and my cousin stayed outside with him. The women said that they wanted us to get married, so they put henna on my hands. I had no contact with my cousin as I had no cell phone but I trusted the family as I had been taken there by my cousin. Next day, my cousin's friend said that somebody wanted to meet me. When I got there, I found a strange man there. He asked me if I knew him. Seeing my ignorance, he introduced himself as the *wadera* of my village. He told me that the problem was over and that my grandmother had agreed that I could marry my cousin, so he had been sent by my grandmother to take me back to the village. When I asked about my cousin, the *wadera* and my cousin's friend said that he had already reached my village and that when I got there we would be married. I trusted the *wadera* as my cousin's friend was also with him. I only realised the conspiracy when I reached my village. My cousin's friend had deceived us. When I reached my grandmother, she beat me a lot and I was made kind of prisoner there. The Baloch family came and my grandparents forced me to marry the man they had engaged me to. His family had already paid the 100,000 rupees to my grandmother.

Q:　　What was life like after your marriage? How did you get on with your husband and in-laws?

A:　　From the first day I was the target of physical torture. My sisters-in-law and parents-in-law were always urging my husband to hit me or beat me. My in-laws didn't give me a single penny. They didn't let me talk to anyone in the village. From the very first day of my marriage, they called me a *kari*. I said 'If you knew I was a *kari*, why did you accept me then?' My husband replied that it was because he wanted to take revenge on me. For three months after my marriage my in-laws didn't let me go back to my home village. When Eid[72] came, my grandmother came and took me to her village. But the very next day she wanted me to go back to my in-laws. I asked my grandmother to let me stay with her for a few more days but she refused. I kept on asking so my grandfather got angry and scolded my grandmother and said that there was no need to bring me back to the village. He even said that I was a *kari* and that *karis* have no right to celebrate Eid.

Q:　　Can you let me know the reason why are you in this shelter? How did you escape?

A:　　When I came back from my village with my grandmother, my husband tortured me a lot but no-one tried to protect me even though my mother-in-law was watching. She said that because I was a *kari* they would bury me alive. That day, I became very frightened. My husband kicked me and beat me with sticks and his hands. One day, my in-laws went to one of their relatives in the same village and took me with them. I kept thinking about a plan to leave that house as soon as I could, so when I saw that my mother-in-law was busy talking with her relatives and my husband was asleep, I left the house silently without taking any of my clothes so that they would not suspect what I was doing and I ran towards the other village. There I asked many people to help me but everyone refused. I had nothing except my gold-earrings. Eventually a woman took pity on me. She believed my story and took me to a market. I sold my

---

[72] A religious festival.

earrings there for 3,000 rupees even though they were worth about 10,000 rupees. I bought a dress for 500 rupees from that money. The woman left me then and I went by rickshaw to one of the friends of my cousin whom I loved. The friend called him to go there. First he took me to the police station and then through the High Court I have reached here.

Q: Why do your in-laws want to kill you?

A: Because they were calling me a *kari* as they knew that I had wanted to marry my other cousin. They couldn't tolerate that and I was scared that they would kill me as *kari*, so I had to get to shelter at the *darulaman*.

Q: Why do you think that this has happened to you?

A: This isn't just my story. It is happening to every other girl here. Some are sold. Some are called *kari* and killed. Sometimes they are killed for having their own choice. Some girls are given in *faislo* and then no-one knows what happens to them. This is going on everywhere in Sindh. See the *darulaman* is filled with women who have been accused of being *karis* and there are so many other unfortunate women who cannot reach here and are killed without mercy. My mother-in-law came to this shelter and said that if I don't go back to them they will kill me. I said 'Do whatever you want but I will not come to you again. When I was with you, can you name any physical or verbal torture that I didn't have to endure? What do you expect from me now?' I would never go back to them again.

Q: How would you have dealt with all this if you were a man?

A: I wouldn't have married a girl who was in love with someone else. Second, if I found that she was involved with any other men I would have divorced her, but I wouldn't have killed her.

Q: What do you think honour is?

A: When a girl and a boy talk together then honour rises up in men. Honour means that a woman should not think of any other man and should follow the orders of a man.

Q: What is life like at this shelter?

A: I have not lived a better life before. Everyone is nice and helpful here.

Q: How do you see your life after you have left the shelter?

A: I am determined to get a divorce from my present husband and marry my cousin. I will marry my cousin.

Q: Is he unmarried?

A: No. He is married because when my grandmother got me married, his parents also forced him to marry. It is the second month of his marriage. It is my second month here in the shelter, but I am sure he will leave her as he was also forced by his parents to marry a woman whom he did not love.

Q: If you had a choice, what kind of life would you like to live?

A: The best life for a woman is that she has the freedom to choose and to marry a boy of her choice. Only then can you live a happy life. That would be a lucky and perfect life.

Q: What life do you see after you leave this shelter?

A: First, I will get a divorce, then I will marry the man of my choice. People say that the Baloch kill their wives if they marry someone else. I say kill me, but I will not live with my present husband.

Q: Have you had any support from anyone here in the shelter?

A: My mother got to know about my misery and she contacted me through someone. Her message was that she would help me to marry the man of my choice. Now, when the court allows me to marry my lover, I will try to meet my mother as well.

Q: Thank you for talking to me.

A: You are welcome, *adi*. Pray for me.

3: *Name*: Sajida, aged 26

The interview lasted for an hour and twenty-three minutes and took place at a shelter.

Sajida was a talkative, slightly aggressive and optimistic young woman. She said that she had an unconditional love for her parents. Many times her eyes were filled with tears and she obviously found it difficult to talk.

Q: *Assalam-u-alaikum.*

A: *Walaikum-assalam.*

Q: How are you?

A: I am OK.

Q: Let me tell you one thing; whatever you tell me will be used only for the purposes of my research and for related publications.

A: OK.

Q: Are you willing to talk to me?

A: No problem.

Q: Thank you. I am carrying out a research project about honour killing and I need your views about it.

A: You can ask any questions if you think I can help you.

Q: Can I record the interview?

A: No problem.

Q: Can you tell me something about you; your name, age, community, parents and so on?

A: My name is Sajida and I am twenty-six. Our caste is Mastoi and we are from Sindh. My father's name is Allah Bux and he was a small landowner. We had our own house and I have three sisters and four brothers.

Q: Could you tell me about your family, your childhood, your brothers and sisters, school, favourite games and so on?

A: I passed year-five in school. I played many games with my cousins, friends and brothers and sisters. I don't remember any particular game but I remember we played many games happily. I had a very nice and lovely time in my childhood until the age of sixteen or let's say seventeen. I had a good life at my parents' home until my father started gambling and became addicted to drugs. After selling his land and home, he sold my two older sisters for money to pay off a loan.

Q: Tell me about your marriage; the mode of the marriage, the process of getting married.

A: When my father got into debt and the gamblers began harassing him to repay his loans, he asked my paternal cousin if he would marry me for 45,000 rupees. The cousin agreed and paid the money to my father and I was given to him in marriage. For three years I wasn't very upset as my in-laws weren't very bad to me, but after three years they accused me of being a *kari*.

Q: Can you tell me more about what life was like after your marriage? How did you get on with your husband and in-laws?

A: In fact, the reason for their sudden change was my sister-in-law. She was my mother's brother's wife actually, and she had never been on good terms with my mother. When her husband died, she began living with us. She turned my husband against me and gradually my husband started to listen to her. You know relatives come and go and sometime male relatives also come, so my sister-in-law actually started to pick on me. She was always criticising me about why I had talked to that one or this one and she used to exaggerate things to my husband. One night, four men broke into our house. They were thieves. Later they were recognised as our neighbours. My sister-in-law and my husband accused me, saying that they had come or had broken in because of me. I denied it completely as I had had no contact with anyone. Eventually I said to my husband 'OK, if it all happened because of me and you are accusing me, tell me this: if I'm a *kari*, I must be *kari* with one person only, so why did four men break in?' He had no answer to this but it was obvious that he wanted to catch me out in some mischief by his accusations and allegations. As the news spread that a few men had broken into our home and that they had been recognized, some neighbours became involved and brought *niani mer* and explained that it was their boys who had broken in just to steal anything valuable and there was no other issue involved, but my husband refused to talk to them and asked for a *faislo*. In the *faislo*, he accused one of the men of being a *karo* who had entered our home and stolen 350,000 rupees. I was heart-broken, but I carried on enduring every kind of verbal and physical abuse and torture from my in-laws, but one evening my husband beat me very badly. I didn't know what to do because my father was no use and my mother was being forced not to help me; all she could do was weep for me. So finding no other option, I left my house and went to the police station for safety. I knew the system and the ways things work because one of my cousins had gone through a similar process and through the police station she had gone to a shelter, so I knew that this kind of provision was available for women. When the news spread that I had left my house, my father went to the police station with the *wadera* and pleaded with me to go back. I realized the pain and insult that my father was going through, so I decided to go with him. The *wadera* of the village took me to his *haveli*. After twelve days in that house, the *wadera* asked me whether the allegation was true. I replied that it was false and that I needed to live with my parents as I knew that my husband and my in-laws would kill me. The *wadera* reminded me that no-one keeps a *kari*. I said, 'In that case, do whatever you think is better for me'. That evening, he called in a few people who looked at me and one of them accepted me. The *wadera* then sold me to him for 350,000 rupees. While the SHO was about to prepare the necessary papers, he received news from the police that my husband and my in-laws were outside, armed to kill me. At that, the SHO told my father that things were dangerous because there was a chance that as soon as I was out of the police station, my husband would kill me as a *kari*. I took a stand and said that no matter what happens, I would like to go with my father. I was a daughter and could not see my father crying. The *wadera* of the village took the responsibility for my safety and I went off with the *wadera* to his *haveli*. I was in the *haveli* for another twelve days. He asked me where I wanted to go to get married. I replied that there was no choice to be made because the accusation was completely false. I told him that I needed to live with my parents because I knew that my husband would not have me back and that was when he told me that no-one keeps a *kari*.

Q: Where did the money go?

A: My father got 80,000 rupees, 100,000 rupees were given to my husband and the rest went into the *wadera*'s pocket.

Q: How do you know that?

A: I was bound to find out; these things cannot be hidden from a sold *kari*. The buyers keep repeating the price they have paid in order to insult the bought *kari* and keep up the pressure on her.

Q: Can you let me know the reason why you are here?

A: Where the *wadera* sold me, it was like I was married again. It was a kind of slavery. Not only the person who bought me in the name of marriage but his entire family taunted me, accused me, called me *kari*, ugly and slut. They used to make me work for eighteen hours a day inside the house and in the fields. I had to milk twenty buffalos every day. Sometimes I had to go to sleep without food. I was prepared to work for every hour of the day but the verbal and physical abuse was unbearable. Whenever I tried to make it clear that it was a mistaken accusation, they beat me. I tried my best not to give them any chances to be angry but they always found a reason to beat me. Despite all my efforts to be accepted, I was hated, so I had to leave them.

Q: How did you escape?

A: I didn't know anything about the city where I lived with my new in-laws but once with them I went back to my own city and we stayed at the home of some of their relatives. I made a plan. I secretly left the house one evening and went to the same police station where I had gone before. The police registered my case and presented me before the court and in response to my request I was sent to this shelter. For eleven months, nobody came to visit me here. Then, after eleven months, a maternal cousin of my original husband came and offered to let me go with him. I said that my husband should appear before the court and that the court should guarantee that he would not beat or abuse me again. He said that my husband's uncle was ready to take responsibility for my husband's attitude. I said that I would be living with my husband and not with his uncle so I repeated my condition that my husband should appear before the court and register his statement in court. After that, no-one came. I asked the judge to send me to the Karachi shelter. The judge moved me to the Karachi *darulaman* and wrote that whenever I wanted to go, I would be set free. I went to Karachi, where my maternal aunt lived. She had been abandoned by my birth family and nobody had had any contact with her because of her crime of marrying a man of her own choice, so she was not allowed to go to our village or meet anyone of her family. She lived in Karachi; I wanted to live with her but she was very scared of my in-laws and could not keep me. So I decided to go to my father as I wanted to live with my father for the rest of my life to look after my parents and my brothers. I had no intention of getting married again. The lady in charge at the shelter gave me 1,000 rupees. I already had 8,000 rupees. She sent one of the teachers from the shelter with me to the bus station to get a bus ticket for me. She helped me to get a ticket to my village and I went to the home of one of my uncles and asked him to take care of my father and to keep me with him, as I had grown tired of a life full of insults. I wanted to live in peace somewhere. I told him to tell my father that by keeping me in his house, he would have a helper and I would work for him to bring up my younger brothers. I wanted to live with them. He went to my father but soon came back and told me that my father's reply was 'She is dead for me'. I had no other choice then; I left my village for Karachi and went to my aunt's house. She was frightened but kept me in her house. When my father knew that I was living with my aunt, he threatened her and told her to throw me out otherwise she would face bloody consequences. At that threat, my aunt became very upset as she was living with her own young children. She became very scared for their safety. Even so, she helped me and arranged a lawyer for me. The lawyer asked the court to send me back to a shelter, as I had no place to live. The court sent me back to this shelter and this is my sixth month here.

Q: Your new 'husband' bought you and you had been working tirelessly and unconditionally for him and his family, so why didn't they keep you with them?

A: You know why people marry *karis*? It is so that they can have permanent slaves. *Karis* have no relatives on earth because after being accused of being a *kari*, everyone cuts themselves off from them and they have to live at the disposal of their master. My master and his relatives bullied me right from the first day, telling me that if I didn't listen to them, they would torture me to death. They were not my relatives. They had no sympathy for me. They wanted me to work twenty-four hours a day for them like a slave. When a slave gets older they just dispose of her. But before disposing of a slave, they want to get her to do the maximum work. However, a master is always scared that his slave might run away, so they treat them harshly as they did to me, and I had no energy left to bear the unbearable treatment.

Q: Why do you think this has happened to you?

A: In my case, as I told you, the real problem was my sister-in-law; her nature created problems for me. Before her intervention in our family, my life was not miserable. After she started living with us, my husband changed his attitude. Actually she had a problem with my mother but she took revenge on me, and this was the root cause of all my problems.

Q: How would you take up the issue if you were a man?

A: Well … I … being a man I might have had an element of suspicion in my mind about why the men had broken into our house but I would have reacted carefully as who could have any doubts about a simple and decent wife like me? If I were a man, in this regard I think I wouldn't have destroyed my house like this.

Q: What do you think honour is?

A: Men call it honour to threaten, to beat, to abuse and to kill their wives. I ask where honour is in today's world. Everyone claims that he is an honourable man. Do those who sell their daughters and sisters for money have the right to be called honourable? That is business not honour. Fine … if you see a woman of your family with your own eyes committing adultery, then do not leave her alive for a moment, kill her. OK. And if the man involved with your woman manages to run away but your woman is in your hands, then kill her on the spot. But making a conspiracy against women and accusing them of being *karis* and then finding people to blame as *karo* with them simply to get money and women in a *faislo* shouldn't be called honour. And selling your girls, wives, daughters, sisters and taking money from the so-called *karos* is not an honourable deed at all. You sell your women a number of times, collect millions from their buyers and call yourself honourable? This is not honour, this is business.

Q: What is life like at this shelter?

A: It is not too bad but it is not home. There is food, but prison is prison. In my village, when the electricity failed, we could sit in the open air, but in this shelter the supervisor only allows us to sit on the veranda in her presence for an hour once a day. Then we are sent back to these airless rooms and have to use plastic hand fans. We cook food by mutual agreement. We have fixed times to eat our food and have tea. We get fresh food every week and it isn't bad at all, but, you know, the availability of food in prison is not everything: freedom is the big thing.

Q: How do you see your life after you have left the shelter?

A: I need to live in the *darulaman* until my husband divorces me. I have already applied for the divorce with the help of the lawyer who was arranged by my aunt. I am looking for protection from the court. I want to look after my parents for the rest of my life but it would not be feasible as I understand the situation. Second, my father can't understand my love and care for him and our family. He knows that I have no other way to go and must surely go to him. My father has already taken 100,000 rupees from someone. This means that even before I leave the shelter, I am sold. My father has sold me twice now and both times I faced nothing but mental and physical torture. I begged my father and said, 'You should be supporting me. I'll help you and look after all of you, but if you sell me a third time, I won't go with you'. He threatened me with the worst consequences, saying that if I don't listen to him, he will kill me. He said that he would kill me and anyone who tries to help me. I told him that if God has written how long my life will be as my destiny, then no-one will kill me, but if my destiny is to be killed as a *kari*, then nobody can stop it. I told him that I needed to survive but if he wants to kill me, then kill me. My father is a drug-addict and a gambler: he sold my youngest sister for 180,000 rupees. You know what that means? It means that even before I have the divorce papers in my hands, before I am free from this shelter, I have been sold to someone by my father again. I pleaded with him '*Baba*![73] I am fed-up with marriage. It is not necessary to marry me off again. I want to live with you and my mother. I'll look after you and my brothers because they are still very young. Twice now marriage has brought me only pain and suffering so I don't want to be married again. You are my father. You should be supporting me'.

Q: If you had a choice, what type of life would you like to live and with whom?

A: As I told you, I would like to live with my parents and look after them and my young brothers, but my father won't let that happen. If my husband and my father let me stay alive, I'll go to Karachi and live with my aunt. After I am divorced, I'll go to my aunt in Karachi and work somewhere to earn my livelihood just as her daughters also work in different places in Karachi. I can work for a company or in a factory. I want to live in a world which is free of this *karo-kari, faislo, wadera* system, selling women, and labels of *karo* and *kari*. Women should have the right to marry someone of their own choice. Women should have the right to go somewhere without their husband's permission. Life is very difficult in this system. Women cannot laugh, they cannot smile, cannot talk. A woman needs love and care but if a husband comes home and starts abusing or beating her without any reason, who would like to live with such a husband? My aunt is willing to marry her son to me. If I survive, I'll settle down and then I might marry him.

Q: Good luck! Is there anything else you would like to share with me?

A: Not really. I have said a lot and I just want you to pray that I shall live a reasonable life.

Q: God bless you.

---

[73] Father.

4: *Name*: Irum, aged 55

The interview lasted for an hour and twenty-three minutes and took place at a shelter.

Irum's whole body was shaking due to Parkinson's disease. She could not stop crying while talking about her sexual relationship with her husband and she burst into tears when she said, 'I did not ask my husband for a single penny for my personal use' and wiped her tears with her *dupatta*.

Q: Assalam-o-alaikum.

A: Walaikum-assalam.

Q: How are you?

A: Difficult to say, what can I say?

Q: Would you like to talk to me?

A: Yes, why not? You want to know why I am here?

Q: Mainly, yes, if you feel that you can trust me.

A: You look so good, why wouldn't I trust you, *Amman*?

Q: Can I record what you say?

A: Yes, you can.

Q: Can you tell me something about you; your name, your age, your community and your parents?

A: My name is Irum. I think I am fifty-five years old. Our caste is Janori and I am from Sindh. My father's name was Mulla Janori and he worked as a labourer. My parents passed away when I was only seven. My father also worked as a farmer sometimes. My mother was a very hard-working woman. She used to make quilts and Sindhi caps, and she made embroidered shirts.

Q: Could you tell me about the family you grew up in, your childhood, brothers and sisters, school, favourite games and things like that?

A: I have seven sisters and five brothers. We were very poor but lived with love and respect for each other. I'm not educated as in villages there was no concept of education. I was brought up like an orphan. We used to live far down in a mud area where floods often hit us badly; we moved from there and settled in a comparatively better area. But we didn't go to school. None of us ever attended a school. We played with each other with hand-made dolls. My mother used to make beautiful cloth-dolls. We were happy and despite the poverty we lived with peace and love.

Q: Tell me about your marriage; the mode of marriage, the process of getting married.

A: My husband's name is Bux Janori. I have five children. About sixteen or seventeen years ago, my father got me married. My husband was all right with me. He used to give me proper food and was caring as well.

Q: How did you get on with your husband, your children and your in-laws?

A: Until I had two kids, my in-laws were happy with me. Then gradually I developed a kind of disease that made me weaker and weaker. Can you see how my body is shaking? Then my in-laws started beating and hitting me because they thought that I was pretending. I was unable to work in the fields. As a result, I became the target of verbal and physical abuse. Although I was trying to work as hard as I could, I had no strength left to work as much as they demanded. They didn't realise that I really was ill. Then my husband, who was nice, arranged another home for me near to my parents' home and we started to live a nice life again. Everything was going all right, but day-by-day I was getting weaker and weaker. There, I had three more children which meant that we had five children altogether. After the birth of my fifth child, I felt extremely weak and I was unable to walk or talk. My condition was very obvious so it was unfair to accuse me of pretending. I couldn't have intercourse with my husband and that made him angry. He hit my genitalia with a stick and slippers when I couldn't have intercourse. That was when my husband got furious with me and he also started beating and abusing me. He said, 'You are useless. You are not my mother who I have to feed for nothing as you are useless to me'. All the joints in my body were in severe pain. Having sex became impossible. I begged him to let me live at home with my children. My children were worried about me but because they were too young they couldn't change their father's behaviour. Each time he beat me, he shouted and insisted that I should leave his home. I was desperate and I asked him where I could go as I had no parents and no other relative to live with. I said to him, 'Where would I go? If I leave you, you will accuse me of being a *kari* so you can kill me here, but I can't leave your house'. I asked him to marry another woman but not to throw me out as I had no-one else to go to.

Q: Can you tell me the reason why are you here?

A: My husband took me to quite a few doctors but the medicine could only trigger the pain in my body and nothing else. I then decided to go to a shrine. Along with my seven-year-old son and sister-in-law, I went to the shrine of 'Rani Pur'. While I was there, an elderly woman who had come to pay homage saw me and suggested that I should have medicine from her son who knew some holy treatment. The woman and her son were very old and kind people. The woman was even older than my mother. They lived at the shrine. She was very kind and took me, my son and my sister-in-law to her home and gave us something to eat and drink. Her son gave me some medicines and did some holy treatment to me and I felt better. The woman comforted me and said that I would be all right. We went back home the following morning. When we got home, my husband asked about our journey. My sister-in-law lied to my husband and told him that I had had improper relations with someone near the shrine so the woman had taken me to her home and I had had illicit relations with her son. My husband beat me brutally and did not listen to me. I tried to explain to my husband what had happened but he was not prepared to listen to anything I said. He told me that I must leave his home otherwise he would kill me. I said 'Trust in what you see with your own eyes and what you hear with your own ears. If you see something wrong in me, then kill me, but do not believe what anyone else says because I am not in any condition to have a physical relationship with anyone. My eldest son was twenty, but when he tried to stop his father from beating me, my husband kicked him out of our home.

Q: How did you reach here?

A: My husband had the old woman's son arrested and bribed the police to beat him. When I got to know about this, I left my house because that showed that since my husband had accused him as *karo*, now he would kill me and take money from him. I realised that I would be killed soon, so I left and went straight to the police station. The police presented me to the court and through the court I reached here. I asked the court to help me to get a divorce from my husband because he had called me a *kari* and if I were to go out of this shelter he would certainly kill me. I told the judge that my husband had accused an old man of being a *karo* and had put him in the lockup with the help of police, but that the man was innocent. He and his mother had just helped me when I went to the shrine. On the orders of the judge, the old man was set free.

Q: Why do you think this has happened to you?

A: Why do people kill a buffalo or a horse when they become useless for their master and owner? A woman is like that. When she becomes useless for her husband he wants to get rid of her. In Sindhi society, people don't leave their wives for free. They need to earn money even from their dead bodies. By calling them a *kari*, they can either sell them for money or kill them and then make money from the accused *karo*. When my husband came to visit me here in this shelter, I told him clearly in the presence of the person in charge of the shelter to divorce me. He called me a *kari* and that was the result of my whole life's services to him and his family. I said to my husband, 'You tortured me when I became unable to have intercourse with you but you accused such an old, kind and innocent man of being a *karo* and paid the police to torture him. I need a divorce because I cannot live with you now'. I am done with him.

Q: How would you take up the issue if you were a man?

A: I am not so stupid as to have ruined my family and insulted my life partner. Diseases are part of life. It is in the hands of God. Being a good man, I would have taken my wife to a better doctor. Sex is not everything in life. I would respect the compulsion and temporary limitations of my life partner. Can he be called a life partner who is partner in healthy times but turns into a killer at a time of illness? I would not have reacted like him. I am an illiterate villager too but I am not an idiot like him.

Q: What do you think honour is?

A: All dishonourable deeds are labelled honour these days. This is very unfortunate. Is it honour to accuse your wife of being a *kari* because she is unable to have sex with you? Is it honour to accuse an innocent man of being a *karo* to grab money from him? What these people call honour these days is an absolute dishonour. If a woman talks, laughs or wears clean clothes, they call her a *kari*? What type of honour is this? There is no honour in Sindhi men. They are pretending to have honour to make money. Is it honour to torture a wife and degrade her by calling her a *kari* because she is unable to have sex?

Q: How is life at this shelter?

A: I am very poor. I have no money to hire a lawyer. The judge says that I can't leave the shelter without some male relative. I am a hardworking woman. Wherever I go I will work and earn my living. Even with my severe pain and physical problem, ask the people in charge of the shelter whether I have been sitting idle. I have been working here. The judge says that I can't leave the shelter alone so I have been trying to contact my brother so that he can take me, but my brother is a very poor man. He is scared that he might be victimised by my husband if he helps me. Now I have asked the court to give me my independence so that I can go to my aunt who lives further down the area where my parents used to live. She came to the shelter to see me. She is willing to keep me but because she is very frightened, she doesn't want her name to be disclosed in any matter, so I can't give her name in court. But I need to go and live somewhere because I badly need medicine.

Q: How do you see your life after you have left the shelter?

A: I need to go to the shrine again. I need my treatment. I want to be healthy and I want to see my children who are currently living with my cruel husband. I need peace in my life. I want my aunt to be able to give me a little space to live. I have become fed up and tired of this whole struggle. I can't marry now as I am not able to take on the responsibilities of married life.

Q: If you had a choice, what type of life would you like to live and with whom?

A: Women are always in the hands of their masters. The first master is your father, then your brothers and then your husband. How can women ever think of living a life of their own choice? God had created man and woman to live as a pair and be supporters for each other in good times and in bad. Women do so but men can't. The partner who doesn't support the life partner at his or her tough time has no right to be respected. I was left with blame and accusations when I was unable to be used as a wife so now I need a free life. This is my right. I need to be divorced. I want peace and freedom. I can work and live on my own.

Q: I wish you all the best and I am grateful to you for sharing your life story with me.

A: Thank you, my dear. Pray for me. I am tired and I badly need a small place on this earth to live.

Q: God bless you.

5: *Name*: **Amna, aged 30**

The interview lasted for an hour and twenty-eight minutes and took place at a darulaman.

Amna seemed a very frank person. She had an amazing style of telling her life story. He eyes were full of tears. At one point, she raised both hands towards the sky and asked 'where is honour?' She wiped her nose with her *chader*.[74] She tried to flap the edge of her *chader* in order to provide me with some air.

Q: *Assalam-o-alaikum.*

A: *Walaikum-assalam.*

Q: How are you?

A: I am very unhappy.

Q: Would you like to talk to me?

A: Yes. Do you write books?

Q: Yes. But the information you give me will only be used in my research papers and publications.

A: OK, but will people read it in Pakistan and abroad?

Q: Yes, I hope so. Can I record our conversation?

A: OK. Can I hold your recorder?

Q: Thank you. Now, can you tell me something about your background; your name, age, community, parents and so on?

---

[74] A large sheet of cloth to cover the head, face and body.

A: My name is Amna. We forest-dwellers do not keep a record of our ages, but I think that I must be about thirty. I am a Baloch and I live in Obaro; I can only speak the *Seraiki* language. My father's name is Moali and he works as a farmer. My mother is also a very hard-working woman. She worked for our home, for us, for others, she did embroidery, made quilts. I always saw my mother working very hard.

Q: Could you tell me about the family you grew up in and your childhood, your siblings, school, favourite games and things like that?

A: I am uneducated. We were poor people. Poverty does not know education. It demands only food, so I remember in my childhood, all the time I was busy at work. I had six sisters and six brothers. How could a poor child play? I started working at home from the very beginning. I had very tender feelings towards miserable people. I worked for them all the time. My jobs were preparing food, washing dishes and clothes, collected animal dung for fertiliser and whatever jobs my parents gave me. These were my games. This was my life. Sometimes we fought, sometimes we remained happy. That was our childhood, nothing special.

Q: Can you tell me about your marriage; the mode of marriage, the process of getting married?

A: I was married in exchange for another girl who was given to my paternal uncle in marriage. My husband's name is Israr. He is a very simple and humble person. My father-in-law had two wives; my husband was from his first wife and he had a half-brother from his father's second wife. Both of my mothers-in-law had died before my marriage but soon after my marriage my father-in-law also passed away.

Q: What was life like after your marriage? How did you get on with your husband, your children and your in-laws?

A: My father-in-law had left seven acres of land to his two sons. Being clever, my brother-in-law, my husband's half-brother, took the bigger and the better part of the land and gave us a barren piece of land which was a long way away from our house. I asked my brother-in-law to give us half of the fertile land and take half of our barren land but he always fought us. It was very difficult for me to look after four young children as well as the cattle, and to go quite far carrying sacks of dung on my head and shoulders to drop them on our land to be dried. That was too heavy a job for us. It was very difficult to manage. Also, my brother-in-law used to beat my husband for no reason; because my husband was completely innocent and could not fight back, I always defended him and that made my brother-in-law very angry with me. He asked me why I was interfering in the affairs of two brothers and I replied that because my husband was simple and I needed to provide food for my children, we needed a share of the fertile land too. That issue was getting more and more serious. My brother-in-law is in fact a dacoit and kidnaps people for ransom, but only a few people know about that. My brother-in-law was friends with my third brother. My brother was always influenced by him but when my brother-in law told him that I had a bad character, my brother tried to defend my character; I always told my brother to trust only what he could see with his own eyes and not to listen to my brother-in-law because he is our enemy. One day in the late afternoon, I was feeling very sick so I called my niece, who lived next door, to prepare tea for my children while I lay on a *charpaee*. Suddenly, I heard a lot of noise outside. I assumed that my father and uncles were having an argument, so I stood on the *charpaee* and tried to look over to the other side of the wall. What I saw was that my brother and *dair*[75] were loudly calling out my name as 'Amna *kari,* Amna *kari*' and were running towards my house. My *dair* burst in and tried to shoot me but God knows best why the pistol did not work … whether its trigger was jammed or it had no bullets … I don't know. I was shouting back that I was sitting there with my children and niece and that my husband was at home, so how have I been a *kari*? My father, my husband and my uncles appeared and asked my brother and brother-in-law for the proof of my being a *kari*. They said 'She was sitting with her children; her husband was also at home and you killed the man in your *otaque*, who was your guest, so how can you call her a *kari*? Your *otaque* is a long way away from here'. They said 'If you had killed Amna with the man, we would have saluted you and called you a hero, but you have killed the man somewhere else and you ran from that place to here to kill an innocent woman here to give us the impression of *karo-kari*, and that clearly shows that you are lying'. My uncle dragged me to his home and I was hidden there from my brother and brother-in-law. Later, my uncle told me the real story that my brother and brother-in-law had killed a young boy of about eighteen years of age. In fact, they had borrowed a large amount of money from him. On that day, my brother-in-law had phoned the boy and told him to come and collect his money. When the boy arrived on his bike, they took him to their *otaque* and killed him. Then they came to kill me to give the impression that the killings were a *karo-kari*. God knows the truth; I do not know who the unlucky youth was.

---

[75] Husband's brother (brother-in-law).

They wanted two dead bodies of opposite sexes so that they could be praised and admired by the villagers and so that the relatives of the dead boy would have to give in to them and give them even more money. I was lucky that all my relatives had gathered in time and above all that my husband was still at home; and I was lucky too that my brother-in-law's gun did not work, otherwise they would have killed me as a *kari* and would have been strutting around as heroes. My husband cried and shouted 'Don't kill my wife; she is not a *kari* but *garhee*'[76] but nobody was listening to him as he is considered to be a stupid man and an idiot because he is simple. You know what they had thought? They had in mind 'Her husband is crazed and his parents are dead so nobody will listen to him or believe him, so we can kill his wife as *kari*'. In that way they could seize my house and property and money, and girls from the family of the poor boy who they killed as *karo*, and then they would both be treated as heroes and the whole world would have treated them with great respect and said 'Look at the brave men who killed their woman to save their honour!' My justice comes from God, I am looking for God's support and help. My husband and I are simple and innocent people. God knows everything.

Q: Can you tell me why you are here?

A: I was taken in by my uncle's family as *garhee*. No-one believed that I was a *kari*. The murdered boy's relatives were stronger than my parents and my in-laws. They took the police there and had my brother arrested, but my brother-in-law is still free somewhere. The police said to my parents 'You might kill her, so give her to us so that we can send her to the *darulaman*'. I cried for my children but my parents handed me over to the police. My husband was in a very bad condition. He was very scared because I had to leave and I was his only supporter. Nobody listens to him except me. The police presented me before the court and the court sent me to this *darulaman*.

Q: Why do they want to harm you?

A: Now my father has come to visit me and has brought all four of my children here. He didn't tell me anything about my husband, about how he was and where he was, but I know he must be in great trouble. My father just told me that my husband is all right. If he's all right why hasn't he come here to see me? This is my biggest worry right now. My children

---

[76] Not offender (opposite of *kari*).

are too young, they cannot rescue their parents. My father told me that I should ask the judge to allow me to go with my father. My father wants me to go with him to the *sardar* as a *kari* so that the *sardar* can sell me. So now you see they have made another plan. If they don't make me a *kari*, my brother will not be freed from police custody and jail and might be given death penalty, and the police are still trying to arrest my brother-in-law as well. They can only be saved if I am called a *kari*. Then they won't be called killers but honourable. If I accept that I am a *kari*, then they will be freed forever, but can't my father see that his daughter's home will be ruined? Who will look after her innocent children? How will her innocent husband survive? You know the Sindhi proverb, 'Sons means our homes but daughters mean other people's homes'. A daughter has no rights, no family and no home in Sindhi society. Families raise their daughters to sacrifice them to save their precious sons. This nation ruins daughters for the sake of sons. People sacrifice their daughters like goats to save the lives of their sons. They are ready to sacrifice their simple and humble daughters anytime to saving their murderous and drug-ridden sons. This is the destiny of the daughters in Sindh. You know what my father did when he came here? He took all the jewellery that I was wearing because he claimed that the woman in charge of the *darulaman* would steal it from me. He regarded me as the same as an animal ready to be sold.

Q: Why do you think this has happened to you?

A: For greed, for seizing our land and my home. My brother-in-law became my enemy. He wanted to grab my property and everything. Then he borrowed a lot of money from one of his friends and killed him. If he had managed to kill me, then he would have got lots of money from the killed boy's relatives as well. This isn't just happening to me; all over Sindh *garhees* are being killed as *karis*. You probably don't know that my relatives had mercilessly killed many women when the police gave them back. When those women had reached the police station for safety, instead of providing protection and taking them to the court, the police made deals with their relatives and, in return for some money, they were given back to their families. It isn't just me who is facing this disaster. Many *garhee* women have died without mercy at the hands of these heartless people.

Q: How would you take up the issue if you were a man?

A: How could I accuse an innocent woman and kill a man for money? I believe in God and God's vengeance. I wouldn't have gone to those extremes against my own brother and his family. I am sure.

Q: What do you think honour is?

A: Where is the honour in selling a helpless woman? Where is the honour in killing an innocent woman? Where is the honour in shouting accusations of *kari* to a *garhee* women? Young infants' mothers are being killed and sold to the vultures, and the businessmen who profit from this are called honourable. In the name of honour, they do even worse business than a pimp does. A pimp sells others' daughters and calls himself a pimp. Our men do worse than that as they sell their own daughters, sisters and wives and call themselves honourable. Small children's mothers are being killed and sold for money and the businessmen are called honourable. Why don't they accept that they are worse than a pimp? They mustn't call themselves honourable but something else. You tell me; is this honour? My father wants me to leave the shelter so that he can sell me and prove to the world that his daughter was a *kari* just to save his son and get money.

Q: How is life in this shelter?

A: It is OK, but I am desperate for my husband, my children and my home. I know they will not let me live in peace with my family. That is my big concern.

Q: How do you see your life after you have left the shelter?

A: What can I see? The *wadera* and my father will sell me and strange people will take me away. You will see – these wicked people will sell me somewhere. My weak bones are unable to bear physical and sexual cruelty. Where … I cannot predict. How they will keep me I cannot say. The person who buys me – will he ever care for me? How many people will use me I cannot say. My future is in the hands of God. I can only see that my children and husband will be ruined. I will be sent far away from my home. I won't be able to see my children and husband again. My father will win the case by making me a *kari*. His son will be freed from jail and my brother-in-law will also be released from jail. Everything will be settled as the men wish; only my husband, my children and I will suffer forever. Nobody is there to listen to me. There is no justice in Sindh. No-one listens to the crying women. You tell me what I should do. Where can I go, how can I save my family, how can I save myself? My own father wants my family and me to be ruined to save his son's life … he has burnt my life, my home. Only a miracle will let me see my children again. I know the brutes will sell my weak body and my children will never see their mother again. They will sell my daughters and enslave my sons. I need to die before that happens.

Q: If you had a choice, what type of life you would like to live and with whom?

A: I want a free life with my husband and my children. Please save me from being sold. I don't need my property back. I ask the judge to give me freedom and to provide me with security so that I can take my children somewhere. Save me from the tyrants. Save my children. I don't want to be sold. I don't know where the people will take me. This is a curse. Who can save my life? I need only my children and my husband. I cannot live without them. This is too much. My denial of the false allegation will lead me nowhere but to an instant death as soon as I leave the centre. My father is waiting for me outside to hand me over to the *sardar* to be sold in a *jirga*. By selling me as a *kari*, the *sardar* will get money and my father will save his son's life.

Q: I wish you had justice.

A: I know that there is no justice in Pakistan, or in Sindh, but I still hope that God will listen to me and give justice to my family. We are helpless.

Q: God bless you.

6: *Name*: Fareeha, aged 48

The interview lasted for an hour and twenty-two minutes and took place at a darulaman.

Fareeha was very emotional. Despite being very upset, she laughed and smiled and, unlike other women who were interviewed, she described her childhood in detail and with interest. She had toothache. She was wearing a turquoise-coloured dress, had an artificial bangle on her wrist and was holding a small key attached to a thread.

Q: *Assalam-o-alaikum.*

A: *Walaikum-assalam.*

Q: How are you?

A: I am in severe pain.

Q: I'm sorry to hear that. Would you like to talk to me?

A: Yes, that's why I'm here. I want to tell you a lot.

Q: Let me tell you one thing, whatever information you will give me will be used only for the purposes of my research and for related publications.

A: You are studying?

Q: Yes.

A: In London?

Q: Yes, near London.

A: You must promote my case in London; the London police will surely be stronger than the Pakistani police. Please, you should tell the police and the judge not to do anything unjust with me and not to listen to my husband. I'll tell you everything you ask me.

Q: Thank you. I shall write your story and share it with every reader. Would you mind if I record what you say?

A: No. Do it to keep the things I tell you safe.

Q: Can you tell me something about yourself, your name, age, community and parents?

A: My name is Fareeha. We are Baloch from Kandhkot. My father's name is Musharraf and he has some fertile land. I have four sisters and three brothers. I can't tell you anything about how old I am as we forest dwellers don't keep any records of unimportant things like that. I can say that about thirty years ago, I got married. At the time of my marriage I was about eighteen. So you can count the years and it comes to something like forty-eight.

Q: Could you tell me about the family you grew up in, your childhood, siblings, school, favourite games and so on?

A: I can speak only the *Seraiki* language. We enjoyed our childhood, it was full of love and care. We had enough to eat and our parents gave us plenty of time to play with each other. We brothers and sisters loved each other. We used to make small animals such as horses, cows and goats out of clay and play with them for a long time. Us girls used to play with dolls. We sewed clothes for our dolls and made the dolls marry our friends' men-dolls and it was a lot of fun. We used to send dolls' marriage invitations to each other. I am uneducated. In those days, in the old times, who bothered to send their children to school? Only now have people realised that if you have a degree, you can get a job, so people study and send their kids to school now.

Q: Tell me about your marriage, the mode of the marriage, the process of getting married.

A: I was married in exchange for another girl who was given to my brother in marriage. I lived quite well with my husband until my brother died and his wife (my sister-in-law) was widowed and started living with us. That was a big problem for me.

Q: What was life like after your marriage? How did you get on with your family, husband, children and in-laws?

A: My parents were financially better-off than my in-laws but as my in-laws were their relatives, they had had to marry me to their son in exchange for a girl. My husband and I were the same age. We lived happily with each other for some time, but then he soon started to show the violent side of his personality. He started hitting and beating me over very petty issues. Since then, I haven't been able to get any relief from my in-laws. No-one has ever been happy with me. Nobody was there to look after me or hold my hand. You know the Baloch system … I had no-one to complain to. Do Baloch listen to their daughters? They throw their girls away as soon as possible in the name of marriage and then consider their girls dead. Also, as you know, in-laws are in-laws; they can never become your parents. My brothers-in-law, my mother-in-law and my husband beat me for nothing. Hitting and beating me became routine for them. My father-in-law died two years after I was married. My mother-in-law is still alive. I did all the work at their home. From working in the fields to milking the buffalos, everything was my job. I did as much as I could but I could not make my in-laws happy. My father gave me gold jewellery on my marriage. My husband took it from me and started working as a contractor. When he developed his contacts with other people, he got a job as a policeman. My brothers-in-law, my mother-in-law and my husband were beating me for nothing. And when my brother died and my sister-in-law began living with us, the torture got worse. I lived like an orphan with them. I have five sons and three daughters. My daughters were older than their brothers and are all married now. The girls that we got in the exchange for my daughters were given in marriage to my husband's brothers. Two of my sons are twins and are both mentally retarded. They are thirteen now. I feed them with my own hands. I don't know who is feeding them now or whether no-one is looking after them. When my husband bought a bungalow in Karachi, I moved there with my sons as my daughters were married, so who would take care of them but me? As my husband had now become rich, without asking me and without my permission, he got married to another woman. You know women are always after money, so now in my home, where I was supposed to be living, that woman is now living there and no-one bothers about me. I am dying here. Just a few months ago my husband got my son married and I am here in this hell. My son got married without letting me know. They are happy and getting married and enjoying their lives. I weep and I miss my children, my family and my house. Who is feeding my crippled twins? They can't do anything for themselves. I wash their bodies; I take them to the toilet. Now I don't know how they have been living, what that woman is doing to them. Can she take care of them like a mother does? Never.

Q: Can you tell me why you are here?

A: Before he married that woman, you know what my husband did? He sent me to my brothers' house. A few days after I got there, he accused me of being a *kari*. My brothers were surprised and said that I had been with them and they had not seen anything, so how could he accuse me? He phoned one of my brothers and said 'She is *kari* and I will not keep her but I'll kill her'. My brothers were scared and asked me to go back but how and where could I go? I've never seen the boy whom my husband called a *karo* but I have heard that he is about the same age as my son. At my age and time, how can I be accused of being a *kari*? I'm sick. I have diabetes and my teeth are falling out. I have no medicine but my husband is calling me a *kari* to get rid of me. He made a *faislo* with the boy's family. That family wanted to save their young man so they paid my husband about 300,000 rupees. Look at how clever he is. On the one hand he wants to get rid of me by calling me a *kari* and on the other hand he makes money by accusing someone of being a *karo* with me.

Q: How did you reach here?

A: As I told you, when I was accused I was already at the home of one of my brothers and we all were very concerned about the false allegation made by my husband. None of us ever believed it. We all agreed that my husband wanted to get rid of me and that was why he had called me a *kari*, but my brother didn't know where to hide me. When we heard that my husband had made a *faislo* with the man's family, our worries increased. At four o'clock the next morning, my two brothers-in-law, along with a one-armed man, entered my brother's house. Before they went in, they fired some shots outside the house. The noise of the shots made me scared and I thought that they had come to kill me so I ran out of the back of the house. When I was running through the fields, I heard a police siren, so I changed my direction and ran towards it. When the police saw me, they let me sit in their vehicle and took me to the police station. There they asked me questions and I answered everything they asked. On the next day, they sent me to the court and through the court I am here.

Q: Why do you think he wants to kill you?

A: I'm like Benazir.[77] People want to kill me just as they wanted to kill Benazir and I think I'll also be killed like her. How will Zardari[78] and his ruling government give me justice when he can't even catch his wife's murderer? My husband isn't poor any more. My jewellery and my hard struggle during his tough days have made him rich. Now he is a policeman and a rich contractor. Now he needs a new bride, because I am an old and useless woman as far as he is concerned. He can kill me as he is rich and I am a helpless woman. His greed and dishonesty led him to accuse his wife as a *kari* and accuse an innocent boy of being a *karo* whom I have never seen in my life. My brother told me that the accused boy is the same age as my oldest son. God will wreak my revenge on this man. God will give me justice. My husband and his new wife have poisoned my life. They feel nothing for my innocent crippled children or for me. I sent appeals to everyone; from the chief justice of Pakistan to the prime minister and the

---

[77] Benazir Bhutto (daughter of Zulfaquar Ali Bhutto, the very first elected Prime Minister of Pakistan who was hanged by the military dictator Zia-ul-Haq in 1979), was elected twice as Prime Minister of Pakistan, from 1988-1990 and from 1993-1996. She was assassinated on 27 December 2008 while campaigning for the Pakistani general election of 2008 in Rawal Pindi (Pakistan).

[78] Asif Ali Zardari, born 26 July 1955, is a Pakistani politician and the former co-chairperson of the Pakistan People's Party. He served as the eleventh President of Pakistan from 2008 to 2013. Mr. Zardari rose to prominence after his marriage to Benazir Bhutto in 1987, becoming the First Gentleman after his wife was elected Prime Minister in 1988.

president of Pakistan, but it seems that everyone is scared of him and that no-one listens to poor women in this country.

Q: Why do you think this has happened to you?

A: To me? Because I am a woman, because I have no power, because my husband needs a young woman now he is a rich man. He needs to throw me away like a piece of paper. See everywhere this is happening to women. When they get old, their husbands want to get rid of them, but not without making a profit. First they accuse or kill them as *karis* so they can get money from an accused man and then they expect to be honoured like a brave and honourable man. We women are the source of money for our money-grabbing, greedy parents and in-laws.

Q: How would you take up the issue if you were a man?

A: I … what do you mean? I would respect my life partner who had given her energy and youth to my house and life, who had borne my children and looked after them well and whatever else. How could I call some innocent person *kari* or *karo*?

Q: What do you think honour is?

A: Killing poor innocent and helpless women is honour in Sindh these days. Gone are the honourable men in this society. They have died. Honourable men do not exist in our society now. Do you call these Baloch or Sindhi men honourable who accuse their wives as *kari* and make a *khair* or *faislo* with the accused man to grab his money, and after taking the money they become friends again? A curse on this type of honour. If you are honourable, then why do you take money from the person who you think was *karo* with your wife? And after taking money from the *karo*, your honour goes into hibernation. You sell your wife and take money from the man who buys her and call yourself honourable! It is an act of dishonour. I don't call it honour. When you want to get rid of a woman, you plan to kill her and think you are honourable. The real honour is to kill your wife with another man at the moment when you see them doing wrong with your own eyes. Then I will call you an honourable man. But you call yourself honourable when your wife has never seen the man you are accusing her of sinning with. Who can call it honour? Is this honour – you tell me? I know my husband and his relatives will not let me live, but I beg you to let people know not to respect him as a hero because he is not doing it to rescue or protect his honour but to get rid of his old wife and to have a new wife, plus earning money in a *faislo* from the innocent man whom he accused of being a *karo*. Is my husband allowed to do whatever wrong and unjust things he wants to because he is rich? Does the law not apply to rich people? You meet the judge on my behalf or call him on a cell phone and talk to the SSP[79] and DSP[80] Police; how can they not listen to you?

Q: This is not in my control, but I will let your words be read by people, as I told you earlier.

A: Will the relevant authorities read it?

Q: I hope so. How is life at this shelter?

A: Days are passing, food is available and nothing else. I shall have to leave here eventually so I'm worried about what will happen to me then. No-one is bothering me here but I need medicine. I am in severe pain. I am a patient but no medical facilities are available to me here. It is my ninth month in this jail-type shelter. Nobody has come to visit me. What should I say to the judge about where I want to go? I have no option. My children have been brainwashed by my husband. My oldest son has just got married. My daughters can't do anything for me because they are in the hands of others. I have some hope from my brothers. They want to keep me, but I am afraid of my husband and my in-laws since they have accused me of being a *kari* and have taken a lot of money from the other party, so will they let me live?

Q: How do you see your life after you have left the shelter?

A: I am longing for freedom to see my children. I am longing for justice and protection but I cannot see any hope of fairness. For God's sake, help me and get my husband arrested. Is there any authority existing in this country or not? Call someone in authority, get him to sign papers so that my husband will be forced by law and should not think of killing me. I am a poor woman so nobody will listen to me. If nothing happens to him, he will kill me. I want my rights from my husband. I want my husband to be taken to court and he should admit all his wrongdoings. Will someone listen to me or not? He is a corrupt man. I have a lot to tell you and the judges against my brothers and husband and brothers-in-law. My husband

---

[79] Senior Superintendent of Police.
[80] Deputy Superintendent of Police.

has about 400 acres of land in Sindh and I should tell the court this so that he and his criminal brothers can be treated strictly.

Q: If you had a choice, what type of life you would like to live and with whom?

A: I want to see my children first. I am worried about their well-being. I need justice.

Q: I wish you all the best.

A: Pray for me.

Q: I shall.

7: *Name*: **Rabia, aged 18**

The interview lasted for an hour and twenty-one minutes and took place at a local darulaman.

Rabia appeared to me as an amazing, unrecognised flower. I cannot forget her beautiful brown eyes. She was wearing a green and black dress, heavy black bangles and a stylish nose-ring. Her eyes and nose were red because she could not stop crying while she was talking about the torture which her mother-in-law and brother-in-law had inflicted on her. Her face shone when she talked about her dolls.

Q: *Assalam-o-alaikum.*

A: *Walaikum-assalam.*

Q: How are you doing?

A: *Adi*, I am OK.

Q: Would you like to talk to me?

A: Yes. I want to talk to you.

Q: Let me make one thing clear: whatever information you give me will remain secure and will be used only for the purposes of my research and any related publications.

A: What does research mean?

Q: I am studying *karo-kari* so I shall share your story with other people.

A: That is good. City people do not understand the tribal system. Let them know what causes our suffering.

Q: Thank you. Do you have any objection if I record what you tell me?

A: No, why? Do record it. Can I hold your recorder?

Q: Thank you. Now, can you tell me something about you, your name, age, community, parents?

A: My name is Rabia and I am eighteen. Our caste is Malik and we are from Rohri. My father's name was Asif and he worked as a farmer but he has passed away now. I have three sisters and two brothers.

Q: Could you tell me about the family you grew up in, your childhood, your brothers and sisters, your school, favourite games and so on?

A: I am not educated. We were bought up in very strict circumstances and we were not even allowed to go to learn the Qur'an in the mosque. My maternal grandfather and maternal uncles were very cruel and did not let any of us study in school. We weren't even allowed to play with our neighbours. We could only play at our house with each other. With my brothers, I played some games like hide-and-seek and with my sisters I played with dolls. Playing with dolls was my favourite game but my maternal grandfather was very strict and whenever he saw me playing with the dolls he either hit me or broke my dolls. I have been facing disasters and trouble ever since I was a child. My father was a drug addict and a gambler. In one of his drug fits, or for some other reason, he accused my mother of being a *kari* with one of her cousins. He beat her and threatened to kill her. We were very young then. My mother realised that my father would kill her and would get money from anyone whom he would accuse as a *karo*. She was very scared, so she took us to her father's home. But my father soon realized what she had done and told my grandfather to hand his wife back to him. He admitted that he had been deceived by some of his relatives and that his wife was not a *kari*. But then my grandfather refused to hand my mother and us children back, but what he did then was that he sold our mother for 50,000 rupees in some other village. The week after that, my father died of a heart attack. I was just twelve at the time. My brothers, my sisters and I cried and begged our maternal grandfather and uncles not to sell our mother but they did not listen to us and locked us in a room. My mother cried loudly and begged my grandfather to let her work at his home as a slave if he would let her live there with us children. My relatives on that side are very cruel. They didn't listen to our mother or to us and she was sold. My younger brothers were six and seven years old at that time. They were weeping and wouldn't let go of my mother, but my uncles forcibly pulled them away from my mother and the three of us lived and grew up without our mother at my uncles' home.

Q: Can you tell me about your marriage; the mode of the marriage, the process of getting married?

A: Soon after selling my mother, my maternal grandfather sold my elder sister and then me. I'm not sure about the exact amount but it was certainly more than 100,000 rupees. Even before I started menstruating, I was sold in marriage to a fifty-year-old man and I was only thirteen. My husband worked as a peasant but he was addicted to drugs and to gambling as well. He was a cruel man but my eldest brother-in-law was a real menace. My husband was completely drunk most of the time. I was the target of physical and mental abuse by my in-laws, especially by my sister-in-law and brother-in-law.

Q: What was life like after your marriage? How did you get on with your husband and your in-laws?

A: It was a very painful existence. My husband was cruel but my eldest brother-in-law was the real bully. One of my husband's aunts had a television at her home so sometimes after I had finished my housework I used to go to watch television at her house close by. When her other son turned up and saw me watching the television, he grabbed me by the hair and dragged me all the way back home and warned me that if he saw me watching television again he would kill me. He could not bear me smiling or talking to anyone. My husband was virtually a useless tool in that house, it was my brother-in-law who was a kind of ruler at home. Everyone had to listen to him. He was really aggressive. On any petty pretext, he used to grab me and throw me around. He hit me with slaps and kicks but no-one ever came forward to rescue me. I had no-one to complain to; whenever I complained to my husband, he just threatened to divorce me. My husband told me that I should leave home, otherwise he would divorce me. He was not in his right mind. I thought many times about leaving home but I had nowhere to go. In the home of my maternal uncles, both of my younger brothers have a miserable life and I have heard that my maternal grandfather has sold my youngest sister as well when she turned thirteen.

Q: Can you tell me the reasons why are you here?

A: The aunt who had a television loved me and cared for me. Her in-laws had also bought her but she was lucky in the sense that her husband was kind, so she was happy. She sometimes gave me little presents and called me her daughter. Since I had lost my own mother and had no other supporter, I felt like she was my own mother. That made my brother-in-law my enemy. About four months ago, my brother-in-law called that aunt a *kari* and convinced her husband either to kill her or throw her out. When she heard that frighting allegation, she escaped from her house. That made me very sad. I had a picture of her and one day, I was crying as I looked at that picture and my brother-in-law saw me and said that since I was crying for a *kari* I must also have the same character. That day he said that he would do the same with me and throw me to the wolves. My in-laws worked for a *Syed* landlord and had borrowed money from him. I don't know how much but my in-laws often spoke about it and used abusive language towards the *Syed*. They were in fact jealous of the *Syed's* wealth. When my brother-in-law accused me of being a *kari* with the *Syed*, whom I had never even seen, I wept and insisted that I was not a *kari*. Even my husband didn't support me. They all united in order to kill me as a *kari* to get hold of the *Syed*'s money by calling him a *karo*. You know, they took 720,000 rupees from the *Syed*, the largest amount ever taken from a *karo*.

Q: How did it happen? Can you explain the whole thing in detail?

A: Once, I was hanging out the laundry. You know how open the houses in villages are. You can easily see everything over the low fences. Believe me ... I do not know whose car passed outside our house but soon after it went by, my brother-in-law came in and howled that the *Syed* was in the car and I had given him a smile. I took oaths that I was innocent but he beat me heartlessly and told my husband that his wife was a *kari*. I was ready to swear on the Qur'an but he beat me a lot and told my husband that his wife was a *kari*. My husband didn't listen to me either. They called my paternal grandfather and accused me of being a *kari*. I wept and insisted that I was not a *kari*. My grandfather tried to console my husband and my brother-in-law and said, 'Do not accuse the orphan wrongly, she is not a *kari*', but my in-laws didn't listen to him either. For the next three months they remained silent so I thought that they would not harm me but then I realised that I was misunderstanding them. One evening, my youngest brother-in-law's wife told me secretly that my brothers-in-law and my husband had decided to kill me and to do it, they had kept a loaded gun in her room. She said I must run otherwise I would be killed that night.

Q: How did you escape?

A: My sister-in-law gave me 500 rupees and said that she had talked to her mother who was ready to help me. When I saw no-one around, I first went to the kind of the toilet we had at the end of our house and then ran off. My sister-in-law told me that her brother would meet me after I had crossed the road. When I got there, I found him in a rickshaw. He spoke to my sister-in-law on his cell-phone and the rickshaw took us to their mother's house. Her mother was also very scared so she wouldn't let me stay at her house and instead she sent me to the house of one of her friends. I was there for three days. On the third day, the mother of my sister-in-law came and told me that my in-laws were searching for me like hounds. She was very scared of my in-laws but even so she took me to the women's police station. A lady police officer interviewed me. Then she called a photographer who took my photo for the newspapers. I talked to the newspapermen as well. From there, I was taken to the court and the court sent me to the shelter.

Q: Why do they want to kill you?

A: Greed. It is their job to sell their women and take money from men by accusing them as *karo*. If they kill the women they get money. If they don't kill their woman, they get money by selling them. So both ways they get money. If they kill the *karo*, they get money and if they make a *khair* or *faislo,* they get money. So their greed is making them do all that and they are getting money either way. They know that the women are helpless. Nobody will defend them if they are accused of being *karis*, nobody stops men when they kill or sell women, so they are committing every kind of crime without any fear.

Q: Why do you think this has happened to you?

A: My mother was accused as a *kari*. My in-laws had bought me for money so I had no one to support me. I was an easy target in their hands. I was an orphan. My brothers are too young to defend me. My sisters have also been sold. If my maternal relatives like my grandfather or uncles take me from this shelter, they will sell me, so my in-laws want to take me so that they can sell me and get the benefit. This is what is making women *kari* and men *karo* everywhere. It is just greed and nothing else. When a woman is killed, then these men take double the amount from the *karo*. If she isn't killed but her male folk accuse her as a *kari*, then they sell her and get money. So men benefit either way. Whenever my in-laws and my maternal relatives visit the shelter, they threaten that if I don't make a statement in their favour in court, they will kill me. I don't want to go with any of them. My maternal uncles will not kill me but they'll sell me like my mother, and so will my in-laws. I asked my in-laws why their greed is not satisfied after they have taken the greatest amount that has ever been taken from a *karo* in Sindh. What can I see for my future? Where shall I go?

Q: How would you take up the issue if you were a man?

A: The issue, what issue? I am not a *kari*. OK … if I were a man I might have thought the same as they are doing. I might have been selling and accusing innocent women as *karis*. I don't know.

Q: What do you think honour is?

A: What honour is? Whatever it is, the Sindhi don't know what honour is. You know they took 720,000 rupees, the largest amount ever taken from a *karo*, from that *Syed* whom I had never seen in my entire life and he might have never seen me in his life. Is this honour? This is shame and dishonesty. The *Syed* is rich and he owed money to my in-laws so they accused him of being a *karo.* Now the *Syed* will not ask for his money back. He has already paid such a large amount to them to save his life. Where is the honour in that? The Sindhis sell and buy innocent girls, aged twelve and thirteen, use them as concubines, tear their bodies and then call them *kari* and either kill them or sell them to become rich. Would you call that honour? I think the much better business for them is to open brothels and use us there as prostitutes and at least we would not be beaten up there in the name of honour and no-one would kill us. That would be a much more honourable business than this.

Q: How is life at this shelter?

A: Full of problems and very difficult. It is very hot here. The electricity doesn't work. The generators are broken. We can't go upstairs or outside the halls. All the time we have to be locked in. There is no clean drinking water available. No water for having a bath. I ran from my home empty-handed so I have no other clothes to wear. Last week, a girl left the shelter so she gave me two of her dresses. I am wearing them. During the fast, the weather is horrible, but what can I do? Only I know how I am enduring the fast. It is horrible but what else can I do? I want to be rid of my life as there is no peace or hope in life.

Q: How do you see your life after you have left the shelter?

A: Now, my in-laws and my paternal relatives are trying to force me to leave the shelter and to go with them. I don't want to go with any of them. I know they won't kill, me but they will sell me and use that money to buy food. I asked them, 'You have taken the biggest amount ever taken from a *karo*, why is your greed still not satisfied?' My maternal uncles came here to the shelter and threatened me that if I don't make a statement in their favour in court, they would go to the court disguised in a *burqa*[81] and kill me there. I know that the death threat was just a blackmail tactic to put pressure on me. They only kill old and ugly women who can't be sold and I am too young and beautiful to be killed. So whoever of them wins the battle will sell me off. But the good thing is that my mother came to visit me when her husband saw my photo in the newspaper. She was crying to see me here. She wants to help me. My stepfather and my mother went to my maternal grandfather and uncles to ask if she could look after me. My uncles threatened to kill her, her husband and her eight-year-old daughter but she is determined to help me and I would like to go with her. Pray for me, *Adi*, I want to live my life.

Q: If you had a choice, what type of life you would like to live and with whom?

A: My mother is trying to help me. I am happy to know that my mother is living with a nice man who looks after her so well. She has an eight-year-old daughter. I want a divorce from my drug-addict husband and I want to live with my mother. I want to live a peaceful life. My in-laws and maternal relatives are very cruel. They want to sell me. I don't know where they would sell me so I don't want to go with them. I have not seen love from anyone. I was too young when my father died and my mother was sold. Now I have put my life in the hands of my mother. I know mothers cannot think badly about their children. I will live with my mother whatever she decides for me.

---

[81] A long, loose stitched garment which covers the whole of a woman's body.

Q: I wish you all the best and I thank you for sharing your story with me.

A: Thank you, *Adi*. Please pray for me.

Q: I shall.

8: *Name*: **Najma, aged 21**

The interview lasted for an hour and thirty-six minutes and it took place at a darulaman.

Najma cried a lot about everything throughout the interview. She was absolutely beautiful; her little laugh was lovely. She could speak Punjabi and Urdu. She was wearing a maroon embroidered dress with a black *dupatta.* She proudly told me that she came first in her fifth-grade exam.

Q: *Assalam-o-alaikum.*

A: *Walaikum-assalam.*

Q: How are you today?

A: I am fine but, you know, who can really be fine here?

Q: Are you willing to talk to me?

A: Yes. I am. I want to talk to you.

Q: Let me tell you one thing: whatever you tell me will only be used for the purposes of my research and for related publications.

A: Will you write it in a newspaper?

Q: In a research book.

A: OK. I'll tell you my true story.

Q: Thank you. Can I record what you say?

A: Yes, then you can listen to me again.

Q: Thank you. Can you tell me something about you; your name, age, community, parents?

A: My name is Najma and I am twenty-one. By caste we are Panhwar from Punjab. My father's name is Shakeel and he works as a gardener. I have four sisters and eight brothers.

Q: Could you tell me about the family you grew up in, your childhood, siblings, school, favourite games and so on?

A: My childhood was very painful. I do not want to recall anything of my childhood. I used to be beaten by my parents and my older brothers. I was an object of physical and mental abuse at their hands. My crime was that I wanted to study to become either a doctor or a lawyer. Nobody wanted me to go to school because no-one had ever studied in our village before, so it was not acceptable to them. However, one of my aunts who lived in Karachi paid us a visit and convinced my father to send me to school. I didn't like playing any games. I used to work at home and then I studied at school during the break time. Other girls used to play outside but I stayed in, busy studying with the teachers who loved me and encouraged me to study. Because of my good grades, I was given a scholarship by my school. That scholarship was sufficient to buy school uniform and shoes for me. Some of our relatives used to live in Karachi. They came to see us and when they saw my interest in studying they told my father to let me study. After that, my father became a bit more relaxed about the issue of education. When I went into year six, I noticed that one boy used to follow me and make vulgar comments about me. I thought that if I did not let my parents and brothers know about it, it might become worse. When I told my older brother about him, my brother beat the boy outside but he also stopped me going to school. That was a very difficult situation for me. I pleaded and begged my parents and brothers but nobody was prepared to listen to me. Instead, they got me ready for marriage. That was an absolutely unbearable thing for me I had had dreams of a better life. I wanted to study and to become something and to change my life. Full of anger, I left home. I left my home but I didn't know where to go. I didn't know that the world is full of wolves. My initial thought was that I would go to the *data darbar*.[82] I had 600 rupees in my pocket and I paid 280 rupees for the bus-fare to Lahore. The bus got to Lahore at three o'clock in the morning. The driver realised that I was a twelve-year-old girl. I was the last passenger to get off the bus. Out of nowhere, four men appeared. Two of them were policemen. They wanted to take me with them. When I realised the situation I was in I wept. The owner of the bus came and listened to me carefully and suggested that I should go back

---

[82] A shrine in Lahore.

home. Although I was really terrified and regretted leaving home, I had no heart to go back because I knew that my father and brothers would kill me. My father had said many times that if a girl leaves this home and comes back, she should be killed immediately without bothering to find out whether she is pure or not. The owner of the bus handed me over to a man and told me that he would look after me and might convince my father to forgive me. I've never talked about anything that I faced in my life – you are the only person I've shared my story with. I was then in a really problematic situation and eventually, after nine months, a family found me and that family helped me to contact my parents. The family lied to my parents and told them that I had been with them and had not faced any disaster. They got a guarantee from my parents not to kill me and my parents promised them. My parents believed them and let me return home. They talked to my maternal uncle and he was prepared to take me as his daughter-in-law. Although they accepted me and didn't kill me, I was still the target of abuse and everyone in the family was saying that I was not pure, so I had no right to marry. Eventually, the oldest family members agreed to kill me as *kari*. They could not believe that after nine months, a girl on her own in the world without any shelter could still be a virgin. When I was realised that they were definitely going to kill me, I ran away from home and after some difficulties I got to the home of the same family again. They trusted me and when my relatives got there, they didn't hand me over to them. Then I lived there for five years. They got me admission to year six and I took the grade 10 exams. I started to dream again of becoming a doctor and to forget what had happened to me in the past. One day, my father and two of my brothers came to the family's home and said that my mother was in hospital. Hearing that, the family let me go with them because everybody believed that they would not harm me. When I got there, my mother was cooking food! So for the second time my family had ruined my life. This time, they had fixed the date of my marriage and I was absolutely at their disposal. My parents, brothers and other relatives were my enemies and I was treated worse than an animal. I was locked in a room and was given pieces of dry bread through the window.

Q: Can you tell me about your marriage; the mode of marriage, the process of getting married?

A: I was part of an exchange for my mother. When my mother was given to my father in marriage, her father made her marry my father on the promise that my mother would give birth to two girls to be given in exchange for her. I was my mother's second daughter so I was born virtually engaged to my maternal uncle's son. I had no choice but to accept the marriage. My in-laws were visibly very unhappy and aggressive with me.

Q: What was life like after your marriage? How did you get on with your family, your husband and your in-laws?

A: From the very first day of my marriage a life of torture began. My parents didn't come to ask me how I was. I wasn't given any food. After three days of marriage, I became unconscious and started bleeding severely. At that point my in-laws called my brothers. My brothers took me to the hospital. The lady doctor shouted at my husband and other relatives and threatened to call the police. My drunken husband was abused by my brothers and they fought in the hospital. After four days in hospital, I was discharged. My mother and brothers insisted that I should go with them and they asked me to divorce my husband; that was the real torture for me. I said 'When I was begging you before to let me study and not to give me to this addict, none of you listened to me. Now you are asking me to get divorced from him. You won't let me live in peace. After this divorce you will force me to marry someone else and I don't know what will happen to my life; again I have been thrown down a burning-well so just let me live there. This is my destiny now'. At that, my father and brothers abused me and beat me and said that my life was a curse for them; they were really aggressive and swore that they wouldn't even go to my funeral. I had left my parents for that addict who was my husband, but the drunken oaf proved himself even worse than them. He used to beat me after he'd been drinking and many times he threw me out of the house saying that he would like to see who would come to rescue me. For two years I was in that hell. Because of the endless physical torture I had two miscarriages. One day my eldest sister came to me. I wept a lot and told her everything. She forced me to go and meet my mother. My husband wasn't at home. I went along with my sister to see my mother as she was in the same city. On the way back I was alone as my sister had gone to her own home. As soon as I got home, my husband, my father-in-law, my mother-in-law and sister-in-law were waiting for me. Without letting me say a single word, they shouted '*Kari, kari*' and my husband held my hands while my father-in-law struck me with his knife. Life is dear even to animals; I was a human being after all. When I realised that my in-laws would not let me survive, I screamed and bit my husband's hand and ran out through the door that was still open. I rushed to my mother's house. My mother advised me to run away as she was afraid that my in-laws would get there and kill us both. My brother took me to his friend's house. Next morning, his friend sent us to a person who helped me get to a shelter. He was a really kind person; he helped us and let us live in one of his homes. No more than a month later, my husband and my in-laws found the address and came to me again. I didn't open the door and called a man whose number had been given to me by the spiritual leader. The man got there in no time and took them all to the spiritual leader. The spiritual leader clearly told my husband that I was not his wife anymore because he had accused me of being a *kari*. He also threatened him with severe consequences if he even thought of harming me. My husband was prepared to divorce me and I agreed. I couldn't want to go anywhere from there. At that place, the spiritual leader asked me to marry a man who was there and was already married. I accepted the proposal because I had no other option left. Also, I trusted the spiritual leader. They gave me a home and I got married. For the first time in my life I met a loving and humble person. I thought that my days of pain were over. Life became smooth. My second husband was an amazing man. He gave me love, care and respect. He was very sensitive and understood my past. He realised my situation and promised not to leave me.

Q: Can you tell me why you are here?

A: I started to live a very loving and peaceful life. My new husband made a nice home for me. He provided me with everything that a woman could want. About six months passed and I thought that my relatives would never disturb me again as now I was married to an outsider and my cousin had divorced me, but my assumption was wrong. One day, my brother knocked on the door. My husband went out and came back to me with the news that my brother wanted to meet me. I was scared but my husband, being very kind, suggested that I should meet him. When my brother came in, he met me and showed his satisfaction with my present life. We talked very nicely and he stayed with us for three days. I thought that he had accepted my marriage and was happy for me. Then he left us. But when he had gone, my husband said that he had some doubts and believed that my brother had come with some bad intentions. I ignored this thought. But he was right, as after a week. when I was alone at home because my husband had gone to work, there was a knock at the door. When I checked through the hole in the door, I saw that my brother was there. I opened the door and all of a sudden more than five men and my mother rushed in. My father, my ex-father-in-law and three of my brothers forced me to go with them. They said that I was living with a man immorally as I was still in a *nikah* with my previous husband. They all were united and were really furious. I couldn't use my mobile phone in their presence because they wanted to drag me away with them immediately, before my husband came. After a great struggle, I managed to escape and I ran to the house of some neighbours who were aware of the situation. They didn't have my husband's number but they called the police. The police took me in their vehicle to the police station. That evening, my husband got there. He was very worried and wanted me to register a police case against my family and I intended to do so. At that time, I was five months pregnant. However, the police sent me to the *darulaman*. My husband got very worried and arranged a lawyer and I filed a case against my family that they intended to harm my husband and me. My husband was hopeful that he could take me back soon … you know, *bajee*, what happened to me? Four months ago, the brother who had come to stay with me and had showed his satisfaction killed my husband with the help of my ex-husband, when he was sleeping at home. (*She cried loudly*). The neighbours saw my brother coming and my ex-husband running but by then my brother had cut my husband's body into pieces with the help of my ex-husband.

Q: Why do you think this has happened to you?

A: My luck, the ignorance, the system. I do not know why this happened to me but I know one thing for sure; that I was cursed at the time of my birth. I didn't see any peace in my life. I didn't see any happiness in my life. The first time someone loved me and gave me care and a home, my cruel family snatched that away from me. My family and my ex-husband are saying that I have violated the *Sharia* or Islamic law by marrying someone without having a proper divorce from my ex-husband. Did I? Can you tell me if I did? My family is calling me a *kari*? Am I a *kari*, tell me? My life is before you. You have listened and recorded my version – so am I *kari* or a criminal?

Q: How would you take up the issue if you were a man?

A: I don't know, but I wouldn't have killed someone's husband. I am sure about that. I wouldn't have snatched the right to have an education from anyone.

Q: What do you think honour is?

A: Honour means respect, but in Pakistan honour means killing women and using women according to men's wish and will. Their honour is related to the way they treat poor, innocent women. They beat and hurt and kill women in the name of honour. Is this honour?

Q: How is life in this shelter?

A: It is a life of compulsion. Who wants to live in a prison? Unfortunate women who have no other option live here. We can't go upstairs or outside these halls. All the time we have to be locked in this graveyard.

Q: How do you see your life after you have left the shelter?

A: I can't say. It is my ninth month here. I gave birth to my first child here. My child was born here. When he was one month old, his father was killed for protecting the life of his mother. I don't know – will the court do justice in my case and hang my brother and ex-husband?

Q: If you had a choice, what type of life you would like to live and with whom?

A: I still don't understand what the law is, what the regulations are. Who is *kari*, who is *garhee*? Who is *karo* and who is not *karo*? Where can I go now? The world is full of politics and I am too naïve to understand it. I have lost my last rescuer. Now I live only for my son. But they are saying that this is an illegitimate child and that when I leave this shelter, they will kill him and me as well. Where can I go? I have no courage to go out of this refuge, but I intend to go out maybe after seven or eight years to take revenge on my family, but my child is too young now. I cannot commit suicide now … and what can I see? I can't see anything in my life.

Q: I wish you and your son all the best.

A: Thank you. Pray for my son, please.

Q: I will.

9: *Name*: **Rubina, aged 20**

The interview lasted for an hour and eleven minutes and it took place at a darulaman.

Rubina became very sad at my questions about her marriage. She was very aggressive towards God. She burst out crying when she asked why women have no right to live a life of their own.

Q: *Assalam-o-alaikum.*

A: *Walaikum-assalam.*

Q: How are you doing?

A: I am good. How about you?

Q: I am fine. Thank you for asking. Can I ask you a few questions, if you are comfortable about it?

A: Sure. You can.

Q: Let me make one thing clear: whatever information you will provide me with will remain secure and will be used only for the purposes of my research and for related publications.

A: OK.

Q: So, you are OK with that?

A: Yes, you can ask me whatever you like and if I am confortable with it, I will aanswer your questions.

Q: Of course. And if you do not want to answer anything or want to leave the interview halfway through, you are absolutely free to do this.

A: Fine. Ask.

Q: Can you tell me something about you; your name, age, community and parents?

A: My name is Rubina and I am twenty. I am only telling you what my assessment is as there is no record of my birth so I cannot tell you my exact age. My identity card has not been made, so I am not sure what my age is. Our caste is Khaskeli. We are from Sindh. My father's name is Abid. He used to work before he became paralysed. About two or three years ago, he had a stroke which left half of his body paralysed.

Q: Could you tell me about the family you grew up in, your childhood, siblings, school, favourite games and things like that?

A: I have five sisters and five brothers; I am the third.

My childhood was all pain. We had almost nothing to live on or eat properly. We used to fight all the time. We shouted at each other. I remember we pulled each other's hair hard and hit each other. My father was a poor worker and our mother was unable to earn anything, so our childhood was just a mess. Our parents also beat us but the verbal abuse was too much. I really hate my home and my family system. I am uneducated because my father was very strict and ordered that no girl could ever go to school. My brothers went to school but they only studied for a few classes, like up to year five only. Schools are made for boys only.

Q: Tell me about your marriage; the mode of marriage and the process of getting married.

A: I was part of an exchange for my brothers. My older brothers' wives were the daughters of my maternal uncle. I was exchanged for them. When I grew up, like when I was thirteen or fourteen, my uncle forced my parents to marry me to his son. His son was an addict and I didn't want to marry him. I hated that family. My brothers' wives were very rude to me and they always teased me that after my marriage their brothers would take revenge on me. Also, I had my own choice. I wanted to marry someone of my own choice. He was our neighbour: from my childhood I had loved him and he also wanted to marry me. Although we hadn't told anyone about our relationship, my sisters-in-law realised it and forced their father and brothers to take me away from there as soon as possible. When I refused to marry my sister-in-law's brother, my uncle and his elder brother came to my parents' house with rifles and said that if I didn't agree to marry him, they would kill me. I didn't want to marry a man who I didn't like. I begged my parents but they were scared of my uncles, as they were strong and quite notorious for fighting. One of my uncles had killed two people, so everybody was frightened of him. So my parents and my other relatives forced me to marry. I never wanted to marry him. Besides, I thought that I was too young to marry but they didn't listen to me, so under threat of being killed, I was married. My mother said that if I refused the marriage, she would kill me with her own hands. I said 'Why don't you think about my life? I should be able to live my life the way I want'. They replied 'Who are you to think of your life? We elders have to decide everything'. I was given two choices; either to be killed or to marry that man.

Q: What was life like after your marriage? How did you get on with your husband and in-laws?

A: I was married under duress three years ago to my paternal cousin. I have no children so far. My husband tried to strangle me on my wedding night. He said that his sisters were suffering because of me so he would take revenge on me. For three days I faced severe physical and sexual torture. Then I told my mother. She took me to her house and I refused to go back to my in-laws. My sisters-in-law then also left my parents' home and went back to their own parents as it had been an exchange marriage. My brothers again sent me to my in-laws by force. They beat me harshly when they sent me there. All the continuous physical torture made me sick. I couldn't just accept it all as my destiny. My in-laws or my husband could have made me theirs by care and love, but they only hated me, accused me, beat me and nothing else. Throughout those two years, none of them gave me a single penny to spend. What does a woman not need? Sometimes my mother gave me a bit of money or a dress, but nothing else. Why should I live with them, to be abused or tortured or to die sick? During my illness, they didn't buy a single tablet for me or ask me whether I was alive or not. I don't want to go to those barbarians again.

Q: Can you tell me why you are here?

A: Once I was talking to my boyfriend in my room. My older brother caught me. I had a cell phone which my boyfriend has once given me. My brother asked me who I was talking to on the phone but he wasn't satisfied with my answer. He took the SIM-card out of my cell phone and told my father-in-law about it. My father-in-law called my father. My father couldn't walk but he was brought there on a motor bike driven by my brother. My uncle told him that I was a *kari*. When my father asked for the proof, he said that he would kill the boy involved with me within two days as a proof. My father took me to his house and the family of the boy whom I love moved somewhere else during the night, as the news spread that he had been accused of being a *karo* and could be killed any time by the accusers. My father took me to his house at four o'clock in the afternoon and at six o'clock my youngest sister came and told me secretly that my uncle, my husband and his brother were coming with my brother to kill me. I put my *burqa* on and slipped out of the house. I knew the direct way to the police station but I took the other route to avoid being caught. I reached the police station that night and asked the duty officer to help me. Within an hour, my relatives arrived. The police officer asked me if I would meet any of them. When I refused, he didn't insist. After two days, the court sent me to the *darulaman*.

Q: Why did they want to kill you?

A: They called it a matter of honour. When I was begging and crying in front of everybody that I did not want to marry, none of them listened to me. They gave me to an addict who never gave me a single penny in his life. Why would I have lived with them? From the very first day they made my life hell. My husband said that he would beat me and keep insulting me for the rest of my life but would never divorce me so that my life should be hell. Didn't they care that I didn't want to get married? Now they want to kill me and after they have killed me, their honour and respect would be restored. They are ignorant. They are enemies of their girls. They want to use their girls like a goat or a cow. I know that the Qur'an says that before marriage a girl should be asked for her consent. They have their own interpretation of everything that goes against the poor girls.

Q: Why do you think this has happened to you?

A: My bad luck, my fate. Men have authority over women. Women can't even think about their own life and can't take any decisions on their own. Where is God? Does he exist? I would like to ask God why this injustice has been happening to women? Why doesn't the government make laws which let women choose a life partner for themselves? God is responsible for this hell! Why did he let me be born into that family? If I hadn't been born, I wouldn't have gone through all this suffering. This all happened because I was born. My parents are responsible for everything. They had exchanged me for my sisters-in-law. It wasn't my fault; they did it. Then my uncle and his sons forced me to get married. They all are responsible for ruining my life. My mother, my father, my brothers, my uncle, my husband, my sisters-in-law and brothers-in-law all are responsible for the painful life which I have now.

Q: How would you take up the issue if you were a man?

A: You mean if I was a husband? Well, in that instance, I would have given my wife a good life. But why would I marry a girl who didn't want to marry me? OK, after marriage, a woman needs something. My husband only had money for his drugs. He didn't give me anything, ever. Why would I do this to anyone? The best thing is divorce for a woman who doesn't want to live with her husband. If I were a man, I would have certainly have divorced my wife if she didn't even want to see my face.

Q: What do you think honour is?

A: Men's honour lies in the forced marriages of their girls. This is their honour. They say that all women are their property. So they marry them by force, sell them, kill them, in fact do whatever they want to do and when a woman speaks for her rights their honour gets hurt. I have taught them a lesson about what the honour of a woman is by coming here to this shelter. They are now crying and shouting everywhere that their honour has been ruined because of me; I ask them where my honour is. Has that been crushed? First, give me back my honour. They violated my honour first, then I ruined their honour. Does a woman not have a right to live a life of her own choice? Do parents have daughters just to torture them mentally?

Q: How is life at this shelter?

A: Don't ask me. I wish that even my enemy shouldn't have to spend a moment here. There is no water, no air. Day and night we are forced to live in the hot rooms. It is worse than hell probably. All the time I blame my parents and my brothers and pray that they should face the worst curse on earth because it is due to their obstinacy that I am here in this hell. What is there here? We have to survive without light, air and gas. I wouldn't even wish my enemy to spend a moment in it.

Q: How do you see your life after you have left the shelter?

A: What if we escaped? It is just a transitional period. Sooner or later we will all be killed or sold. At least, I am sure that I will be killed as soon as I leave the shelter. I am telling you this. Keep it a record of it. My in-laws will not let me live. I am determined to fight them. I will register a case against my husband and ask for a divorce. My in-laws, my brothers and my mother came to the court last time. They were begging me and wanted me to make a statement in their favour so that the judge should release me and they should take me back to the same torture-cell. I said 'Listen to me; I am already in torture but I am happy that now you are also in a torture-cell and want to kill me!' I would never give them a chance to get out of it. For the first time in my life, I am content that they all are also facing the hell which I have had to endure since I was born. My mother asked me, 'Are you a daughter?' I asked in return, 'Are you a mother?' You don't know what they have been doing to me. I won't leave this shelter until I have the divorce papers in my hands. I am sure they will kill me even after my divorce because my uncle said that if the boy and I both go to hell, he would find us even there and kill us. They are trying to make a fool of me. They swore on the Qur'an that they wouldn't harm me and they asked me to go with them, but I knew they were lying to me. I know that the day I go with them, they would shoot me dead. They are my enemies. My uncle has sold some of his land in order to bribe the police and lawyers so that they should hand me over to him. I said 'If I had the power, I would have had you all locked up in jail forever'. I said to them 'You have all plotted together and made my life hell, so now I shall make your lives hell. I don't want to see any of their faces again in my life'. They are the worst people. I can't trust them. Now they want me to make a statement in their favour so that the judge will allow me to go with them and then they will kill me and the boy whom they have called a *karo* to grab money.

Q: If you had a choice, what type of life you would like to live and with whom?

A: I would get a divorce from my husband through the court and marry the boy of my choice. I know that he will marry me. He came to visit me here in this shelter but I had to tell him plainly not to visit me here as my relatives would kill him whenever they see him. If my parents had listened to me, would I have had to live in this disaster? I will try to live a good life with the boy I love. He will marry me. His family is willing to see me but all they are scared of my relatives. The boy will take me to some other country. He has promised to take me to another country where we can live in peace. I don't want to see the face of anyone in my family.

Q: Thank you for sharing your story with me.

A: You are a very good woman. You pray for me.

Q: Yes, I will.

10: *Name*: Shaheen, aged 23

The interview lasted for an hour and eighteen minutes and took place at a darulaman.

Shaheen was wearing brown dress with a bright pink *dupatta*, a nose-pin and dangling earrings. Throughout the interview she was scratching her nails.

Q: *Assalam-o-alaikum.*

A: *Walaikum-assalam.*

Q: How are you doing?

A: You can see, what can I say?

Q: Let me make one thing clear: whatever information you give me will remain secure and will be used only for the purposes of my research and for related publications.

A: Tell everyone. I want everyone to hear what is going on in Sindh.

Q: OK. So can I record the interview?

A: You can, if you like.

Q: Can you tell me something about you; your name, age, your community and your parents?

A: My name is Shaheen and I am twenty-three. My caste is Khaskeli. We are from Jacobabad. My father's name is Usman and he works with a horse and cart. We are originally from Sindh.

Q: Could you tell me about the family you grew up in, your childhood, brothers and sisters, school, favourite games and so on?

A: My father married twice. His first wife died and he had two children from her. Then he married the woman who is my mother and from her there are six children, two sisters and four brothers. I am uneducated. I went to school and spent three years there. Now I can read quite a few words in newspapers but I can't write. You know how in the system of education here in our village either the teachers don't come or the schools aren't open, so how could I study? No-one was there to look after it so whenever we went, we normally found it closed. I didn't learn anything from school. I played many games with my brothers and sisters and our neighbours. I used to fight physically, like wrestling, and I always tried to win every fight and every game. I enjoyed playing wrestling as well and many more games. I was very fast at running so I used to beat the boys and hit them and I didn't listen to anyone. No boy could have ever beaten me in a race. I used to play with dolls as well. I had three female dolls and one male doll, made of clothes and sticks. Because my mother did not let us do marriages of dolls, the male doll was my female dolls' brother who used to take them shopping and to visit other relatives' homes. Because I didn't like my brothers, I only made one male doll to play with the three female dolls. I had a wooden box for the dolls' clothes and I sewed lots of dresses for them.

Q: Tell me about your marriage; the mode of the marriage and the process of getting married.

A: When I was sixteen, I was married to Ihsan. The mode of our marriage was *watto-satto*. They were not our relatives but were of the same *zaat*[83] and the people who arranged the marriage deceived my parents by saying that the boy was a civil servant. In fact, he was a drug addict and jobless but my parents believed those people. My parents gave me some dowry but I didn't get anything from my in-laws.

Q: What was life like after your marriage? How did you get on with your husband, children and in-laws?

A: After my marriage I realised what my in-laws really were. My husband had no job. He took drugs and was a kind of useless cabbage at home. He used to beat me every day for no apparent reason. They used very abusive language to me. The main reason was that I had six sisters-in-law; one was my brother's wife but the other five were unmarried and my husband worked as a pimp for them. He used to bring men home and called them uncles, but I knew what was going on in their home. The men were from cities other than our own city. My husband called them uncles in front of others but I knew what was going on in their house. One man tried to have an illicit relationship with me too. I strictly refused. At that, my husband beat me brutally and I got badly injured. My head was bleeding but no-one took me to hospital. Their home was kind of a brothel and this was their business. These men used to give them clothes and other household stuff. My husband didn't give me a single penny to spend. I became pregnant but had nothing to eat. My child died in my womb due to malnutrition. I developed bad asthma but I had no money to buy medicine. My parents were also poor. They gave me some money but how much could they give me? I used to work outside at various homes as a maid. They were rich people so they used to help me with some bread, vegetables, soap and other regular stuff. My husband always threatened that he would kill me as a *kari*. He always said that he would divorce me if I did not listen to him. I complained to my parents but they didn't do anything as his sister was my brother's wife and my parents did not want her to leave their house. It was like hell to live in that house. I was a

---

[83] Caste.

simple and decent woman. I considered the life as my destiny. I worked at various houses to earn my living and I would have still been living with them if they hadn't accused me and threatened to kill me as a *kari*.

Q: Can you tell me the reason why are you here?

A: My in-laws and my husband wanted to kill me as a *kari*. The reason was that there was a man, their relative, who used to come to their home. Believe me, I didn't have any link or any contact with him. He was a good and polite man and had respect for me, but my all in-laws started calling me a *kari* with him. My husband said that I had to sell my body to others. The beatings happened every day. The man stopped coming to our house but my husband and my in-laws said that he was a *karo* and all the time called me *kari*. Once my husband beat me really hard and ripped my clothes and said that it was my last day because I was a *kari*. I cried and screamed but no-one helped me even though my mother-in-law and sisters-in-law were watching him hitting me. That day I wanted to commit suicide. I ran out and wanted to jump into a river that was not very far from our house. Our neighbours heard me screaming and knew what was going on; some of them followed me and held me by my arms to stop me from jumping in the river. The same man also came and said that he was willing to marry me as he was accused by my husband of being a *karo* so he was left with two options, either to be killed or to pay money in a *faislo*. He sent an auto-rickshaw to me and I went to a shrine with one of his friends. In the morning, the man came to the shrine with the *wadera* of the village and said that the previous night, the police had arrested his father and brothers so he had to appear before the police station and the court to make a statement in their favour so that the arrested male members of his family could be released. I was then taken to the police station. From the police station, I came to this *darulaman*. This is my third month here.

Q: Why do they want to kill you?

A: Because I didn't want to be a prostitute. I wanted to earn money with honour and respect. I hated the way my in-laws were earning money. When my husband realised that I wouldn't sell my body to everyone, he planned against me. In that way he would have killed me and then taken money from the man he was calling a *karo* without committing any offence. They are dirty and greedy people. You know I was not a *kari* and neither was the man a *karo* who was accused of being *karo*. He saved my life so I asked him to marry me, otherwise I had nowhere to go. I have applied to the court for a divorce from my husband. Now a *faislo* has been made by the *wadera* and the accused man will have to pay them 200,000 rupees. He is arranging the money and soon he will pay them the amount.

Q: Why do you think this has happened to you?

A: My destiny … because my parents had trusted the middlemen and did not enquire about my in-laws. They thought that their daughter would have a nice life but they didn't know what type of people they were giving their daughter to. Sindhis do not think about their daughters, so why would my parents have made any enquiries? Sindhis throw their daughters away as soon as they start menstruating, no matter whether dogs catch them or wolves. I cry on my own. Can any woman leave her home happily? No, she can only do so when she is extremely unhappy and has no other choice. A woman can live in very poor conditions, but only if respect is there. A woman leaves home in great pain and agony. Sorrows and pains compel her to leave her home.

Q: How would you take up the issue if you were a man?

A: I would have earned money for my wife. I would have not forced her to sell her body. I would have respected her and loved her.

Q: What do you think honour is?

A: Money is not honour; even poverty has an honour if someone understands it. My husband's honour was to work as a pimp and bring men for his mother and sisters to earn money. He is known as a pimp in the whole city. Honour means one should have some principles in life. Die with hunger, but he should not sell his females' bodies to vultures. Honour is to earn with struggle and to spend with care. Honour is in working. Do your work and feed your family; this is honour. There is no honour in selling the bodies of women. The small amount of food which is earned by working is much better than the luxury food earned by dishonouring your relative's bodies. Look at my husband. He is a pimp and he calls himself an honourable man. This is honour in Sindh now – when a woman refuses to become a prostitute, accuse her of being a *kari* and kill her. These corrupt men claim that their honour lies between their women's legs, so why did my husband want me to present his honour to strangers?

Q: How is life at this shelter?

A: Not good at all. What is there here? There is no light, no air, no gas. The water is really dirty. Look at my body; my skin is coming off. There is no water for having a bath. The water we have to drink is very contaminated. I wish I had something to kill myself with. We do not have clean water to drink. Look at these children around. The poor children are in real trouble but there is no good system to look after them.

Q: How do you see your life after you have left the shelter?

A: I have applied for a divorce. I'll marry again and I hope I'll have a good life this time; at least an honourable man who will keep me at home and earn for me.

Q: If you had a choice, what type of life you would like to live and with whom?

A: I assume it would have been without jail, this shelter and torture. Is this a life? I have been living with only pain, only torture and insults at every step. The man whom I am going to marry has promised to keep me happy and give me respect. I don't need much. I just need a small home where I can live respectfully.

Q: I wish you all the best and I thank you for sharing your story with me.

A: Thank you for listening to me, *Adi*.

11: *Name*: Asma, aged 22

The interview lasted for an hour and twelve minutes and took place at a darulaman.

Asma was wearing a nose-pin, a pendant and small earrings, and she wore a few artificial rings on her fingers. Her dress was orange and grey. A band made of colourful threads was around her wrist. She looked neat and clean but very pale.

Q: *Assalam-o-alaikum.*

A: *Walaikum-assalam.*

Q: How are you doing?

A: I am OK, *Adi*, God's will be done.

Q: Let me make one thing clear: whatever information you give me will remain secure and will be used only for the purposes of my research.

A: But someone told me that you would write about honour killing.

Q: That's right. I shall write a book on honour killing. So can I record your interview?

A: You can, *Adi*, no problem.

Q: Can you tell me something about you; your name, age, community and parents?

A: My name is Asma and I am twenty-two. Our caste is Bhattar and we are from Sindh. I was eight when my father died; he worked as a woodcutter.

Q: Could you tell me about the family you grew up in, your childhood, siblings, school, favourite games and things like that?

A: I was the youngest child in my family. I was the eleventh. My five brothers and five sisters were older to me. When I was born, they were all married. I was brought up by my sisters-in-law. I was the most loved child in my family. My parents and my sisters-in-law were very kind to me. My brothers were very strict and from my childhood they stopped me from going outside to play. I had the opportunity to study until I was five but when my father died my brothers didn't let me carry on at school. Even so, I finished learning the Qur'an with a *molvi*[84] at a nearby mosque. I played at home with my sisters-in-law and others. I had no other friends around but it was still a nice childhood. Everyone loved me. Until my father died, everything was settled and organized but after he died, chaos spread in my family and nothing got settled after that.

Q: Tell me about your marriage; the mode of marriage and the process of getting married?

A: Seven years ago, I was married to my paternal cousin. The mode of my marriage was *watto-satto*. My brother married the exchanged girl, who was my cousin. My brother didn't want to get married to her as he was an educated person and she was not, but because my father said so and he feared my father, he agreed to the marriage and when I was hardly

---

[84] Islamic religious preacher.

seven my brother got married to her. He didn't like her and subjected her to mental torture, but even so she was very nice and kind to me. She always cared for me. When I grew up and turned fifteen, my mother gave me in marriage to the brother of my exchanged sister-in-law.

Q: What was life like after your marriage? How did you get on with your family, your husband, children and in-laws?

A: My uncle's family, who became my in-laws as well, were very unhappy because of the way my brother treated their daughter, so they started taking revenge on me. They said that since their daughter was not happy, why should they keep someone else's daughter happy. The first two years were very difficult. Nobody behaved nicely to me but since I was always humble by nature, I remained down-to-earth. After two years of my marriage, my husband realised that his sister was loved by everyone at our home except for my brother, and then he changed his behaviour and so did my mother-in-law. After that, and the better behaviour of my in-laws, my life became bearable. My in-laws were quite poor and my husband worked as a labourer, but they were simple and gentle people. I knew that one day I would win their love so I didn't complain about them to my parents. This endeared me to them.

Q: Can you tell me the reason why are you here?

A: In five years of marriage, I couldn't conceive a child. I was quite desperate about it. My husband took me to various doctors but it was no use. My older brother had seven children and his wife was pregnant again, so she wanted an abortion. When I got to know that, I asked her not to have an abortion but to deliver the child and give it to me. She agreed. I was very happy in those days and waited for the time. When she had the child, she and my brother both flatly refused to give their child to me and said, 'Who gives their child to someone else?' That was a shock for me because while she had been pregnant they had both been prepared to give the child to me. So I stopped going to my mother's home for a year after this very frustrating time. After a year or so, my mother came to me and took me to her house. I didn't know that my brother had some grievances against me after he had refused to give me his child. After about three months, there was a neighbour's marriage party in our village. My husband had bought a lovely pair of gold earrings for me and I went to my mother's house to go to the wedding. I wore the lovely pair of gold earrings which my husband had bought for me and I went to the marriage party in my mother's neighbourhood. When I left the wedding, I gave the earrings to my mother who put them in her box and we went to sleep. Around three o'clock in the morning, my brother started shouting that he had seen a man in the house. We all woke up and switched on the lights, but couldn't see anything except the broken latches of my mother's box and we found that my earrings had been stolen. Soon afterwards, the secret was revealed when the goldsmith to whom my brother had sold my earrings told my husband about it on condition that his name remained a secret. I was very upset and I went to my mother but she asked me to stay silent and not to fight with my brothers, but I argued with my brothers. That night, after the quarrel, I slept at my mother's house. In the middle of the night, my brother arrived holding a torch and shouted that he had seen a man coming out of the room where I was asleep with my sister and her two young children. He called me a *kari* and said that the man had come for me. I didn't know that my brother could go to that extreme. I simply denied his allegation but before dawn, my five brothers had all called me a *kari*.

Q: When you found that your brother had stolen your jewellery, did you go straight to him to ask him about it?

A: No, when I realised that my own brother had done this to me, I was very upset and so I didn't go to them for another three months. I kept crying. My husband was loving and tried to persuade me to forget about the jewellery but I couldn't. After three months, I decided to tell my mother and brother that I knew what had happened to my jewellery and to ask them either to give it back to me or pay me what it was worth; I went to my mother's house and I argued with my brothers and the others. My mother then insisted that I shouldn't blow the issue up because she knew that nothing positive would come out of the quarrel. But because of these heated arguments, I got sick, so the next day, my mother took me to the doctor as I was not feeling well. The doctor told me that I was pregnant. I was really excited and I shared the incredible news with my husband over my mobile. He was overjoyed and insisted that I should let him come over so that he could take me back to our own house. As it was getting dark, I told him that I would go home the next day with my mother. That night, one of my sisters was also at our mother's home as she had come to visit me. After hearing such big news from the doctor, I decided to bury the issue of my lost jewellery and I slept. During that night, I felt torchlight on my face. I woke up screaming and saw my brother, the one who stole my jewellery, standing near my bed holding a torch. I asked him what he was doing there at that time but he didn't reply, he just left. I went back to sleep. After, let's say, half an hour, my mother came in and called to me. I woke up and asked what the matter was. She said that my brother had sent her to see whether I was asleep there or not. I got angry and asked why were they upsetting me and disturbing my sleep. At that, my mother went back and I tried to go back to sleep but after a little while my brother again entered in my room, where my older sister and her two children were also asleep. Soon my mother followed my brother. He switched on the light, opened the door of bathroom, checked inside and looked under the beds where we were sleeping, and then he went out and shouted outside the room that there was a man in the house who had come for me. My mother asked me and I told her that I simply had no clue about his accusation. I recalled that my brother had only come into the room, shone his torch on my face and then had sent my mother in, nothing else. It hardly took a few hours and before dawn came I was a *kari*. My sisters and mother couldn't do anything for me. My brother got everyone awake and was angrily shouting that I was a *kari* as he had seen someone coming out of my room. He called my husband on his mobile and told him that his wife was a *kari*. My mother, sisters and sisters-in-law were crying and denying the allegation, but all my brothers ganged up and called me a *kari*. My husband talked to them logically and said if that was the case, I would have been killed on the spot, and that the previous night I had told him that I was expecting, so how could I do anything like this. However, in the morning, my brothers went to the *wadera* of the village and asked him to intervene. When my husband got there, the *wadera* called him and ordered him to divorce me as I was a *kari*. My husband denied the charges so my brothers beat him brutally and told him to divorce me. The man who was accused of being a *karo* with me was also our relative. His father and two brothers were beaten cruelly and their three buffalos were shot dead. The boy himself ran away in time. The reality, in fact, is that my brothers owed their business partner 20,000 rupees. A few days before they had accused me, this business partner had told them to pay back the loan. During an argument, they went wild and hit each other. My brothers wanted to teach him a lesson. Since they already had grievances with me, they felt it was a good opportunity to accuse me of being a *kari* with their business partner. We all understood the matter but were helpless because my five brothers were very forceful and the *wadera* was also on their side. My husband came to take me home but my brothers locked me in a room and told him either to kill me or divorce me. He cried a lot and begged my brothers but they didn't listen to him and sent him back. The same night, my husband brought his mother to my brothers' house. My mother-in-law was also weeping and crying and swore on the Qur'an that I was not a *kari* and that it was a false accusation, but my brothers didn't listen to anyone. My husband asked my brothers why they hadn't killed me and why they wanted him to kill me. He asked for proof of my being a *kari* but they had no proof. My husband said 'I would not let anyone kill my wife, neither would I kill her'. The *wadera* put pressure on him and forced him to sign the divorce papers. Within two hours, my brothers, with the help of the *wadera*, had coerced my husband and made him sign the divorce papers. When we heard about this, my sisters advised me to leave the house at once otherwise the men would kill me. My mother took me to the house of a woman who was a social activist and a member of a political party. She already knew about my situation but she told us that the police in that area would not listen to her because of the involvement of the influential *wadera* in the matter. She kept me locked in her room and stood strong before the *wadera* and my brothers and did not hand me over to them. Eventually she managed to call a police mobile unit which took me to the police station.

Q: How did you escape?

A: My mother very sensibly took me to the social worker's house. As soon we had got to her for safety, my brothers also got there with the *wadera* and insisted that she hand me over to them. The brave woman flatly refused to do so and locked my mother and me in her room and asked the *wadera* not to commit an injustice. The *wadera* told her that I had been declared *kari* by my brothers, that my husband had divorced me and that no-one had the right to keep a *kari*. In that locked room, I was able to hear the exchange of arguments from both sides, and when I realised that the political worker was becoming weaker before the six men, I told myself that no-one could save my life. That was the exact time the police mobile arrived. The *wadera* talked to the police as well but the police officer said that the matter had reached higher authorities so they were helpless. First, the police sent my brothers and the *wadera* away, then I opened the door-latch from inside and went with the police in the police vehicle. Before long, the *wadera* reached the police station but the police officer refused to hand me over to him. Then my brothers-in-law came to the police station and told me that my husband had been compelled by my brothers and the *wadera* to sign the divorce papers and that was why he had signed. Anyway, the activist woman helped me. She arranged a lawyer for me who appealed to the court on my behalf and then I was sent to this *darulama*. When my mother got back home, my brothers locked the door of the house from the inside and didn't let her in. She spent the night at my sister's home, as it wasn't far from her house. But that continuous pressure and fear made her very fragile. She was under so much pressure and pain that in the same night she had a heart attack and by the morning she was dead. When my sister called my brothers, they refused to take my mother's dead body and said that they had no relationship with her.

Q: Why do they want to kill you?

A: You know any woman can be called *kari* if her husband, father or brother is in debt. We have no redress; our lives are at the mercy of this structure controlled by these men. In my case, my brothers forced my husband to divorce me, accused me of being a *kari* and accused an innocent man of being a *karo* because the boy was their business partner and they owed him money. They wanted to sell me as a *kari* and get money. Then the *karo* would not dare to ask for his money back from them. You know, they got 500,000 rupees from the accused *karo* in a *faislo*. Now they have become popular and could become the leaders of the people around. Now everyone will be scared of them. They will be considered brave and honourable. The *wadera* has come to the shelter twice to visit me. He said that if I make a statement in his favour, he would help me to get married to the *karo*. I told him straight that I need to live with my husband and that I had no link with the *karo*. I said 'If you want to help me, send me to my husband as I can live only with my husband. If you give a written statement in the court that you will send me to my husband, I can go with you'. He refused to do that so I refused to go with him. The *wadera* terrorised my in-laws to the extent that nobody will visit to me in the shelter. When he was assured that I had no supporters and that I had virtually nothing, he brought two dresses for me to the shelter and said if I agreed to obey him, he would give them to me. When I refused, he took the dresses away with him. The *wadera* was trying to bribe me so that I would trust him and go with him so that he could sell me for money.

Q: Why was the *wadera* so interested in you particularly?

A: Not just in me. The *waderas* are interested in every *kari,* to sell them and get money. The *wadera* knows I'm beautiful and young; so he will keep selling me as many times as possible from one man to another by continually calling me a *kari*.

Q: Why do you think this has happened to you?

A: It has not happened to me only but it has been happening to many women in Sindh. The *wadera* knows that I'm saleable because I'm beautiful and young; he will keep selling me off from one man to another by calling me a *kari*. The *wadera* wants to sell women only for the profit he can get, not for any honour-related issues. He is interested in every woman who is accused of being a *kari*, so that he can sell her in order to get money.

Q: What do you think honour is?

A: The people who know and would sacrifice their lives to save their honour have died long ago. Now, in this world no-one is honourable. Fathers are selling their daughters to become rich. Brothers are accusing their sisters to pay off their debts. Husbands are accusing their wives to make way for second marriages and calling their enemies *karo* to take revenge. What type of honour is this? They have been using the name of honour to cover their crimes. Where is honour? Who is honourable now?

Q: How is life at this shelter?

A: Life is extremely difficult here. I left my home in the dress I am wearing now, with no money. My sisters brought me another dress and helped me with some money but they cannot afford to give me any more because they are also very poor. I work for other women; wash their clothes; look after their children; sew their clothes and they give me a bit of money for that. I have no other means to earn money. I have heard that the government provides some funds for women in the shelters but I haven't received any. I was pregnant when I came here. Because of the lack of proper food and medical facilities, my child died in my womb in the seventh month of my pregnancy. The administrators didn't call a doctor for me. I gave birth to a dead child. I don't know how I survived. Here in the shelter I have heard that the government sends some funds for *darulaman* dwellers, but I haven't had any money. My sisters are also very poor. They rarely come to visit me. Sometimes they give me just 200 rupees, sometimes 500. My brothers-in-law are very scared of my brothers, but even so, two of them came once and gave me some stuff to use here along with some money. They were weeping. They told me that my husband is in a very pathetic condition. You know my brothers have given a picture of my husband to the guards outside this shelter so that if he comes, they should inform them. My brothers-in-law told me about this. My brothers-in-law explained that my brothers have pressurised and threatened them with severe consequences if they contact me.

Q: How do you see your life after you have left the shelter?

A: My in-laws and my husband are ready to take me back but they are very scared of my brothers and the *wadera* of the village. The divorce papers are with my brothers. If I make a statement in favour of my husband and go to him, my brothers would kill him. They will never let my husband take me back. For that, they will kill him and me as well. I have registered a case against the *wadera* when the woman activist provided me with a lawyer. The lawyer asked me why I had made all those statements in the favour of *wadera* and against my husband. At that I was puzzled and I told him that from the time it all started, I have been making statements in favour of my husband and against the *wadera* and my brothers. At that, the lawyer told me that the *wadera* had given money to the statement-taker in the court and he had changed my statements and now my recorded statements show that I trust the *wadera* and have been requesting the court to hand me over to the *wadera* so that he can save my life from my brothers. People say that it is not advisable to live in these shelters for long periods, but I have nowhere else to go. If I go to my brothers, they will hand me to the *wadera* and I will be sold. If I go to my husband, my brothers will kill him too. It all seems dark for me.

Q: If you had a choice, what type of life you would like to live and with whom?

A: I would love to go and live with my husband but it seems impossible now. Please keep me in your prayers so that I can go back to my home and live in peace.

Q: My best wishes for your safety and your future. Thank you for sharing your life story with me.

A: Thank you, *Adi*.

12: *Name*: Ghazala, aged 27

The interview lasted for an hour and fifteen minutes and took place at a darulaman.

Ghazala was wearing a black embroidered *chader* over her brown dress, which covered her head and body. She was not wearing any jewellery but had a thread around her neck. She was looking very lonely and sad. She could not stop crying even for a moment.

Q: *Assalam-o-alaikum.*

A: *Walaikum-assalam.*

Q: How are you?

A: What can I tell you? I am crying over my destiny.

Q: Would you like to talk to me?

A: Yes, whoever wants to help me, I can talk to them.

Q: Let me tell you one thing, whatever information you give me will be used only for my research purposes and for any related publications.

A: OK. I'll tell you everything that has happened to me.

Q: Thank you. Would you mind if I record what you say?.

A: No, you can, if you want.

Q: Thank you. Can you tell me something about yourself; your name, age, community and your parents?

A: My name is Ghazala and I am twenty-seven. By caste we are Khuwaja. I am from Larkana. My father's name is Bakhshan and he is a small landowner. We had a good life and had never been very poor.

Q: Could you tell me about the family you grew up in, your childhood, siblings, school, favourite games and so on?

A: I'm not educated. In those days, who used to send their daughters to school? But I can recite the Qur'an that was taught to me by my father-in-law. My father had two wives. From these wives he had three daughters and five sons. My father was a very honourable and strict man. He had killed my older sister when she was only thirteen because she had sat with her cousin on the same bed. The cousin whom she had sat with was only twelve at the time. We could not play any games in our childhood because of the strict regime at home. Even my mother was not allowed to go to her parents or other relatives. I used to do housework ever since our childhood.

Q: Tell me about your marriage; the mode of the marriage and the process of getting married?

A: I was married to Ata. My husband worked as a labourer on daily wages. Sometimes he got work and sometimes not. The mode of our marriage was *watto-satto*; my brother married my husband's sister.

Q: What was life like after your marriage? How did you get on with your husband, children and in-laws?

A: My husband was a weak and feckless person. I had to look after and feed my children so I worked all the time. I would embroider clothes for other people and I made quilts to sell. I am a very hard-working woman. My mother in-law and my father-in-law died soon after my marriage. Then all the responsibility fell on my shoulders. I gave birth to four children. My husband didn't share in any of the responsibilities. I was always alone in all the troubles, whether it was a matter of food or medicine for the children. I lived a very difficult life with him. You know how everyone understands that what kind of man's home is there and then people pay due respect to the person. People around knew what type of person lived there. I asked my parents to give me a calf. I looked after her and she grew into a cow. One night when I was asleep with my husband in the same bed, I heard a noise. I asked my husband to check and we saw a man's shadow outside the room near my cow. My husband quickly took his rifle and fired at him. The bullet hit the man in his leg and he rushed out where three other people were waiting for him. My husband caught him but with the help of his companions he managed to run away. The police soon came as the police picket was near our home. People who lived around us woke up and the police arrested my husband. The man had broken into our house to burgle us, but when the police arrested my husband, he shouted that he was innocent and that the man had come in because of me. I cannot believe how all of a sudden, my husband began shouting that I was a *kari* and had tried to shoot me before the police arrested him. The neighbours kept quiet and didn't come forward to help me or to utter a single word in my favour. At that, the police suggested that I go to the police station with them otherwise my relatives would have killed me. I couldn't understand anything that was happening. I told my husband that I had been asleep with him and that my children were also sleeping near us. I had woken him up after hearing the noise from outside, but he didn't listen to me and had shouted at me that I was a *kari*. The police took me to the police station. The man who broke into our house with the intention of stealing from us was from quite a powerful family, so my husband was arrested. The police told me that my husband would kill me as soon as he was released because the man he had shot was only injured and not dead. In that case my life was at risk. The police only allowed me to take my two younger children with me. Both are girls. One is seven and the other is six. My ten-year-old son and eight-year-old daughter are at home. The police took me to court two days later and the court sent me to the *darulaman*.

Q: Why do you think your husband wants to kill you?

A: My husband hated me because he wanted to marry another woman. He never gave any money to me or my children. Because I am a righteous woman,[85] I didn't complain to anyone but I accepted his supremacy as God's will. I laboured and provided food for my children. I didn't give him any cause to kick me out. But, look at my destiny; a burglar broke into my house and gave my husband a golden opportunity to get rid of me by calling me a *kari* with a thief who I had never seen. God has listened to him now. He will kill me to prove that the man who broke into our house was a *karo* in order to get a girl from the *karo*'s family and get money for my dead body. Who will listen to me? No-one will believe me. Who believes a simple and innocent woman like me? A police officer who came to me along with the *wadera* of the village asked him to keep me as a *sam* but the *wadera* wouldn't take me. The policeman said that I was a decent woman but even then the *wadera* didn't take me with him to his *haveli* because I am an old woman. I am not young or beautiful. Nobody will buy me if the *wadera* tries to sell me so why would he take me? *Waderas* are interested in young girls so that they can sell them and get money. They only want young girls because nobody buys old women. So I will be killed. I have nowhere to live. Nobody will own me and I can't live here in this shelter either. How long can you live in these shelters? I know that no-one would believe a simple and innocent woman like me. But if I had had an opportunity, I would have strangled my husband. I hate the bastard. He is very mean. I hate the pimp.

Q: Why do you think this has happened to you?

---

[85] The Qur'an gives a detailed description of an ideal woman: 'Therefore, the righteous women are devotedly obedient, and guard in (the husband's) absence what Allah would have them guard (Qur'an, 4: 34). Muslim scholars (men) interpret the verses of the Qur'an so as to institutionalise the image of Muslim women. For instance, Imam Ghazali (1058: 111), one of the most renowned and widely read Muslim scholars, explains the behaviour of an ideal woman in the following words, 'One who remains in her private quarter and never neglects her spindle'.

A: My husband didn't like me from the start. He knew that I was an orphan and that my brothers wouldn't intervene no matter whatever happened to me, as they were under their wives' thumbs, so he always hated me. It was a forced marriage as my father-in-law and my father were friends and they decided on the marriage. My husband didn't want to marry me. After our marriage he didn't like me at all but I had no other place to go. He didn't give me money for our home and children but I was the daughter of respected parents so I didn't complain to anyone. I worked; I laboured and provided food for my children. I didn't give him any reason to get rid of me, but look at my destiny! My husband is the most shameful man. The poverty wouldn't have killed me; this accusation has killed me. Without any sin or mistake of mine, I have been called *kari*. Is there someone to listen to me or provide justice in my case? Now my brothers and my husband would kill me. My husband will get another wife in the *jirga* and money from the *karo*. Is this justice? My children will be ruined. How would a stepmother look after my children? Yesterday, a policeman came to see me here. He said that my husband has decided to take my children from this shelter and to kill me as *kari*. I cried in front of the policeman and said that this is injustice. My house and children have been affected. A thief entered my home and I am accused of being a *kari*. Where is the law? Is this the law? I said 'Give my husband the Qur'an and ask him to speak the truth'. The policeman said that he was helpless as my husband is determined that the man had come for me.

Q: Do you think that if the burgler had not broken into your house, your husband would not have threatened you with death as *kari*?

A: One thing is certain, that he wanted to get rid of me but he had no clue as to how he could throw me away because I wasn't giving him any reason to point a finger at me. Even so, I knew that he could do anything with me. Besides, is it necessary to have a *karo* to hand? Our dishonourable men can produce many *karos* at once. Any innocent man can be picked and killed or accused of being a *karo*. Creating *karos* has never been a problem in Sindh.

Q: How would you take up the issue if you were a man?

A: In this case, I would not even have any kind of doubt about my wife. When I was sleeping on the same bed as him, how could he accuse me? If I was out of the room or was found coming in from outside, my husband would have had a right to accuse me. The man didn't come for me, and I hadn't gone to him either, so what kind of accusation can be justified? He simply jumped at a chance to get rid of me. At first, he shouted 'Thief, thief', and ran after him and shot him. I was still in the room with my children. How can he accuse me?

Q: What do you think honour is?

A: I am an honourable person. I have lived with honour all my life with such a dishonourable man, the most dishonourable pimp who doesn't understand what honour actually is. Honour is to live honourably with your family and honour your wife. My husband is accusing me of being a *kari* because he has no honour for me or for himself either.

Q: How is life at this shelter?

A: There is no peace, no rest. I can't stop weeping even for a minute. I am burning up inside. I can't eat anything. What can I do, where can I go? The police let me take only my two younger girls aged six and seven. My ten-year-old son and eight-year-old daughter were crying for me but I couldn't take them. I don't know what has happened to them. I have no-one's mobile number to call and ask someone. Nobody has come to visit me. My husband has spread the news about me everywhere. I don't have parents and my brothers won't come to see me, as now I am a cause of insult. I had to leave my two children there. Who is preparing food for them? I don't have a single penny here. My two children and I have nothing to wear. I have nobody's number to call and ask for help. I want to contact my brothers to get them to come and listen to me at least before deciding my fate. What can I do? Will the earth rip open or the sky fall in? Where can I go?

Q: How do you see your life after you have left the shelter?

A: I can't see anything. With great difficulty, I made my home; I bought some small things to decorate my home. Now people might have ruined it. I have lost my home forever.

Q: If you had a choice, what type of life you would like to live and with whom?

A: At least with an honourable man who knows what honour is.

Q: Thank you for sharing your story with me. God bless you.

A: You listened to me and I hope people will listen to you.

13: *Name*: Tahira, aged 27

The interview lasted for an hour and fifteen minutes and it took place at a darulaman.

Tahira seemed very disturbed and depressed. She cried and wept for her daughters and showed her concern for their safety. She was of the opinion that it is impossible to improve Sindhi society.

Q: *Assalam-o-alaikum.*

A: *Walaikum-assalam.*

Q: How are you doing?

A: I am very depressed.

Q: Please know that whatever information you give me will remain secure and will be used only for the purposes of my research and for related publications.

A: OK.

Q: So you know that I will record your interview?

A: OK. Why record it?

Q: To write the interview down and analyse what you have said.

A: People will read it?

Q: Yes.

A: Tell people that we women in Sindh have been living in hell. Do something.

Q: I shall write down as much as I can. Can you tell me something about you – your name, age, community and parents?

A: My name is Tahira and I am twenty-seven. My caste is Khoro. I am from Larkana. My father's name is Punhal and he is a small landowner.

Q: Could you tell me about the family you grew up in, your childhood, brothers and sisters, school, favourite games and things like that?

A: I am not educated. We are six sisters and four brothers and we are all illiterate. We didn't play much as our house was very small and we had quite a few goats and cows so we normally looked after them and I helped my mother to dry the dung of the animals and to do other housework. We were serious children. While I and my mother worked inside the house, my brothers remained outside playing with their friends most of the time.

Q: Tell me about your marriage; the mode of marriage and the process of getting married.

A: My father indeed got me engaged to my paternal aunt's son. This cousin, my fiancé, then became involved with one of his other cousins and tried to marry her, so he refused to marry me and my engagement was broken off. My father was very angry and cut off all relations with his sister, the one whose son I was engaged to. After that, my father got me engaged to my maternal uncle's son. When I grew up, my father died. My maternal aunt had died as well. After the deaths of my father and my aunt, my older brother tried to reunite the broken relationship between the two families; ours and my aunt's whose son I was previously engaged to. After getting the relationship better, my brother broke my engagement with my maternal uncle's son because he wanted to get married to the daughter of my paternal aunt, the family where I was engaged first. So he made me engaged again to the same cousin who had refused to marry me when my father was alive. I was really unhappy as my cousin was too old for me and he had already refused me once. I am now twenty-seven but he is fifty. My brother did it by force. The mode of the marriage was *watto-satto*. I wanted to marry my maternal uncle's son who I had got engaged to by my father. My mother cried a lot but what could the poor woman do before her son forced me to get married?

Q: What was life like after your marriage? How did you get on with your husband, children and in-laws?

A: I got constantly tortured there. After just one month of marriage, my husband beat me up. He was very short-tempered and on every small issue he used to create lots of mess. Every time, after beating me he would throw me out of his house. He said that he had not wanted to marry me, but was forced to marry me, and that he hated me. He threatened me with *talaque*.[86] Once, I went to my brother and told him what I was enduring. My brother didn't listen to anything but got angry at me and told me that I must be at fault and that's why my husband beat me. I thought that after having children, my husband would change his behaviour. I gave birth to two daughters but his attitude remained the same. He wanted to marry his cousin as she had not married because of him. I was caught between the two of them. Besides, my sister-in-law was a very argumentative woman. She was married but had no children. Her husband had disappeared after some mental illness and had never been found since then. She used to stir my husband up against me and he would get mad and beat me and threaten me with divorce. I was so scared that if he divorced me I would have nowhere to go. My sister's home was just opposite their house but he didn't let me go there and didn't let her come to see me.

Q: Can you let me know the reason why are you here?

A: Once, when my husband was not home, I went to my sister's house because her son was very ill and I wanted to see him. I just came back after half an hour. When my husband came back, my sister-in-law told him that I had visited my sister's home in his absence. He became extremely angry and started beating me. He shouted that I was a *kari* with my sister's husband, otherwise how would I go without my husband's permission. He shouted that he would kill me as *kari* and my brother-in-law as *karo*. In that fury, he repeated the word '*talaque*' over and over. I begged him not to *talaque* me as I had no place to go. I was afraid that my children would be ruined. Where would I take them? I became convinced that my husband would kill me any day, any time, so when he was out and his sister was having a bath, I left the house. I took shelter at my uncle's home, where I heard that my husband had stated in court that I had been abducted. So my uncle produced me before the court. I stated before the magistrate that I had not been abducted by anyone but that my husband wanted to kill me as a *kari* with my sister's husband, so I had escaped.

Q: How did you escape?

A: I was really scared, so I ran to my brother's home. He also became angry and said that they would not interfere in my affairs. When my brother refused to let me into his home, I had nowhere to go. So I went to an old friend's house. She wasn't at home but her mother gave me some money and I used an auto-rickshaw to reach to my maternal uncle's home.

---

[86] Divorce.

Seeing no other alternative, I went to the maternal uncle whose son I had been engaged to before this marriage. He rescued me, but the next day my husband registered a case against them for the abduction of his wife. My uncle then produced me before the court. In the court, I gave statement against my husband and made it obvious that I had not been abducted by my uncle but that my husband had divorced me and wanted to kill me as a *kari* with my sister's husband. The man he accused and I are absolutely innocent. The police then sent me here to this *darulaman*.

Q: Why does he want to kill you?

A: He was bored with me. He still wanted to get married to the woman he loved and wanted to get rid of me. He would do anything to clear his way. I told him that I hadn't asked him to marry me. It was all decided by my brothers and him; nobody had asked me about my marriage, but he didn't listen to me.

Q: Why do you think this has happened to you?

A: Girls are not asked about their choices in our families. If a girl opens her mouth to let someone know about her own choice, her relatives get up to kill her. Many killings on such issues have happened in my family before. Parents and brothers don't want girls to think about their own marriages. Even if a rumour spreads that a girl wants to marry someone of her own choice, they just kill her, and even if she survives she remains the target of constant abuse from both her in-laws and her parents. This is what my sin was; I had just wanted to marry the cousin my father had engaged me to.

Q: How would you take up the issue if you were a man?

A: I wouldn't have married a woman who didn't want to marry me. I wouldn't have ruined her life. If the marriage was inevitable, then I would have respected her and my children. I wouldn't have beaten her up every day and threatened her with the worst consequences or kicked her out of my house. Even the Qur'an does not say anything about killing a woman for honour, so why do they make their own laws? It is not honour, it is selfishness and greed for money. *Karo-kari* is a curse in the name of honour.

Q: What do you think honour is?

A: I don't call it honour to make accusations of *kari* and *karo* about innocent men and women and kill them to get a second marriage and for the sake of money. This is not honour. Honour for parents is to look after the happiness of their girls too, and not just their boys. If they start thinking about their girls' choices, issues like this will be far fewer. Don't force girls to make them rebel; girls should be consulted about their marriages. That's what the Qur'an and Islam say. Men are our protectors and control women so that their women can remain pure. Men's responsibility is to keep an eagle eye on the sexual and moral conduct of their kinswomen, whether wife, mother, sister or daughter, to ensure that they behave well. Killing an adulterous woman is an act to please God and a man must perform it in order to fulfil his religious duty. The men have the right to beat and kill if a woman violates the code of honour, but they have no right to kill or threaten to kill an innocent woman. You don't know what is going on in Sindh in the name of honour. You sell your wives, daughters, sisters and mother a number of times, collect millions from their buyers and call yourself honourable? This is not honour. OK, if you see a woman of your family with your own eyes commit adultery, don't leave her alive for a moment; kill her instantly with the man to please God, but conspiring against women and accusing them of being *karis* and then finding innocent men to accuse as *karo* should not be called honour.

Q: How is life at this shelter?

A: It is very painful. It's my third day here but I miss my children and need to see them as soon as possible. I don't know what they will do to my children. As my husband has accused me of being a *kari*, they must be calling my daughters 'the daughters of a *kari*'. I miss them and want to get out of here as soon as possible. I would have taken my children with me had I had enough money to pay their fare.

Q: How do you see your life after you have left the shelter?

A: I shall go with my maternal uncle and marry his son, who was my real fiancé, as he is still unmarried. But before leaving the shelter it is essential for me to get my children back from my husband. He has given me a divorce but people like this twist and turn in front of other people, so I want a divorce paper from the court. Then I will leave this shelter.

Q: If you had a choice, what type of life you would like to live and with whom?

A: I would have married my maternal uncle's son. My father got me engaged to him and he is the same age as me. I want to live in peace with him and get rid of my husband.

Q: Thank you for talking to me about this issue.

A: You are welcome. But please, you educated people should tell the government to change the system and the law as whoever wants to get rid of his wife accuses her of being a *kari* with an innocent man and then gets a huge sum from various corners. When will the system be changed and we can also be considered human beings?

Q: I will try my best to let as many people as I can hear your voice and to let your words be read.

A: Thank you.

Conclusion

You have gone through twenty-six accounts of men and women whose lives have been affected by honour killings, without any interference from any researcher or analyst as I believe that readers must be the real judges; you know best how to analyse the individual stories and the verdicts which are made. I have tried my level best to translate the interviews as accurately as possible and to retain the actual definitions of the typical vernacular words used by real people in their own cultural context. Because of the nature of the subject, there is bound to be a sameness in the stories which have been told, but if there is a sameness in the way that the stories are related which is a consequence of my translations, I apologise for it. Some of the interviews are longer than others but the time spans seem similar. The reason for this is that some interviewees spoke quickly, some slowly; some took time to control their emotions. Those who sobbed and wept during the interview spoke less but took more time. The moments of crying and sobbing are not recorded in the interviews, but pauses during the conversations are shown by three dots. In these accounts, you come face to face with tribal enmities, personal interests, greed and financial gain, the results of illiteracy and unemployment, ignorance, gender inequality, the strength of tribal and cultural traditions, the complexity of the concept of honour, the scarcity of the basic necessities of life, the criminal negligence of the state and the corruption endemic in the law-enforcement agencies, the role of powerful tribal leaders, the unavailability of any justice system, the dearth of a welfare system, the communal solidarity with the killers, the compulsion to kill for the sake of honour and the acceptance of its consequences, the strong hold of the unlawful justice system, and the strong chain of an inexorable system in which a single man's or a family's reaction is not only valueless but also punishable. These interviews were recorded and preserved. Listening to them, reading them is not easy. All the names, villages and other identifiable elements have been given pseudonyms and although cities, tribes and castes have been named, they give no clues to enable any individuals to be traced.

Initially, I had planned not to write anything as a conclusion but to let you scrutinize, explore and dissect the accounts for yourself in order to understand the phenomenon of honour killing in this particular region, but then I thought it unfair not to discuss some of my own thoughts with you: I sat with these people, looked them in the eye, watched them, waited while they formed their responses, and my reactions are naturally part of the context in which these accounts were gathered. In my book *Honour Killing in the Second Decade of the Twenty-first Century*, as a researcher I analysed the accounts of my interviewees in some detail and discussed the menace of honour killing with the help of previous research on this complex and emotive subject. In this current book, even though you now have more power than me to evaluate the subject which you have read about, I would nevertheless like to share my views and how I see the whole situation – but with no intention of imposing any of my findings and conclusions on your own personal discoveries and assessments.

As in other Islamic societies and also in Sindh at large, honour killing is considered an honourable deed. Honour killing, in a strict historic sense, is an act of extreme violence in which, if a kinswoman is found guilty of a pre- or extra-marital relationship, men's honour is challenged and they immediately kill the adulteress or the couple. The classic notion and a common perception of honour killing, that when a man sees a female relative in a compromising situation with someone, he considers it a threat to his honour and therefore reacts spontaneously in a violent way, has acquired great value in terms of endorsing man's superiority. The concept is effective in maintaining a feudal, tribal and male-dominated patriarchal society. Thus Hanmer (1996: 15) rightly pointed out that "the strength of the cultural boundaries for women raises the issue of what are the boundaries for men". Some advanced countries which have strived hard to formulate their laws on the basis of gender equality have set the boundaries for every citizen irrespective of their gender. But in those countries which are still governed by primitive laws and traditions, the solution to this question is still hidden in a heap of research papers.

All the participants in my study, irrespective of their gender, grew up in a narrow sphere with strict tribal norms. Whether it is a matter of home, food, relationship with parents or siblings, childhood happiness or sorrows, games, education, marriages and moral values, poverty and violence are deeply embedded in their lives. The consequences of poverty may vary in scale but its negative effects are clearly visible in the accounts related by my participants, whatever their gender or status. Having very few options other than to live in the prevailing unjust agricultural society, the interviewees lived in mud-houses which lacked the basic necessities of life, with no sanitary system. Safiruddin (2005: 29-30) explained how these homes are built and what materials are used:

Mud, rice straw and wooden logs constitute the main materials for the constructions of the mud house. Mud and rice straw are locally available in abundance, and the wooden logs are collected from nearby forests. First, a wooden frame is prepared for the construction of walls. Wooden logs are fixed 4 feet apart to a depth of 3-4 feet. The height of the logs is about 10 feet above the ground level. Wooden frames are erected at the four corners of the rooms; logs serving as pillars are fastened to horizontal logs up to roof height. The wall frame so formed is thick. It is then filled with a mixture of mud and rice straw, leaving spaces for provision of doors, windows and ventilators. The roof of a mud house is normally flat.

While I was interviewing my participants, identification on the personal level appeared to be a very insignificant matter. Poverty interconnects numerous issues and increases troubles in multiple directions. The persistent state of the scarcity and lack of education increased moral and ethical corruption, crime rates, drug addiction and violence, and all of this makes people's simple survival even harder.

My interviewees' accounts provide substantial and often shocking evidence that violence is endemic within and outside the domestic boundaries. Because they have very little access to the outside world, the inhabitants of this region consider their traditional tribal culture to be the only honourable way of living. In fact, the whole system in upper Sindh functions through violence. The agrarian, economic and tribal social structures have established a strong gendered division which strengthens discrimination by maintaining separate spheres for women and men; thus, boys and girls are treated differently from their earliest childhood onwards.

The occurrence of violence in everyday life in this strongly patriarchal culture makes women completely powerless and isolated; women's suffering begins in their childhood and when they leave their natal families, frequently when they are still in their teens, it continues within and after marriage. Whether their marriage is an exchange, bride-wealth or a form of consanguineous arrangement, violence is always the main component. In the name of marriage, women are sold, exchanged and coerced, and they face physical and mental violence from their in-laws and their husbands. The responsibility of saving the honour of a family or clan is not restricted only to husbands; any men of a family can kill a disloyal kinswoman, becoming a saviour of the family's honour. Each man of a family has a right to save the honour of the family by killing any kinsman's wife. As a mutual duty, it is considered a praiseworthy deed. The strategy helps the men to maintain control over each other's women.

Omar, at the age of sixteen, killed his male cousin on the spot when he saw him in a compromising position with his sister-in-law. Overall, people – both men and women – in such a traditional society are confined to a narrow domain where they do not know what their rights are, or how to emerge from their socially and tribally constructed restrictions.

When it comes to the tribal traditional justice in cases of honour killing, gender inequality seems to be the most significant factor. For an act in which the involved man and woman should be held equally responsible, they can receive very different treatment. The family of the *karo* man tries its best to save his life whereas the family of the *kari* woman leaves no stone unturned to kill her. A man's family tries to save him by any means and if he is murdered as a *karo*, his family launches an against his murderer because in this male-preference culture, men are precious but women have no respect or value. A common perception of the *karis* is that it is not murder but more like cutting off a malign finger. Najam (2011) commented that "Nobody mourns for them or honours their memory by performing their relevant rights. *Karos* by contrast are reportedly buried in the communal graveyard".

Various tribes have various methods of dealing with the *karis* who, for one reason or another, cannot be killed on the spot but somehow manage either to get back to their natal families or to take shelter. Women who declared *karis* are thrown away without mercy; the state, their immediate surroundings and the traditions which rule the society deal violently with women who have been deprived of economic, social and cultural rights. Economic dependence and inadequate welfare provision force women to endure inhumane torture and often they have no shelter to provide rescue. A few tribes in upper Sindh, such as the Mehars, do not physically kill women accused of being a *kari*, instead they banish them, marrying them off into faraway tribes. Their original community must never see a banished woman again and she must never visit her family. In a world where individual identity is closely linked to being part of a community, such banishment can be experienced as an extremely harsh punishment. "You know why people marry *karis*? To have slaves for ever. But a master remains scared that his slave might run away, so they treat them brutally" (Sajida). In some areas, such women are sold. 'A diseased finger should be amputated', says a proverb in Lal Garh of Dera Ghazi Khan. It is a common practice that a sold woman is abandoned by her family.

If a *karo* (whether or not he is actually guilty of what he is accused of) manages to escape, then the men of the family who declared him a *karo* live in great anxiety and feel humiliated until the *karo* is killed. Atif said: "People got to know that we have killed one of our female children but it was insulting for us that we only killed a woman of our family and not the person involved in this disgrace. Even so, the killing conveyed a message to the boy's family about how far we will go to maintain our honour and they have understood what we will do to their son".

You will have realised through their accounts the power of the word 'honour', and that if a man accuses someone, irrespective of their gender, he gets a licence to kill. And the accused person, especially if she is a woman, virtually has no escape, and from that very moment that she is convicted without any trial. Shah (1998) stated that in Northern Sindh, "women live in terror that any man of their family can kill a man outside it because of rage, enmity or over some dispute, simply by declaring any woman of the family as *kari* with the killed man, and consequently kill her too".[87] Shah (1998) explained that women are caught unaware most of the time as they are going about their daily routines. She named a few women who were killed unaware of their crime: Khursheed, a Langah woman from Khairpur, was killed while she was asleep, so were Farida and her young daughter Maujan; Hasina's sister was killed when her hands were full of a load of fodder; Janat's aunt was killed while she was kneading dough, eighteen-year-old Waziran was watching a play on television. Thirteen-year-old Sarah was asked to make tea for her brother who drank it, took a gun, killed two boys outside and came back to kill his sister while she was chaffing wheat (Shah, *Dawn*, 19-25 November 1998).

In the shelters, the women who had been threatened with death were usually waiting for some expected or unexpected decision to be made by the court. Because of the inadequate welfare provisions, women who were seeking and obtaining redress for the abuse and torture that they had suffered faced insurmountable obstacles and deprivation. The shortage of everyday amenities, electricity failures, the non-existence of any form of entertainment, liberty or freedom, the lack of health facilities and financial assistance all added immense difficulties to the lives of women who were already depressed and tense. It is a legal requirement that a woman cannot leave a shelter without a man *wali*, either from her birth family or from her in-laws, so the women have to accept one of two equally painful situations.

---

[87] My translation.

The distressed women concluded that the whole system, from family politics and financial depravity to the principles and punishments of honour, is nothing but a scheme for keeping women underprivileged and slaves. Radford (1992: 6) suggested that "the patriarchal oppression, like other forms of oppressions, may manifest itself in legal and economic discrimination, but like all oppressive structures, it is rooted in violence". The women were convinced that men are the guardians of their kinswomen's virginity, fidelity and chastity. They considered it to be men's responsibility to keep an eagle eye on the sexual conduct of their kinswomen, whether wife, mother, sister or daughter, and in particular to ensure that they do not engage in extra-marital relations. The female participants accepted men's right to kill on grounds of infidelity; what they objected to was being falsely accused. In addition, they could not understand how men's extreme rage over a perceived violation of honour can subside once money is taken from the person who had violated their honour. The cries, tears, pain and helplessness of these women made me realise my own limitations as well. I could only use words to console them but there was nothing practical that I could do for them. Each one of the women had a fear of being killed or sold, and while I am writing these lines, I am still wondering what fate these broken women met.

The women knew that after an accusation, they had to live out their lives suffering from social stigma and facing hatred from all sides. In fact, even a minor action by a woman, such as going out alone or visiting her natal family without the consent of her husband, especially if the husband or in-laws are not on good terms with her natal family, can bring such a terrible accusation, as happened in the case of Tahira who told me about the way she had been called a *kari*.

The pressure and restrictions imposed by husbands on their wives not to meet their parental families represent an attempt to keep the women in further isolation so that whatever the circumstances, the women should not be able to gather sympathisers from any corner. If the wives continue visiting their parents or siblings, the husbands not only physically abuse them and threaten them with divorce but can also go to appalling extremes. For example, Najma had gone with her sister to see their sick mother. On the way back, she came alone because her sister had gone to her own house. As soon as she entered the house, she saw her husband, father-in-law, mother-in-law and sister-in-law waiting for her. Her husband held her hands and her father-in-law struck her with a knife. Because of the suddenness of the attack, Najma was unable to explain anything. Domestically, honour-related violence is mostly against women and in many cases the women of the family also side with the men. According to a report published by the Asian Human Rights Commission (2009), male relatives are usually authorized by their families and the community to take any action if a female is deemed to have compromised the family reputation. In fact, other women tend to join with men to foster the traditional values of honour and show their uprightness in regards to the cultural norms. For example, when I asked Sajid whether he had confirmed the allegation presented to him, he said: "When my mother-in-law told me about her, my wife was sitting on my right-hand side on a *charpaee.* She could have said to her mother, 'No that's a lie!' Instead she remained silent and when I looked into her eyes she could not face me, which strengthened my mother-in-law's claim". Khan gave two potential explanations for that: "The mothers may live in fear of family men or they may have been socialized in a repressive manner and have internalised the notion of family honour, thereby accepting the existing traditions and customs which control the young females of the family" (Khan, 2006: 51).

In addition, in the tribal culture, a married woman is supposedly protected whereas an unmarried woman is vulnerable. The women believe that only men can provide them with financial and social security. Despite the fact that the basis of their turmoil is connected with the institution of marriage, marriage nevertheless still seems to be the only way for them to live a safe and prosperous life. In other words, they see protectors in predators.

However, the divergent accounts of some of my interviewees tell stories about pre-planned murders in the name of honour. My main concern is whether killings on the pretext of honour really are honour killing or whether some other motives lie hidden behind them. The women who were in the shelters clearly said that they respected men's emotions in regard to honour, but that what they objected to was the use of honour as a pretext to accuse women of being *karis* in order to satisfy their malign interests. Najma, like a number of the other accused women, did not even know who she was accused of being a *kari* with.

To understand men's violent attitude in relation to anger, Campbell (1964) argued that, for men, aggression is usually instrumental. They use aggression as a method of exerting control over other people when they feel the need to reclaim power and self-esteem. The violent behaviour of men in this tribal society is a prized attribute. In addition to their domestic violent behaviour, sexual violence also carried minimal importance. For example, to the prison inmates forced rape was not an arguable issue. Men have absolute rights over women's bodies once they have a signed piece of paper called a *nikah*. Bruises and scratches on the faces of married women were not uncommon.

A study of sexual violence in the districts of Johannesburg, South Africa (2000) revealed that "the women, especially those who are living in poverty, tolerated sexual violence and discrimination to a surprising degree".

Jackson (1977: 37) made a very insightful general observation about sexual behaviour which seems very true when applied to the sexual or honour-related behaviour common in upper Sindh. She wrote: "Sexual behaviour is social behaviour: though it may appear to be a private matter, something uniquely personal, each sexual relationship is structured by the cultural values of the society in which it takes place". Since writing about and discussing sex or sexual behaviour is a strong taboo in Pakistani society, researchers are reluctant to carry out research into marital or sexual relations in these tribal-oriented cultures. If this were not the case, analysing honour killing through psychosexual behaviour could lead to opening another dimension of this extreme violence.

Women have been suffering through violence for generations, but the women whom I interviewed were not as submissive, timid or meek as the previous literature affirms. They were asking me questions about their rights. They raised questions about the unfairness of their gender-biased society. They denied the common belief that nature or God want men to wreak injustice on them. I could clearly see rage in their eyes. They were shouting, sobbing and weeping.

Killings on the pretext of honour are a sign of bravery and high morality in upper Sindh. When Arshad told me the story of the cold-blooded murder of two young people, I could not stop myself from asking, "Didn't the girl try to scream?" "Not at all", he replied (how confident he was!), "She was too terrified. She just uttered a sentence, 'He held me forcibly', which was of course a lie". A report by Amnesty International (2001) stated that "Women are more likely to be accused of moral crimes than men". A deeply ingrained thought about the character of a woman is that she must be a liar. The centuries-old expression 'Frailty, thy name is woman!'[88] is still unchallenged in many parts of the East and the West. Such myths grant liberty to the perpetrators of violence, abuse, assaults and rapes and narrow the space for targeted women.

---

[88] A famous line from Shakespeare's tragedy, *Hamlet*, Act 1, Scene 2.

The social reaction and honour killing are two intermingled phenomena. The people of upper Sindh have learned the word 'honour' with a very strong meaning attached to it. A killer who kills in the name of honour has a clear conscious conviction that all sections of the society will support, even approve of, his act. Arshad told me that "Well, normally a killer is treated more honourably than an ordinary man. You know in this society, if not every other then at least every third person is a killer, so now it is a kind of race. One thing is for sure, people try to avoid conflicts with a killer because they know that the man who has already killed one or two might kill the third and the fourth as well, so for a killer, dealing with other people becomes comparatively easier". Hanif, who killed his wife and her friend at the spot, said:

> It is obvious that a woman after marriage becomes honour for the man and this is dishonoured if she does something other than with her own husband. This damages a man's honour. Honour is passion. It cannot be controlled easily and it cannot be controlled after seeing something like what I saw. Now I feel honourable. I have done an honourable deed. I walk around honourably not cowardly. People respect me. If I had not killed them I would have never been able to live with honour. You know the cruel world and its system. The insulting remarks kill people from within and they do not remain normal. A person who cannot defend his honour is called a pimp and a coward in this society. To avoid a shameful life it is essential to save your honour. Now the blessings of God are on me that I am saved from comments like these. I am considered an honourable man by society. I feel refreshed. There is no such burden on my head. I believe that evil deeds invite disaster. So whoever does evil, they face the punishment. My act was in accordance with Islam and *sharia*. Islam does not permit anyone to do such shameful acts as I witnessed.

Sixteen-year-old Omar, who killed his cousin after seeing him with his sister-in-law, admitted the sympathetic attitude of everyone towards him, including the police in the jail. Omar said: "Her husband, my father and my uncle appreciated what I did. It was an honourable deed so I was appreciated. All around people appreciate me and call me an honourable person" (this reaction is not restricted just to the community: the police are part of the same social setup and they respect honour killers (Khan, 2006)); "in jail, even the policemen and other prisoners look on my act as an honourable deed". Anwar was in jail for killing his wife but denied the killing; he too was happy about the attitude of the police; he said, "The police were so respectful towards me that I felt proud of myself!" Anwar and Omar both appreciated the conduct of the police. The men and women who live in this area strongly believe that the concept of honour is strictly related to the conduct of the females of their family and that God has authorized them to be the caretakers of the actions and the behaviour of their women. Omar said: "A woman is given to a man in marriage by her parents so it becomes her responsibility to look after her husband's honour. When she violates it, then a man's honour is aroused and he kills her. Those who have honour and respect an honourable life kill, otherwise many dishonoured people see this and leave their wives alive. They do not kill because they do not have honour". Arshad too said that "Not to kill the person who is bringing shame or a stain to his honour makes a man the most dishonoured person in the world. You have to save your honour at any cost".

Zafar said: "Honour is a passion. It emerges when it sees that something is going wrong. If a person tries to tarnish your family's respect or values, then honour arises and you have to take revenge. If somebody touches or looks at our females with bad intentions, will honour not arise? Will honour not burn? Will honour not force men to react and kill those who challenge our honour? Why does a stranger or a man who does not belong to our family, our caste and has no blood relation or family link … try to disrespect our family?"

Atif said: "We call honour killing a *jihad*.[89] Those who have no energy, no power or are scared of the police or maybe others, they do not kill: only powerful, brave and honourable Baloch kill. Only strong people with a strong will, with strong faith in God and the day of judgement, kill". When I asked him what would happen to him if he were to repeat the same act, Atif's immediate reply was: "Do you think I will let honour down? I will repeat the same thing over and over again if it happens again, but now no-one would dare even to look at our family because they have learned the lesson and understand that honourable Baloch live there".

Usman said, "To save honour, an honourable man must cross all limits". Adnan said, "If I had not killed the man, our cruel society would not have let me survive. I would have been the target of insult and abuse". For these men, honour killing was a way of surviving. Shah (1998) explained that "A man's ability to protect honour is always judged. The trigger point of a man's passionate urge to kill could just be a comment that he might hear in the marketplace. This is called a *tano*, a Sindhi word for insinuation and insult mixed together. It renders a man 'socially impotent'. The *tano* would be very subtle but for any *mard* (man) it would be enough for him

---

[89] Fight in the name of God.

to declare war on the culprits". Arshad said, "Whatever tradition is persisting and comes down to us from our forefathers, it is our duty to maintain it. I can never think about or even imagine tarnishing my culture".

Chasing a man who has escaped death after being accused as a *karo* is also a strong tradition and it seems to become the mission especially of a family which has killed a woman in their family as a *kari*. Atif explained that "five or six years is a normal time for searching for a *karo*. We have not seen anyone who had been rescued after an allegation of *karo*. A *karo* or *kari* definitely have to be killed, no matter how much time passes. They cannot hide anywhere on earth from a true Baloch. The guilty one has to be found. That is a real obligation. A *karo* has to be killed, a *kari* has to be killed … No way out, no rescue. Today, tomorrow or the day after tomorrow, but they have to meet their punishment. The is no mercy for a *karo* and *kari*. But nobody else will kill a *karo* except a legitimate relative of the guilty girl".

The men had religious justifications for their killings in the name of honour. Omar said, "You know I did the act in accordance with Qur'anic teaching, so I was satisfied that I had performed my duty honourably". Religious commentators' interpretations of the particular Qur'anic verses and *Sunnah* to which he was referring are at times misogynist and favour the supremacy of men over women. Thus Mirza (2008) explained that, "Women in Islam are considered half human and in the Qur'an women have half the rights of men, sister has half the rights of brother and women are considered deficient in intelligence".

Through their justifications of honour killing, it appeared that various tribes have various levels or degrees of honour. The most honourable person in this society is one who kills on a petty suspicion, the moderate honourable man is one who takes a reasonable time to gather some evidence, sees some suspicious acts with his own eyes and then kills. The lowest level of honourable men is those who delay and think, and then kill. And the sign of a dishonourable person or a family is one who does not kill the honour-breaking woman. Sometimes, even a small gesture such as a smile or an indication by a woman that she has a soft feeling for some man can pose a threat to men's honour.

The question might be asked whether the meaning of honour will ever be redefined in a way which is not gender-biased as it is at present. Such a query might lead us to discover or might even create a balanced meaning of honour.

The stories related by the interviewees, therefore, certainly seems to confirm that under the guise of honour, a variety of ulterior motives are also being served, such as greed, jealousy between siblings and simple dislike of someone, but that the perceived preservation of honour can obscure these personal and frequently entirely dishonourable motives.

Welchman and Hossain (2005) argued that "the whole concept of honour is based on a tribal, pre-Islamic world view in which a woman is considered as a chattel with no mind or will of her own". In ancient times, if a woman was raped, honour killing was considered a merciful act to save her from dishonour, but if a female relative was found guilty of adultery, male family members were obligated to punish her otherwise they were themselves prosecuted. So men have to set boundaries and limit women's actions in order to keep their families' honour safe. The UN reached an agreement against gender discrimination which is known as the *Universal Declaration of Human Rights* (UDHR). It clearly lets people, without any gendered discrimination, do whatever they want to, within the framework of humanity and the law, and as long as no other person's human rights are infringed: "Everyone has the right to freedom of thought, conscience and religion; this right includes freedom to change his/her religion or belief, and freedom, either alone or in community with others and in public or private, to manifest his/her religion or belief in teaching, practice, worship and observance". Under this accord, it is the responsibility of every state to protect the rights of women and to enable them to be given rights equal to those of men. In other words, women are as honourable as men are. Killings in the name of honour must therefore be considered crimes not only against the individual but also against the state and humanity as a whole. Strong actions to introduce more comprehensive laws against honour killings are badly needed to end violence against women under the socially approved phenomenon of honour killing and to ensure that those who kill for so-called honour are given the punishments which they deserve.

Crimes are committed everywhere in the world, but states bring the criminals and offenders before the courts and get them punished. By this means, crime rates are decreased and social order is maintained. The reasons are not difficult to understand. But the common thing within the sphere of the different names for the same act is that in some jurisdictions, the act of murder with the association of 'honour', in fact, is not considered a criminal act but rather is patronized by power-grabbing authorities from the cultural and moral points of view. In the local markets of upper Sindh, even inexpensive plastic toys for children are not available, but the shops have many sharp axes[90] on display. Sharp axes and guns are readily available in shopping centres. These are districts where bookshops and libraries are seldom visited. Furthermore, the strict tribal system in northern Sindh is producing and nurturing dacoits (bandits), criminals, thieves and killers who contribute much to raising communal enmity.

The immense power given to men by the religious, legal, social, tribal, communal, and domestic systems in this strictly patriarchal culture make women an easy target for oppression. All the systems support men, whether it is domestic violence against women or the killing of women in the name of honour. Unfortunately, in Pakistan violence in the name of honour is not only acceptable, it is actually appreciated. Killers are treated like heroes and they are given extra importance by their society as a whole. The respect which the killers receive from the various social corners encourages others to follow the pattern.

The particular accounts recorded in this book are examples of how men have exploited this perverted understanding of honour and of the responsibilities expected from men to maintain the tribal concept of honour. The various emotions which I experienced during the interviews let me feel that I have somehow understood the viciously knitted web of honour killing and the mental capability of the killers within a larger social context. I felt that the discourse has to be widened and that instead of hatred and denying facts, things have to be judged realistically in order to discover the main flaws which have been giving such strong ground to this slaughter in the name of tradition.

The roles of the *wadera* and the tribal *sardar* are very notorious indeed. They consider themselves petty kings of their jurisdictions. The reality is that getting justice from Pakistani courts is very expensive. A lot of money is needed to hire a lawyer and wait for justice. In some cases, the waiting has become fatal when the other party involved settles the score in his

---

[90] The flag used by Sindhi nationalists (separatists) shows an *axe* in opposition to the most popular Muslim Sufi symbols of *Ajrak* and Sindhi *Topi*. It represents how the axe can be used in peace but that if someone tries to interfere with our rights, we will even shed our blood for our beloved Sindh, which is symbolised by the red colour of the flag.

tribal way and the disaster leads to more casualties. Poor people are therefore understandably reluctant to go to court. In the supreme courts of Pakistan, the *jirga* system of tribal customary justice has been declared unlawful and there is a restriction on conducting *faislo* in *jirgas*.[91] Nevertheless, many cases are still being decided by these *jirgas* under the supervision of the powerful *sardars* with the persistent tribal justice system. The affected parties, whether they agree or not, are bound to abide by the decisions made by the members of the *jirgas*. There are many stories of those who have rebelled against *jirga* decisions and have seen dire consequences. Examples of this make people too frightened to go against the tribal values.

Interestingly, a *faislo* cannot be arranged or carried out without a *sardar* if the affected family has no money. The *sardars* and *waderas* hold the power when they want to exercise their influence and authority. They feel themselves invincible. Only the rule of law can curb their powers. It is when the rule of law is dysfunctional that such a show of masculine power appears.

The interviews revealed how people look at the role of the *wadera* of their village. Sajid said:

> … after killing her [his wife], I became a little relaxed. I took the axe and I went out. It was nearly morning; villagers saw me, came near me and asked what had happened. Some of them tried to stop me going out in those [bloodstained] clothes. I had so much power in my body that I wanted to kill all who tried to stop me. Anyhow, the *wadera* arrived. He expressed his appreciation of me loudly before the people, took the axe from my hand and took me to his *otaq*.[92] But … I need to tell you that is a conspiracy by the *waderas*; by admiring the killers they want to be in the limelight and make the police feel that they are loyal to the police and that villagers are criminals. The *waderas* are still our enemies and rather they have become stronger and more cunning.

Omar said: "Now people are suggesting that we do *khair* with the boy's family so our elders have asked the area *sardar* and hopefully things will be settled by him. The case will be over soon. As it was a case of honour, I

---

[91] A two-member bench of the Supreme Court, headed by Chief Justice Iftikhar Muhammad Chaudhry, heard a petition filed by the National Commission on the Status of Women (NCSW). Chairperson Anis Haroon called the *jirga* system illegal, unlawful and against the canons of law, and she urged that it should be prohibited and stopped immediately (Khan & Khan, *The Express Tribune*, 17 March 2012).

[92] A drawing room for men only.

do not expect any big or long punishment. God will help us. We will succeed". Adnan, who had killed his male cousin, told me that he was arrested for the murder by the police because the murdered boys' parents were influential and rich. Then Adnan's father and other relatives went to the area *sardar* and requested a *faislo*. The *sardar* called the boy's relatives and told them that the murder was right as their son had been at fault: "He clearly told them that that the slain boy was at fault". So the *faislo* was in Adnan's favour; the dead boy's relatives withdrew the case and he was set free.

A *sardar* is usually contacted when someone needs to make a *faislo* with a slain man's family, but if only a woman is killed on a charge of honour killing then a *sardar* is not contacted. When I asked Atif (who had killed his cousin with the help of her male relatives) whether any *sardar* had contacted him in that matter, his immediate response was "No, why would a *sardar* contact us? As I told you, she was our child, we were responsible for her life and we killed her. Why would a *sardar* interfere in that?" Adnan's story was slightly different. He said:

> Actually, what I feel now is that it is a fault of our tribal system. If a little attention were given to these issues, the problems would not have been aggravated to this level. No-one makes any attempt to resolve the issue peacefully and it results in killing. I assume that if people start thinking about these issues in a gentle way or a humane way, there wouldn't be any cases of *karo-kari*. I don't think that killing should be the only option. In cities, if wives are involved with someone other than their husband, they get divorced, right? But in our tribal culture they kill because after killing the women, men are considered honourable. This is not justifiable.

Adnan's detailed account describes the ineffective state of the law-enforcing agencies. He shot his victim, as Usman did, in a busy market where people were watching him and some of them tried to stop him but did not succeed. The state's inaction in this way plays a vital role in the cumulative build-up of murders in the region.

The tragedy in Pakistan is that for the past many years, families belonged to the *wadera* (feudal) classes which have been ruling the country, and under that system, poor and oppressed people are deprived of their basic rights. The country's fundamentalist forces and the army generals protect this medieval feudal system and are therefore against those who speak out against oppression (Khan, *On line magazine*, 2 March 2011). Khan (2006: 284) wrote that "Violent customs and the code of the honour and the shame schema are implicitly and explicitly upheld by the economically determined social system, endorsed by religion, confirmed by law and facilitated by the state institutions".

The statistics show that the number of women being killed in the name of honour over the last four decades has risen with each passing day. With such an alarming rise in honour-killing cases in Pakistan, there are a number of questions that need to be explored. For example, why are the killers not being given the deserved punishments and what reasons and circumstances make killing the only source of restoring honour? (Mirza, 2008). It is difficult to deny that women in every Muslim country in general, and in every Islamic paradise (a country where Islamic *shariaat* is enforced) in particular, are severely subjugated, oppressed and considered less than second-class citizens.

My findings support the view that although anti-women practices such as *sati* and *jauhar* (motivating women to commit self-immolation for one purpose or another) were prevalent in the sub-continent for centuries, the first evidence of honour killing in Sindh is a law which was introduced during the British rule to curb killings in the name of honour (*see* Napier, 1851: 303) which testifies to the fact that honour killing was evident during the Baloch reign, that is, from 1783 to 1843. The strict implementation of the law eradicated this practice as it did *sati*. Almost a century after the law was passed, Pakistan came into being, but the tradition of honour killing had never even been heard of by most of the population. In fact, the tribal tradition revived itself with the implementation of the *Hudood* Ordinance (1979) and the *Qisas* and *Diyat* Ordinances in September 1990. Thus, for the last few decades, honour killing has been practised mostly amongst Baloch and Sindhi tribes in those districts of Sindh which are adjacent to Balochistan. This is long enough for the next generation to be convinced that it is a long-standing tradition which has been unchanged for centuries. Despite some serious attempts by some political parties to change the notorious laws and to make honour killing an unpardonable crime, no government has so far been successful. Sarwar (2004) added that

> Many lawyers and human rights activists believe that there is no need to define *karo-kari* murders separately, as the existing provisions of the PPC and the Criminal Procedure Code (CrPC) are sufficient, provided that such murders are registered as murder. In cases where guilt is established, through confession or trial, the perpetrator must be convicted at least on paper, even if there is a *razinama* (compromise), so that a criminal record is established.
>
> (*IRIN* Asia, 27 October 2004).

A survey conducted by the Thomson Reuters Foundation Trust (2011) placed Pakistan at number three on the list of the world's most dangerous countries for women. On 29 January 2010, President Asif Ali Zardari, who led the Pakistan People's Party government, signed the Protection against Harassment of Women in the Workplace Bill 2009, which the parliament adopted on 21 January 2010. On 19 December 2011, the Sindh Assembly unanimously adopted a resolution to treat *karo-kari* as a non-compoundable and unpardonable offence and demanded of the federal government that *karo-kari* cases should be handled under Section 302 of the Pakistan Penal Code as murder. It was further demanded that the cases must be lodged by the police and prosecuted by the courts. Chandio (2011) reported that the Pakistan Peoples' Party's senior minister, Pir Mazhar-ul-Haque, became the spokesman for nearly all human rights organizations' long-demanded mantra by saying: "Whosoever is a killer, he should be charged under Section 302 of the PPC and a murder should be treated as murder". The amended resolution, which was eventually passed, reads:

> This assembly resolved that the Sindh government approaches the federal government to treat murder committed in the name of honour *karo-kari* as culpable homicide and amounting to murder and the culprits be charged and prosecuted under Section 302 of the Pakistan Penal Code and it should not be made compoundable. (Chandio, *The Nation*, 21 December 2011)

The President also signed two additional bills in December 2012, criminalising the primitive practices of *wani*, *watto-satto* and marriage with the Holy Qur'an, which used women as tradable commodities for the settlement of disputes. In addition, the punishment for acid throwing was made stricter and was increased to life imprisonment, and the government further established a special task force in the interior Sindh region to take action against the practice of *karo-kari*, establishing helplines and offices in the districts of Sukkur, Jacobabad, Larkana and Khairpur. The Sindh Assembly passed a Domestic Violence (Prevention and Protection) Bill on 8 March 2013, but a report published in *Dawn* in the following year said that as many as 421 cases of violence (Bhagwandas, 2014) were reported against women in just three months (July-September) of 2014. According to the report, 76 women were murdered for different reasons, with the number of those killed under the pretext of honour being 57 (Kumar, 2015). Despite the rising number of reported killings, activists have praised the Sindh parliament for passing this bill, which is aimed at strengthening women's protection against abuse. However, human rights activists say that the government should do more to ensure that women subjected to violence, harassment and discrimination have effective access to justice. Perhaps, as Pakistan and its laws are fluctuating, shuffling and being interpreted in opposing ways between democratic government and dictators, it is difficult to see substantial progress being made regarding the implementation of appropriate amendments to the relevant laws in terms of eliminating honour killings. Even so, the present step taken by the Sindh Assembly is a long-awaited move in the right direction. It gives hope that the federal government will consider the change and listen to the voice of civil society to make the laws effective in protecting women from suppression and violence. Domestic violence in Pakistan is seldom recognized as a crime. Socially and officially it is viewed as a private, internal, family matter, which should not be interfered with. This is emphasized by the fact that Pakistani law is even more inadequate in protecting women victims of domestic violence and penalizing culprits. Not explicitly prohibited by any specific targeted or distinct set of laws, most acts of domestic violence are encompassed by the *Qisas* and *Diyat* Ordinance of 1990, a body of Islamic criminal law dealing with murder, attempted murder and the crime of causing bodily harm.

REFERENCES

Amnesty International (2001). *Broken Bodies, Shattered Minds: Torture and Ill-Treatment of Women.* Oxford: The Alden Press.

Asian Human Rights Commission (2009). 'Recent cases of 'honour killing' in Sindh Province, Pakistan'. Available at: www.humanrights.asia.3 (3) [Accessed 21 January 2015].

Bhagwandas (11 October 2014). 'Sindh records 421 cases of violence against women in three months', *Dawn*. Karachi. Available at: www.dawn.com/ - Pakistan. [Accessed 11 April 2013].

Campbell, J.K. (1964). Honour, Family and Patronage: a Study of Institutions and Moral Values in a Greek Mountain Community. London: Clarendon Press.

Chandio, R. (21 December 2011). *The Nation*, Pakistan. Available at: www.nation.com.pk. [Accessed 19 April 2013].

Hanmer, J. (1996). 'Women and violence: Commonalities and diversities'. In: *Violence and Gender Relations*. London: Sage.

Jackson, S. (1977). *The social context of rape: Sexual scripts and motivation.* Wrexham: Certrefle College.

Khan, A.H. (2011) 'Women in Sindh', *Islam Awareness.* Available at: http://www.islamawareness.net/Marriage/Quran/sindh.html. *[Accessed 12 January 2012].*

Khan, T.S. (2006). *Beyond Honour: a Historical Materialist Explanation of Honour Related Violence.* Karachi: Oxford University Press.

Kumar, M. (23 March 2015). 'No justice for Tahiras of Sindh', *Dawn*. Karachi. Available at: www.dawn.com/ - Pakistan. [Accessed 14 July 2015].

Mirza, S.K. (16 January 2008). 'Islam under scrutiny by ex-Muslim: 'Honor killing' is absolutely Islamic!' Available at: www.islam-watch.org/syedkamranmirza/honor_killing.htm. [Accessed 1 November 2013].

Najam, N. (2011). 'Honour killings in Pakistan'. Available at: www.islamawareness.net/HonourKilling/pakistan.html [Accessed 7 October 2013].

Napier, W.F.P. (1851). *History of General Sir Charles Napier's Administration of Scinde.* London: Chapman and Hall.

Pakistan; Integrated Regional Information Networks Pakistan: 'New 'honour killing' law does not go far enough', Human Rights Groups (27 October 2004). Available at: http://www.irinnews.org/report/26440/pakistan-new-honour-killing-law-does-not-go-far-enough-rights-groups. [Accessed 3 October 2013].

Radford, J. (1992). Introduction. In Radford, J. & Russell, D. (eds) *The Politics of Women Killing* (pp.3-12). New York, NY: Twayne Publishers.

Safiruddin, M. (2005). 'Folk houses in Sindh', PhD thesis, University of Karachi.

Shah, N. (19-25 November 1998). 'Honour killings: Code of dishonour', *The Weekly Review, Dawn.* Karachi. Available at: www.oocities.org/jeaysindh_org/articles/13.html. [Accessed 13 May 2012].

Shah, N. (1998). 'Faislo: The informal settlement system and crimes against women in Sindh'. In *Shaping Women's Lives: Laws, Practices and Strategies in Pakistan.* Lahore: Shirkat Gah.
www.wluml.org/node/1689. [Accessed 15 February 2012].

Thomson Reuters Foundation Trust (2011). 'The world's five most dangerous countries for women'. Available at: http://www.trust.org/documents/womensights/resources/2011WomenPollResults.pdf. [Accessed 2 September 2015].

United Nations Organization (1948). Universal Declaration of Human Rights (UDHR). Available at: www.un.org/en/documents/udhr/. [Accessed 28 March 2013].

Welchman, L. & Hossain, S. (2005). *Honour: Crimes, Paradigms and Violence against Women.* London and New York, NY: Zed Books.

APPENDIX A

INTERVIEW QUESTIONS FOR THE FEMALE INHABITANTS OF THE SHELTERS

All the questions were put to each interviewee but the way in which they were asked varied in order to meet the different emotions, levels of comprehension and reactions which were perceived.

Theme: How violence, honour and collusion are embedded in their lives (how they have been threatened with death in the name of honour).

Sub-topics: Tribal and parental background, life before marriage, life after marriage, perception and viewpoint about men, honour killing and pride, major flaws in life, reasons for being in the shelter house and vision for the future.

1: Can you tell me something about you (your name, age, community and parents)?
2: Could you tell me about the family you grew up in (your childhood, siblings, school, favourite games and so on)?
3: Tell me about your marriage?
4: What was the life like after your marriage? How did you get on with your family (husband, children and in-laws)?
5: Can you tell me the reason why are you here?
6: Why do they (why does he) want to kill/harm you?
7: How did you escape?
8: Why do you think this has happened to you?
9: How would you take up the issue if you were a man?
10: What do you think honour is?

11: How is life at this shelter?

12: How do you see your life after you have left the shelter?

13: If you had a choice, what type of life you would like to live and with whom?

APPENDIX B

INTERVIEW QUESTIONS FOR THE KILLERS WHO KILLED FOR HONOUR BY KILLING *KARI*, *KARO* OR BOTH

All the questions were put to each interviewee but the way in which they were asked varied in order to meet the different emotions, levels of comprehension and reactions which were perceived. The questions also might differ slightly for two further reasons; first, depending on who he had killed (mother, sister, wife, daughter or any other female relative), and second, whether he had killed both karo *and* kari *or just one of them.*

Theme: How violence, honour and collusion are embedded in their lives (how they have been killers/perpetrators).

Sub-topics: Tribal, parental, educational and professional background, family/married life, thoughts about women, honour and pride, concept of adultery and the killings justifications.

1: Tell me something about your background (your name, caste, community, parents).

2: Would you like to tell me some more about yourself (your childhood, siblings, favourite games, education, profession and so on)?

3: Can you tell me something about your married life (the mode of marriage, your wife, children, relations with in-laws and things like that)?

4: Why did you kill them/her? (maybe wife, mother, sister, daughter or someone else from family or from outside the family)

5: How did you feel after you had done it?

6: Who looked after or was supporting you and your family while you were in jail?

7: What was (is) it like being in jail?

8: Looking back on the killing, how do you feel about it now?

9: Why do you think did she what she did?

10: If your wife had seen you in the same position, how would have she reacted?

11: How do you think other people view your act (family, others in the community, people in general)?

12: What is your concept of 'honour'?

13: Imagine, you are in the past and the same situation has arisen, how would you react?

APPENDIX C

THE NAMES OF THE INTERVIWEES

(*all of these names and the names od the fathers, husbands and other relatives who they spoke about are pseudonyms*)

Female Participants; Darulaman A

Saba

Saira

Sajida

Irum

Amna

Female Participants; Darulaman B

Fareeha

Rabia

Najma

Rubina

Shaheen

Asma

Ghazala

Female Participant; Darulaman C

Tahira

Male Participants outside jail

Sajid

Hanif

Arshad

Zafar

Atif

Adnan

Usman

Male Participants in jail

Naeer

Omar

Saeed

Ata

Ayaz

Anwar

APPENDIX D

CHARACTERISTICS OF THE FEMALE PARTICIPANTS

No	Name	Age	Caste	Siblings	Area	Marital Status	Alleged by
1	Saba	25	Bur-ro	4	Jacobabad	Married	Husband
2	Saira	18	Aagani	3	Larkana	Married	Husband
3	Sajida	26	Mastoi	8	Larkana	Married	Husband
4	Irum	55	Janori	13	Khairpur Mirus	Married	Husband
5	Amna	30	Shar	13	Obaro	Married	Husband
6	Fareeha	48	Jaskani	8	KandhKot	Married	Husband
7	Rabia	18	Malik	6	Rohri	Married	Husband
8	Najma	21	Panhwar	13	Sadikabad	Married	Brothers
9	Rubina	20	Khaskli	11	Jacobabad	Married	Husband
10	Shaheen	23	Khaskli	7	Jacobabad	Married	Husband
11	Asma	22	Bhutter	7	Jacobabad	Married	Brother
12	Ghazala	27	Khuwaja	9	Larkana	Married	Husband
13	Tahira	27	Khoro	11	Larkana	Married	Husband

Appendix E

Characteristics of the Male Participants

No	Name	Age	Caste	Siblings	Area	Marital Status	Killed
1	Sajid	83	Aagani	5	Larkana	Married	Wife
2	Hanif	36	Baloch	7	Larkana	Married	Wife with a man
3	Arshad	37	Rind	7	Jacobabad	Married	Cousin with a man
4	Zafar	22	Rind	6	Jacobabad	Married	Cousin with a man
5	Atif	26	Baloch	11	Jacobabad	Married	Cousin
6	Adnan	38	Baloch	9	Jacobabad	Married	A boy
7	Usman	29	Lohar	7	Jacobabad	Married	Wife with a man
8	Naeer	65	Baloch	11	Jacobabad	Married	Wife with a man
9	Omar	16	Shaikh	9	Jacobabad		A man
10	Saeed	26	Mangi	3	Jacobabad	Married	Denies killing
11	Ata	22	Mugal	8	Chajro	Married	Denies killing

| 12 | Ayaz | 45 | Kori | 12 | Larkana | Married | Denies killing |
| 13 | Anwar | 34 | Korai | 13 | Ghotki | Married | Denies killing |

APPENDIX F

BIOGRAPHICAL SKETCHES OF THE FEMALE INTERVIEWEES

1: *Saba*

Saba (25) got married four years previously to Saeed Rasool and had no children. She was allegedly called a *kari* by her husband and was therefore sent to a *darulaman* by the court. She has not decided anything yet, but she needed to live in the *darulaman* until protection is provided by the court. She was a bold, talkative and determined woman who saw 'killing' as a 'routine' business in Sindh. She used the word 'friend', an unusual word to be used by a woman for a man.

2: *Saira*

Saira was eighteen. Her father had died before she was born. Her mother was sold (married to another tribe for money by her paternal grandparents). She had one sister and one brother. She left home with her cousin after her forced engagement to a man for money. She was contacted and taken back by the *wadera* of the village. Her grandparents married her by force three months previously. She was scared of being killed as *kari* so she had taken shelter of her own accord at the *darulaman*. She was determined to divorce her present husband and marry her cousin.

3: *Sajida*

Sajida (26) was the daughter of a small land-owner and had three sisters and four brothers. She was having a good life at her parents' home until her father became an addicted gambler. After selling his land and home, he sold his two oldest daughters for money, and later Sajida was also sold for 45,000 rupees to her paternal cousin. She was accused as a *kari* by her husband after five years of married life. She has no children. She went to one *darulaman* but subsequently moved to one in another city. She needed to live in the *darulaman* until she could obtain a divorce. She was looking for the protection from the court. She was a courageous and verbose woman.

4: *Irum*

Irum (55) was brought up as an orphan. She had seven sisters and five brothers. Her husband's name was Bux Janori and they had five children. She was alleged to be a *kari* by her husband and so had been sent to the *darulaman* by the court. She was unable to decide about anything except for getting a divorce from her husband. She had no lawyer to fight her case. She was worried about her protection if she were to leave the *darulaman*. She appeared very gloomy, upset and sick and needed to receive medical support.

5: *Amna*

Amna (30) was a daughter of a farmer. She had six sisters and six brothers. She was married by *watto-satto* in exchange for another girl who was given to her uncle in marriage. Her husband's name was Israr and she had four children who were all with her in the *darulaman*. Her brother and brother-in-law had killed a man and accused her of being a *kari* and therefore she had been sent to the *darulaman* by the court. She wanted to live with her husband and had requested protection from the court. She was determined to go with her husband and not with her father. She became offended and asked me if I could redefine the meaning of honour.

6: *Fareeha*

Fareeha (48) had four sisters and three brothers. She was married by *watto-satto* in exchange for another girl who was given to her brother in marriage. Her husband had been a farmer but worked as a contractor. She had three daughters and five sons. Her thirteen-year-old twin boys were crippled. No children were with her in the *darulaman*. Her husband had alleged that she was a *kari* and accused another man of being a *karo*, so she had been sent to the *darulaman* by the court several months previously. No relative had so for come to visit her. She was longing for freedom to see her children. She was diabetic and upset and asked for justice and protection but saw no hope of fairness. The interview lasted one hour and twenty-two minutes.

7: *Rabia*

Eighteen-year-old Rabia's father worked as a farmer. She had three sisters and two brothers. When she was twelve, her father had died and her maternal grandfather sold her mother for 50,000 rupees in another village. Her mother was accused of being a *kari* with one of her cousins. When Rabia became thirteen, she was given to a fifty-year-old man in marriage. Her husband worked as farmer but was addicted to drugs and gambling. She had no children. She was the target of physical and mental abuse by her in-laws and eventually her husband and a brother-in-law had accused her as a *kari*. Consequently, she had been sent to the *darulaman*. Her mother had tried to help her. She needed a divorce and wanted to go to live with her mother. All she wanted was to live a peaceful life.

8: *Najma*

Najma (21) was fluent in Urdu and Seraiki. Her father worked as a gardener and she had four sisters and eight brothers. She told me a very complex story and asked me if her life story made her a *kari* or a criminal. She did not know whether she had violated any *sharia* or Islamic law. She was married but her brother had killed the man she was living with. She had a one-year-old son with her in the *darulaman*. She does not know about her future. She said that she was too simple to understand the world and its politics. She wondered if any court is the world could provide justice in her case.

9: *Rubina*

Rubina was twenty. Her father was paralysed and she had five sisters and five brothers. She had married her paternal cousin three years earlier and they had no children. Her husband's physical torture of her had made her sick. She had been caught talking to her boyfriend on her cell-phone and had been called a *kari* by her husband, brothers and other relatives. She escaped and eventually reached the *darulaman*. She was determined to divorce her husband and marry a man of her own choice. She was aggressive about why authorizations are only specified to men and asked me whether God exists. She had grievances against the laws which do not let women choose a life partner for themselves.

10: *Shaheen*

Shaheen (23) had two sisters and four brothers. Her father worked with a horse and cart. At the age of sixteen, she married as part of a *watto-satto* exchange, girl for girl. She had no children. Her in-laws abused her and she suffered from asthma. She admitted her contacts with a man. Her in-laws and husband wanted to kill her as a *kari* but she had run away from home and reached the *darulaman*. She was determined to divorce her husband and was sure that her boyfriend would marry her. She was a happy, joyful and carefree person and laughed at the persistent concept of honour.

11: *Asma*

Asma (22) was a daughter of a woodcutter. She had five sisters and five brothers. Seven years earlier, she had married her paternal cousin in a *watto-satto* exchange and her brother had married the exchanged cousin. She had no children. Her brother and the *wadera* had accused her of being a *kari* but her husband had denied their charges. She escaped death and reached the *darulaman*. She wanted to go and live with her husband but was scared, saying "The *wadera* knows I'm beautiful and young, so he will keep selling me off from one man to another by calling me a *kari*".

12: *Ghazala*

Ghazala (27) was the daughter of a small landowner. Her father had two wives who had between them produced three daughters and five sons. She had married a labourer named Ata. The mode of the marriage was a *watto-satto* exchange. She had four children, two of whom were with her at the *darulaman* and two were with their father. A dacoit had got into their home at night, so her husband had accused her of being a *kari*. The police had sent her to the *darulaman*. She sobbed and wept and called her husband "the most dishonourable pimp who doesn't understand what honour actually is".

13: *Tahira*

Tahira (27) had six sisters and four brothers. After the death of her father (a small landowner), she had been forced to marry a fifty-year-old paternal cousin. The mode of the marriage was *watto-satto*. She had two daughters but they were not with her at the *darulaman*. She had been beaten by her husband and in-laws from the first day of her marriage and had been threatened with *talaque*. Eventually, she was accused of being a *kari* by her husband. She left home and reached the *darulaman*. She seemed very disturbed and depressed. She wept for her daughters and showed her concern for their safety.

APPENDIX G

BIOGRAPHICAL SKETCHES OF THE MALE INTERVIEWEES

1: *Sajid*

Sajid (83) could recite the Qur'an. He was the oldest of all the interviewees. His farmer father had died when he was eight years old. He had two brothers and two sisters. He got married to his first cousin when he was very young. He had killed his pregnant wife when his mother-in-law had told him that his wife was a *kari*. He had one son from the wife whom he killed who died later. He want to jail for life but was released later. He married again and had eight sons and two daughters. He said that friendships formed in hospitals and jails are everlasting. At his age, he felt sorry and did not see any honour or humanity in honour killing.

2: *Hanif*

Hanif (36) had achieved a secondary pass at school. His father was a bus driver. He had three brothers and three sisters and he worked as a taxi driver. He had married in 2007 after paying 80,000 rupees to the bride's parents. They had no children. In 2011, he came home late one night unexpectedly and found his bedroom locked. He kicked the door open and when he saw his wife with another man, he opened fire on both of them and killed them. He had never been arrested for these killings. He believed that what he had done was in accordance with Islam and *sharia*. He felt that evil deeds invite disaster and that if he had not killed them, he would not have been able to move in society with honour.

3: **Arshad**

Arshad (36) had taken his matriculation in 1996. His father had fifteen acres of land which Arshad was looking after at the time of the interview. He had three brothers and four sisters. In 199, he had married a cousin, his paternal uncle's daughter. They had one daughter and one son. He cut the throats of his wife and a suspected boy with a sharp dagger. He admitted that he had previously had a dispute over some land with the murdered boy. After the killings, he ran off to Balochistan. On a *sardar*'s instruction, he had handed himself in to the police. The *sardar* had decided the case and the slain boy's relatives had changed their statements in court and he had been freed from jail. He asked "Who can challenge a *sardar*'s *faislo*?" I interviewed him in a hotel.

4: *Zafar*

Zafar (22) had two brothers and three sisters. His father had died when he was five years old and he had started toiling from his childhood to earn a livelihood for his family. He killed his cousin (his paternal uncle's daughter) and the suspected man. After the killings, he and the brother of the killed girl went home and informed their elders. Their elders were happy and praised them for repeating the great saga of the Balochi nation. He went to the police with his weapon and faced nine months inprison. In the meantime, a *faislo* was made by the *sardar* and he was freed. He felt that if he had not killed them, he would have been unable to live with honour in society.

5: *Atif*

Atif (26) had achieved a secondary pass at school. His father had been a policeman but now looked after his land. He had six brothers and four sisters. He had killed his sixteen-year-old cousin (his paternal uncle's daughter) in 2007 after she had left her home. She was brought back and had admitted that she wanted to run away with a boy. She was given some drugs (available easily everywhere in the country) in tea. When she became unconscious after drinking the tea, she was strangled with her own scarf. He said that that was the right Balochi punishment for such a crime. The suspected man had not been seen since then, but Atif was sure that he would find him sooner or later as the world is not too big to hide him.

6: *Adnan*

Adnan was 38. His father had a low-level government job. He had three brothers and five sisters. He had been in the district hockey team and used to play at the positions of full-back and goalkeeper. He had married a cousin (his paternal uncle's daughter) and they had three sons and a daughter. Before killing his cousin (who had confessed to illicit relations with Adnan's sister) in a market, he had tried to ask the boy's family to let the couple get married, but the boy's parents had refused and had insulted him. He had spent seven years in jail. Eventually, with the help of the area *sardar,* he had been released. He felt that honour-related issues are not impossible to resolve and that killings are not the only option, saying that education is essential to change the system.

7: *Usman*

Usman (29) had four brothers and two sisters. Their father worked as a farmer. He was captain of his village's cricket team. After matriculating, he had left his studies because of the family's poverty. He married a cousin (his paternal aunt's daughter) in 1997 and they had three sons and a daughter. He had killed his wife and her boyfriend and then gone to the police. The police held him on remand three times. Eventually, with the intervention of the *sardar,* the issue was sorted out and he had been set free from jail. After returning home from the jail, he had obtained admission into year nine and at the time of the interview he was intending to graduate. He had married again. The interview was conducted at a hotel.

8: *Naeer*

Naeer (65) had had three brothers and seven sisters. His father had a dairy farm. He had married a cousin, his paternal uncle's daughter, 35 years previously in a *watto-satto* exchange. They had three sons and four daughters. He had shot his wife and her man friend with a pistol at an inn. In his opinion, an honourable man is supposed to react according to Islamic teaching not to be ashamed on the Day of Judgment. He had handed himself over to the police and had been in jail for four years. He felt sad when he thought about his ruined family life and his lost business. The interview was conducted at a jail.

9: *Omar*

Omar (16) had run away from school in year four after being beaten up by one of his schoolteachers. His father was paralysed. He had five brothers and three sisters. He used to work at someone's house as a servant. He had killed a man after seeing him in an obscene position with his older brother's wife (she was the daughter-in-law of his paternal uncle). He had tried to kill her as well but had missed and had then run out of bullets. He believed that he had acted in accordance with Qur'anic teaching and was satisfied that he had performed his duty honourably. He was a bit worried about his parents' wellbeing but otherwise jail seemed fine as he liked the food there, but electricity failures bothered him.

10: *Saeed*

Saeed (26) was a married man with an impaired limb. He had a three-year-old son and an eleven-month-old daughter. His father was also in jail with him. Both his siblings had died. His sister had been married to his paternal uncle's son, but when she died, his uncle had asked for money on the grounds that the girl had died and since he was under an obligation to provide a girl for his son, he had asked either to be given another girl or money for his son to remarry. He denied killing his uncle's son and had accused his uncles of lodging an FIR against him so that they could grab a piece of land which he owned. He sobbed and cried that his mother and wife were alone with two young children.

11: *Ata*

Ata (22) had worked as a shepherd in his childhood. His father had had a low-level government job and had had two wives; Ata had four brothers and three sisters. He produced rice from his seven-acre land holding. At the age of eighteen he had married a cousin (his paternal uncle's daughter) with a commitment to give his firstborn baby girl back to his uncle. He had one daughter and two sons. He denied killing his brother's wife and claimed that she had committed suicide by shooting herself in the head and that his enemies had taken out an FIR against him.

12: *Ayaz*

Ayaz (45) was facing life imprisonment on charges of double murder. His father was a farmer and he had eight brothers and three sisters. He had worked as a labourer at different places. He had married in a *watto-satto* exchange and had a daughter and a son. He had been arrested with his father and after paying a bribe of 70,000 rupees to the police they had been released, but then has been arrested again. He denied killing his brother's wife and another man and said that it had been a conspiracy of the landowners of his area. He claimed that he had confessed to the killings under torture. He had been convicted by the court and sent to jail for life.

13: *Anwar*

Anwar (34) had six brothers and six sisters. His father was a policeman. After passing intermediate level at school, he had passed an entrance test for the Academy Artillery Centre and had been selected for the army. During the training, he had received news that his wife had been killed. He was arrested for her murder as soon as he reached home. He denied killing his wife and said that the landowners of his area had taken revenge on him for a long-standing enmity. He was asked by the police to pay a large bribe to be released but he had nothing to pay it with. He claimed that he had been tortured as a convicted killer. He said that the jails are full of innocent people but that criminals and killers enjoy a free life.

Glossary

Aapa	Respected sister.
actus reus (Latin)	A physical criminal act (see *mens rea*).
Ada	Brother.
Ado-bado (see *Watto-satto*)	Exchange a girl for a girl.
Adi	Sister.
Ahl-e-Bait	Family of the prophet.
Amman	Mother.
Ammar	Mother.
Aqeedah	Beliefs.
Assalam-u-alaikum	Peace be upon you.
Azan	Call to prayer. In Islamic countries, *Azan/Adhan* is delivered five times a day in mosques in order to call people to offer prayer.
Baba	Father, and an elderly man.
Badl-e-sulh	In lieu of peace.
Bajee	Elder sister.
Baloch	People belong to Balochistan (one of the main four nations of Pakistan).

Bari	Gifts in a form of jewellery, clothes and other items from a bride's family for the bride.
Bhajaee	Brother's wife.
Brothery	People belong to the same caste.
Burqa	A long, loose stitched garment covering the whole of a woman's body.
Chardiwari	Four walls of a house.
Chacha	Uncle (father's brother).
Chader	A large sheet of cloth to cover a woman's head, face and body.
Charpaee	A bed, and by extension a decorated, often emboidered Sindhi bed cover or bed-spread.
Chattee	A fine.
Dadi	Paternal grandmother.
Dair	Husband's brother (brother-in-law).
Darulaman	Refuge, shelter.
Deeni madrassah	Religious school.
Diyat	The financial compensation paid to the victim or heirs of a victim in cases of murder.
Dohi	An accused but not proven offender.
Dupatta	A long scarf-type cloth-sheet to cover a woman's head and chest and to wrap the body.
Ehteram-e-Ramadan	Reverence of fasting.
Eid	One of the religious festivals in Islam.

Faislo	A decision taken in a *jirga*.
Garhee	Not an offender (opposite of *kari*).
Ghairat	Honour.
Hadd	The limit or prohibition, or punishment for *zina* under Islamic law.
Hadith	A saying or tradition of the Prophet (peace be upon Him).
Haq mehr	Dowry given to a bride by her bridegroom.
Haque	A right thing.
Haque Bakhsh	Waiver from the right to marry (marriage with the Qur'an).
Hari	Peasant.
Haveli	Palatial type of house.
Hudood	Limits or restrictions.
Izzat	Dignity.
Jahad or *jihad*	Fighting in the name of God.
Jahez	Dowry.
Jauhar	Ability (the act of self-immolation).
Jirga	Tribal court (illegal in Pakistan).
Kachehry	Court not sanctioned by law. Also, in the local vernacular of Pakistan the word is used for informal meetings with friends.
Kalashankov	Weapon, firearm, gun.

Kalima	A noun referring to something which is uncountable.
Kari	An adulteress, a fallen, blackened woman.
Karo	An adulterer, a fallen blackened man.
Karo-Kari	*Karo-Kari* is an act of murder in which two people are killed for their actual or perceived immoral behaviour.
Khair	Agreement.
Khata	Accident.
Mehram	Close blood relative.
mens rea (Latin)	Intention to commit a crime (see *actus reus*).
Masoom-ud-dam	Innocent.
Moen-jo-daro	Indus valley civilization.
Molvi	Islamic religious preacher.
Muhajirs	Immigrants.
Muhsan	Married.
Niani mer	A group of girls or women.
Nikah	Marriage contract.
Nizam-e-Mustafa	Establishing an Islamic state.
Otaque	A living room for men only.
Panah	Shelter.
PancZafar	An illegal court.

Pet likhi dean	Literally 'writing a womb'. Committing an unborn child to a marriage.
Phupho	Paternal aunt, father's sister.
Qanun-e-Amna	Blasphemy, the act of insulting or showing contempt for God.
Qatl-e-amd	Intentional murder.
Qawam	Authority.
Qisas	Retaliation.
Rajam	Stoning to death.
Sadri	Large-sized square handkerchief.
Sahaba	Companions of the prophet (peace be upon Him).
Sahi	Authentic.
Sahih Bukhari and *Sahih Muslim*	Two major authentic *hadith* collections.
Salam	An Arabic word, used for 'Hello'. The short form of *Assalam-u-alaikum*.
Sam	To provide shelter or to keep somebody's precious thing(s) with care for some time.
Sardar	Tribal leader.
Sat Quran	A Sindhi term used to refer to a virgin girl (equal to seven Qur'an).
Sati	A chaste woman (the act of self-immolation).
Sha'ar-i-Islam	Islamic symbols.
Sharia	Islamic law.
Shia	One of the two main branches of Islam.

Siah-kari	Honour killing.
Sindhi	People belonging to Sindh, one of the main nations of Pakistan.
Sindhu	Indus river.
Sunnah	The practices and saying of the Prophet Muhammad (peace be upon Him).
Sunni	One of the two main branches of Islam.
Ta'zir	Penalty.
Talaque	Divorce.
Tano	A Sindhi word for insinuation and insult mixed together.
Taurtoora	Honour killing
Valvar	Exchange for a set amount.
Wani	Giving girls to someone for seeking pardon or peace.
Vikro	Sell.
Wadera	Feudal leader.
Wali	An adult legal heir.
Watto-satto or Watta-satta or ado-bado	Give and take, exchanging girls for marriage between two families.
Zaat	Caste.
Zameen	Land.
Zamindar	Landowner.

Zan	Women.
Zar	Wealth.
Zina	Adultery; unlawful sexual relations between Muslims.